SCHOLASTIC

DAILY
Word Ladders

Grades 1–2

by Timothy V. Rasinski
Kent State University

New York • Toronto • London • Auckland • Sydney
Mexico City • New Delhi • Hong Kong • Buenos Aires

Teaching *Resources*

To my own children—Mike, Emily, Mary, and Jenny—
Word Wizards in their own right.

A father couldn't ask for better kids.

Scholastic Inc. grants teachers permission to photocopy the reproducible pages in
this book for classroom use. No other part of this publication may be reproduced in
whole or in part, or stored in a retrieval system, or transmitted in any form or by
any means, electronic, mechanical, photocopying, recording, or otherwise, without
written permission of the publisher. For information regarding permission, write to
Permissions, Scholastic Inc., 557 Broadway, New York, NY 10012-3999.

Edited and produced by Immacula A. Rhodes

Cover design by Brian LaRossa

Cover and interior illustrations by Teresa Anderko

Interior design by Sydney Wright

ISBN-13: 978-0-545-07476-6
ISBN-10: 0-545-07476-2

Contents

Welcome to Word Ladders!

In this book you'll find more than 150 mini-word-study lessons that are also kid-pleasing games! To complete each Word Ladder takes just ten minutes but actively involves each learner in analyzing the structure and meaning of words. To play, students begin with one word and then make a series of other words by changing or rearranging the letters in the word before. With regular use, Word Ladders can go a long way toward developing your students' decoding and vocabulary skills.

How do Word Ladders work?

Let's say our first Word Ladder begins with the word *walk*. The directions will tell students to change one letter in *walk* to make a word that means "to speak." The word students will make, of course, is *talk*. The directions for the next word will then ask students to make a change in *talk* to form another word—perhaps *tale*, or *tall*. Students will form new words as they work up the ladder until they reach the top rung. The final word is in some way related to the first word—for example, *run*. If students get stuck on a rung along the way, they can come back to it, because the words before and after will give them the clues they need to go on.

How do Word Ladders benefit students?

Word Ladders are great for building students' decoding, phonics, spelling, and vocabulary skills. When students add, take away, or rearrange letters to make a new word from one they have just made, they must examine sound-symbol relationships closely. This is just the kind of analysis that all children need to do in order to learn how to decode and spell accurately. And when the puzzle

adds a bit of meaning in the form of a definition (for example, "make a word that means to say something"), it helps extend students' understanding of words and concepts. All of these skills are key to students' success in learning to read and write. So even though Word Ladders will feel like a game, your students will be practicing essential literacy skills at the same time!

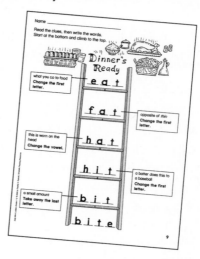

How do I teach a Word Ladder lesson?

Word Ladders are incredibly easy and quick to implement. Here are four simple steps:

1. Choose a Word Ladder to try. (The first five feature easier ladders, so you may want to start with those.)

2. Make a copy of the Word Ladder for each student.

3. Choose whether you want to do the Word Ladder with the class as a whole, or have students work alone, in pairs, or in groups. If students are emergent readers, you might read the clues to them and use a think-aloud method to model how to complete the activity. In addition, you might display a copy on the overhead

projector to demonstrate how to fill in the word on each rung. As their skills develop, students can begin doing the Word Ladders independently.

4. At each new word, students will see two clues: the kinds of changes they need to make to the previous word ("change the first letter," "change the vowel," and so on), and a definition of or clue to the meaning of the word. Sometimes this clue will be a sentence in which the word is used in context but is left out for children to fill in. Move from word to word in this way, up the whole Word Ladder.

Look for the **Bonus Boxes** with stars. These are particularly difficult words, or words with multiple meanings, that you may want to preteach. Or you can do these ladders as a group so that children will not get stuck on this rung.

That's the lesson in a nutshell! It should take no longer than ten minutes to do. Once you're done, you might extend the lessons by having students sort the words into various categories. This can help them deepen their understanding of word relationships. For instance, they could sort them into:

- Grammatical categories. (Which words are nouns? Verbs?)

- Word structure. (Which words have a long vowel and which don't? Which contain a consonant blend? Which begin with a vowel? Which end with a silent *e*)

- Word meaning. (Which words express

what a person can do or feel? Which do not?)

Additionally, you can create your own Word Ladders using copies of the blank puzzles on pages 166–168. Or you might invite students to make their own puzzles to exchange with classmates.

Tips for Working With Word Ladders

Try these tips to give students extra help in doing the Word Ladders:

- List all the "answers" for the ladder (that is, the words for each rung) in random order on the board. Have students choose words from the list to complete the puzzle.

- Add your own clues to give students extra help as they work through each rung of a ladder. A recent event in your classroom or community could even inspire clues for words.

- If students are stuck on a particular rung, you might simply say the word aloud and see if students can spell it correctly by making appropriate changes in the previous word. Elaborate on the meanings of the words as students move their way up the ladder.

- Challenge students to come up with alternative definitions for the same words. Many words, like *bat, pet, bill,* and *lot,* have multiple meanings.

- Once students complete a ladder, add the words to a word wall. Encourage students to use the words in their speaking and writing.

Name _____

Read the clues, then write the words.
Start at the bottom and climb to the top.

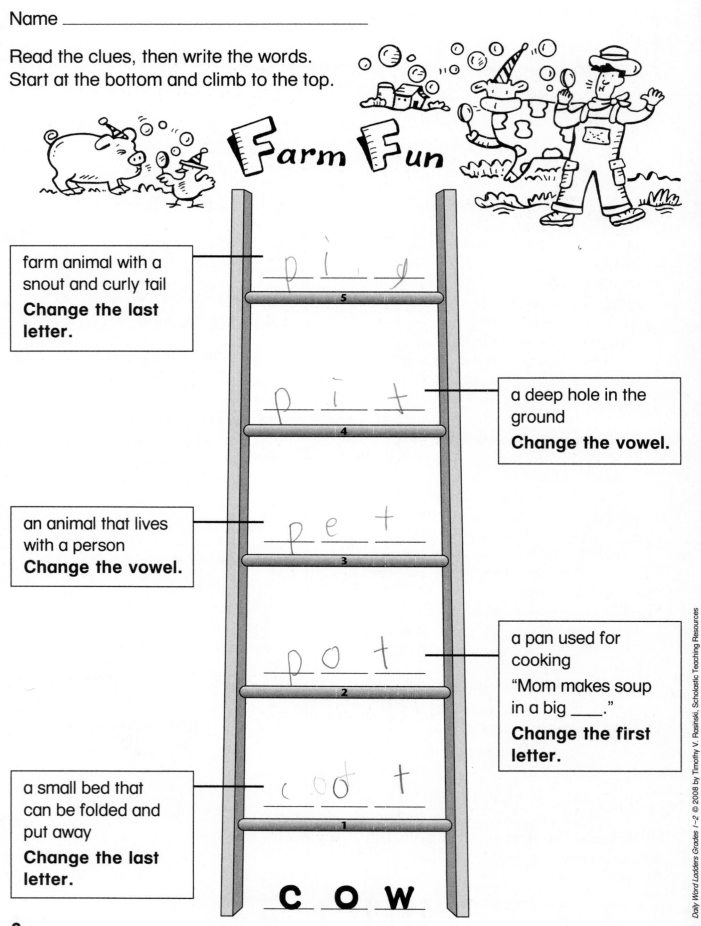

Farm Fun

farm animal with a snout and curly tail
Change the last letter.

p i g — 5

a deep hole in the ground
Change the vowel.

p i t — 4

an animal that lives with a person
Change the vowel.

p e t — 3

a pan used for cooking
"Mom makes soup in a big ____."
Change the first letter.

p o t — 2

a small bed that can be folded and put away
Change the last letter.

c o t — 1

C O W

Read the clues, then write the words.
Start at the bottom and climb to the top.

Dinner's Ready

e a t

what you do to food
Change the first letter.

5

F a t

opposite of *thin*
Change the first letter.

4

h a t

this is worn on the head
Change the vowel.

3

h i t

a batter does this to a baseball
Change the first letter.

2

b i t

a small amount
Take away the last letter.

1

b i t e

Name _____

Read the clues, then write the words.
Start at the bottom and climb to the top.

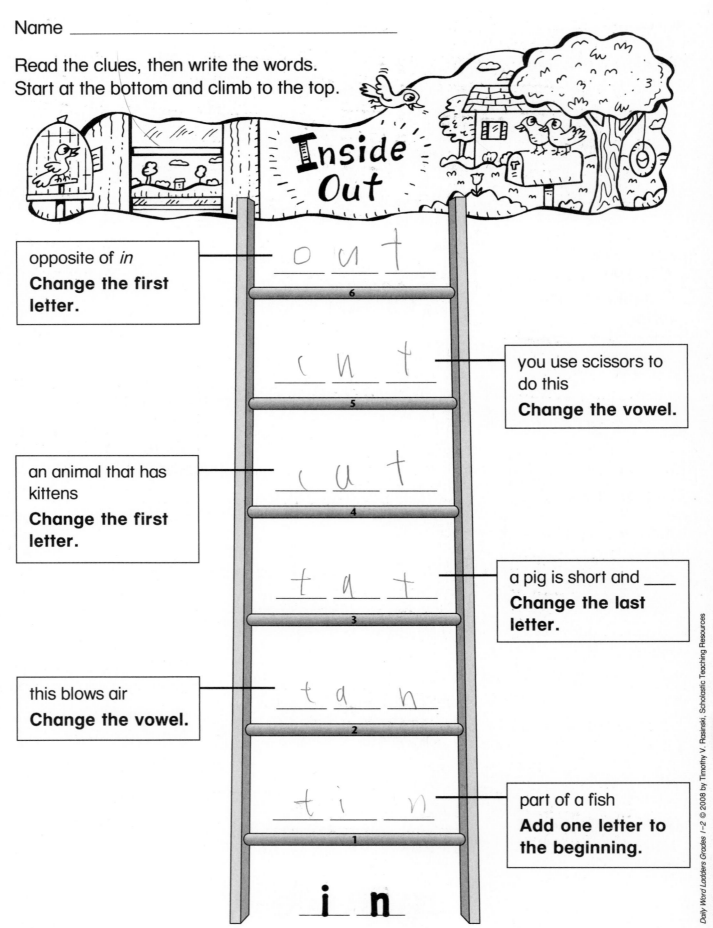

Inside Out

opposite of *in*
Change the first letter.

o u t

6

you use scissors to do this
Change the vowel.

c u t

5

an animal that has kittens
Change the first letter.

c u t

4

a pig is short and ___
Change the last letter.

t a t

3

this blows air
Change the vowel.

t a n

2

part of a fish
Add one letter to the beginning.

t i n

1

i n

Name _____

Read the clues, then write the words.
Start at the bottom and climb to the top.

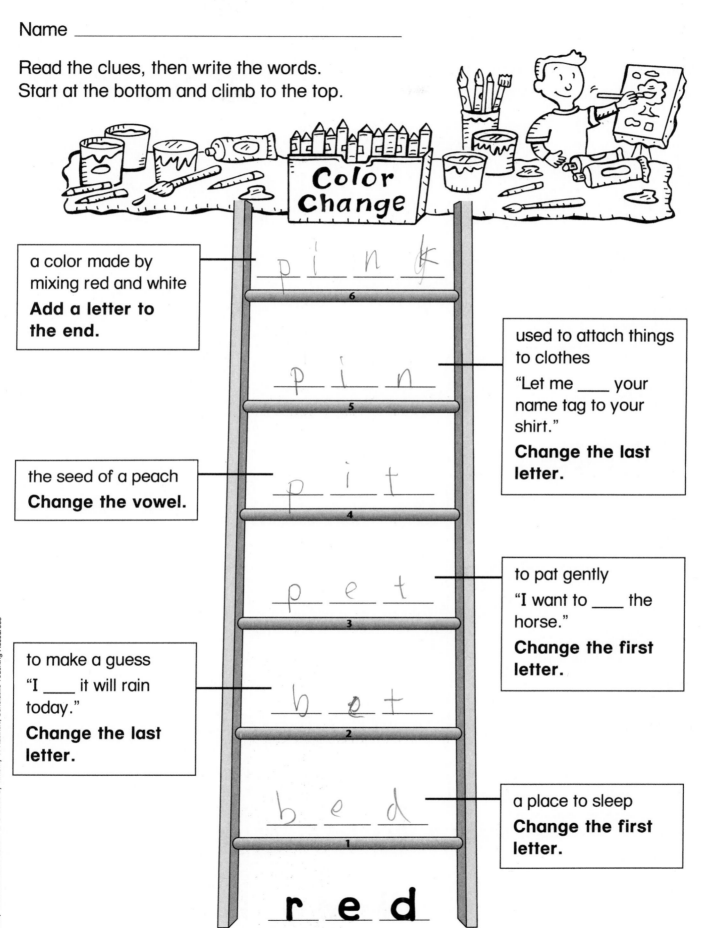

Color Change

a color made by mixing red and white
Add a letter to the end.
→ p i n k *(6)*

used to attach things to clothes
"Let me ___ your name tag to your shirt."
Change the last letter.
→ p i n *(5)*

the seed of a peach
Change the vowel.
→ p i t *(4)*

to pat gently
"I want to ___ the horse."
Change the first letter.
→ p e t *(3)*

to make a guess
"I ___ it will rain today."
Change the last letter.
→ b e t *(2)*

a place to sleep
Change the first letter.
→ b e d *(1)*

r e d

Daily Word Ladders Grades 1–2 © 2008 by Timothy V. Rasinski, Scholastic Teaching Resources

Name _____

Read the clues, then write the words.
Start at the bottom and climb to the top.

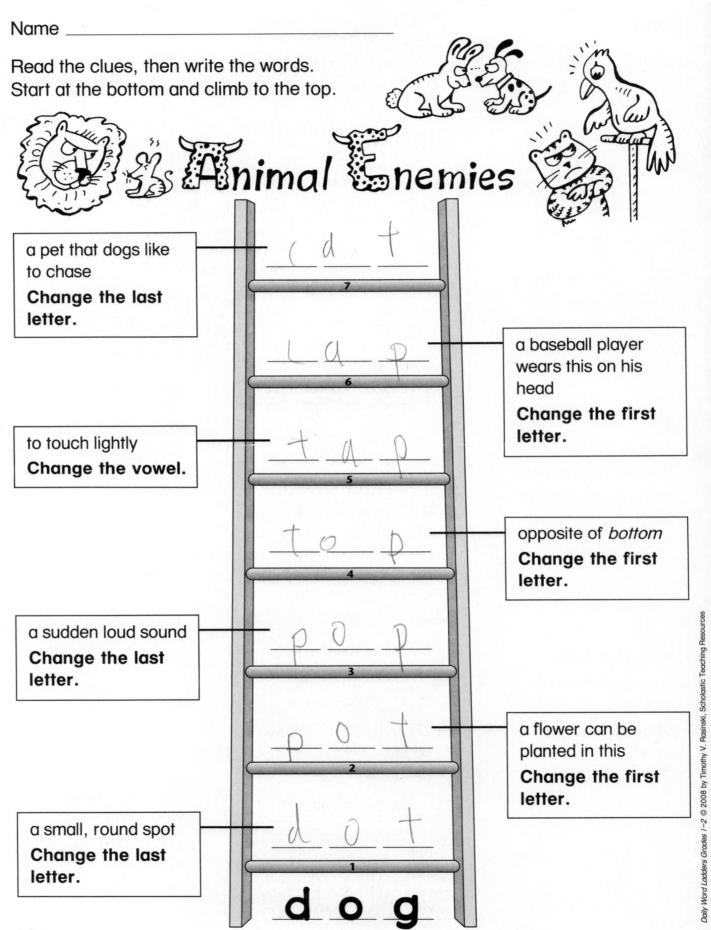

Animal Enemies

a pet that dogs like to chase
Change the last letter.

7   c a t

a baseball player wears this on his head
Change the first letter.

6   c a p

to touch lightly
Change the vowel.

5   t a p

opposite of *bottom*
Change the first letter.

4   t o p

a sudden loud sound
Change the last letter.

3   p o p

a flower can be planted in this
Change the first letter.

2   p o t

a small, round spot
Change the last letter.

1   d o t

d o g

Daily Word Ladders Grades 1–2 © 2008 by Timothy V. Rasinski, Scholastic Teaching Resources

Name _____

Read the clues, then write the words.
Start at the bottom and climb to the top.

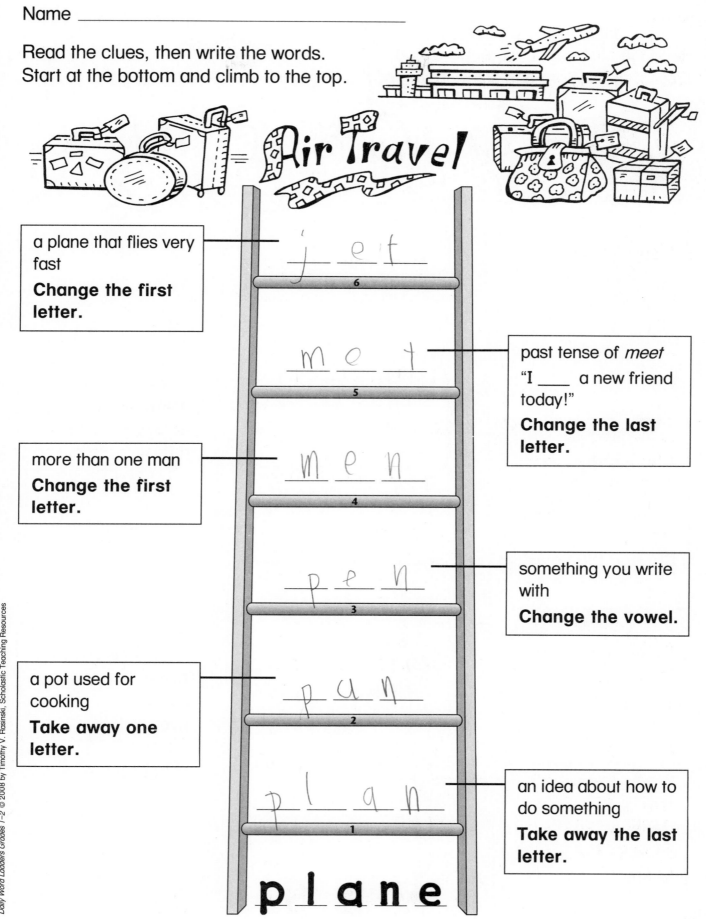

Air Travel

a plane that flies very fast
Change the first letter.

j e t

6

past tense of *meet*
"I ____ a new friend today!"
Change the last letter.

m e t

5

more than one man
Change the first letter.

m e n

4

something you write with
Change the vowel.

p e n

3

a pot used for cooking
Take away one letter.

p u n

2

an idea about how to do something
Take away the last letter.

p l a n

1

p l a n e

Name _____

Read the clues, then write the words.
Start at the bottom and climb to the top.

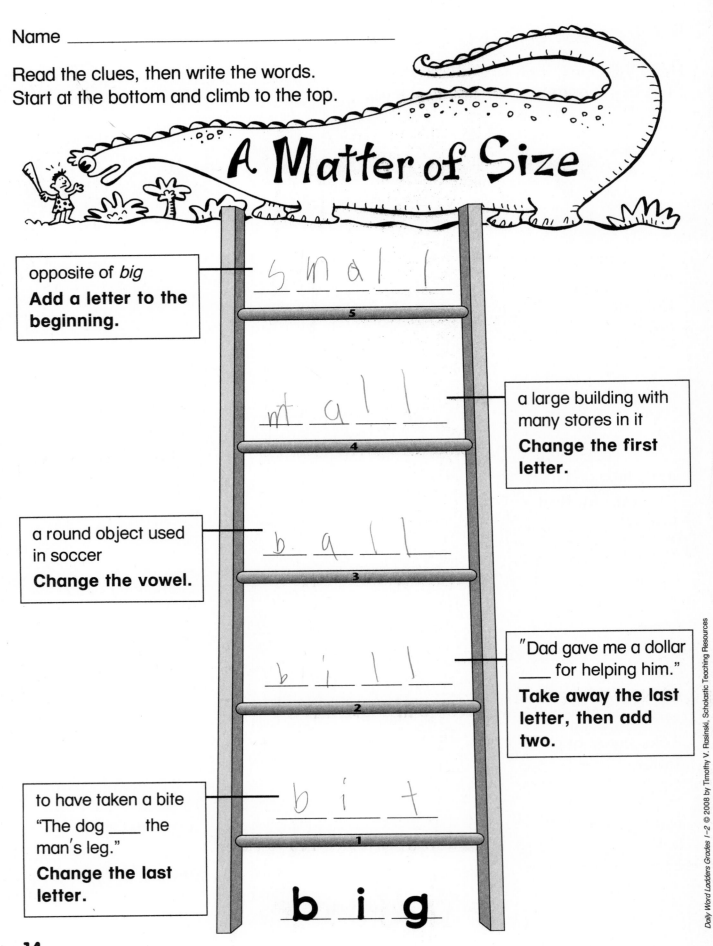

A Matter of Size

opposite of *big*
Add a letter to the beginning.

s m a l l

5

m t a l l

4

a large building with many stores in it
Change the first letter.

a round object used in soccer
Change the vowel.

b a l l

3

b i l l

2

"Dad gave me a dollar ____ for helping him."
Take away the last letter, then add two.

to have taken a bite
"The dog ____ the man's leg."
Change the last letter.

b i t

1

b i g

Daily Word Ladders Grades 1–2 © 2008 by Timothy V. Rasinski, Scholastic Teaching Resources

Name _____

Read the clues, then write the words.
Start at the bottom and climb to the top.

Around the Clock

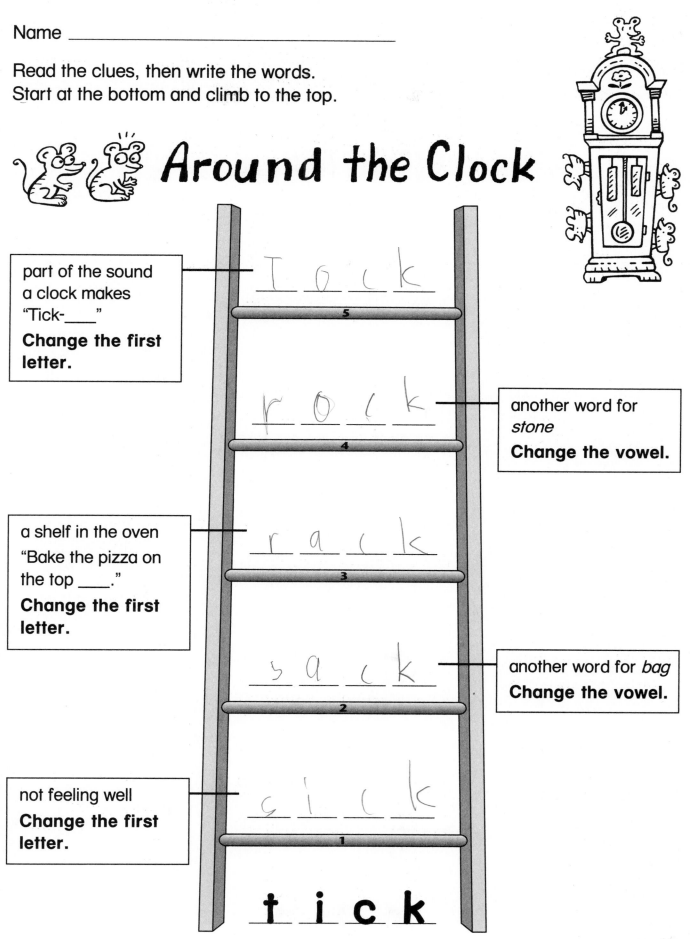

part of the sound a clock makes "Tick-___"
Change the first letter.

Tock

another word for *stone*
Change the vowel.

rock

a shelf in the oven "Bake the pizza on the top ___."
Change the first letter.

rack

another word for *bag*
Change the vowel.

sack

not feeling well
Change the first letter.

sick

tick

Name _____

Read the clues, then write the words.
Start at the bottom and climb to the top.

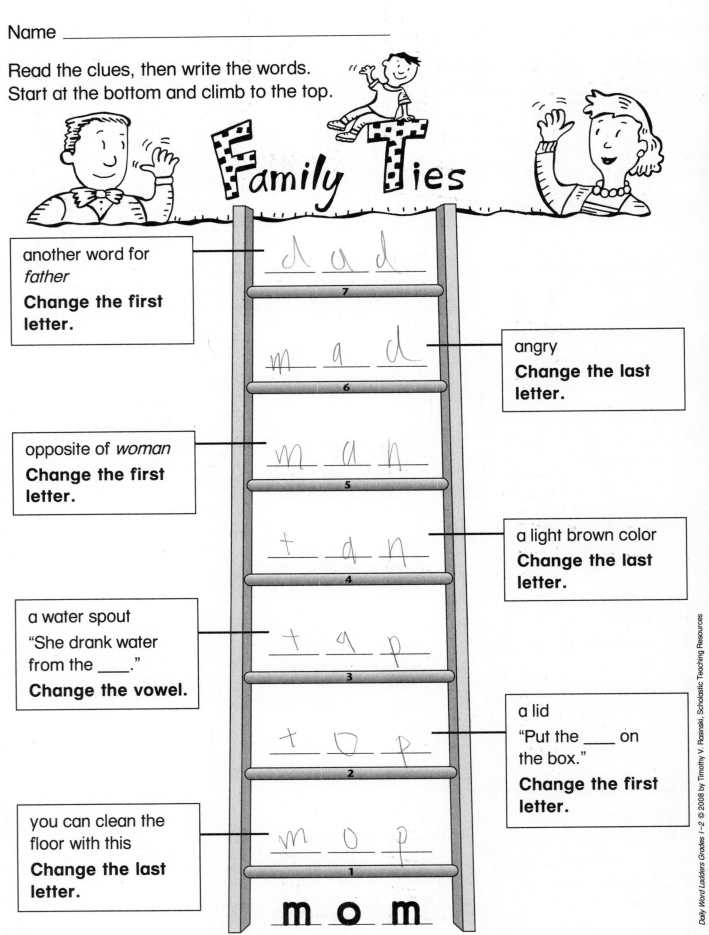

Family Ties

another word for *father*
Change the first letter.

d a d
7

angry
Change the last letter.

m a d
6

opposite of *woman*
Change the first letter.

m a n
5

a light brown color
Change the last letter.

t a n
4

a water spout
"She drank water from the ___."
Change the vowel.

t a p
3

a lid
"Put the ___ on the box."
Change the first letter.

t o p
2

you can clean the floor with this
Change the last letter.

m o p
1

m o m

Daily Word Ladders Grades 1–2 © 2008 by Timothy V. Rasinski, Scholastic Teaching Resources

Name _____

Read the clues, then write the words.
Start at the bottom and climb to the top.

Fun on a Bun

a pet that barks
Change the vowel.

d o g

7

d i g

6

to make a hole in the ground
Change the first letter.

pork comes from this farm animal
Change the last letter.

p i g

5

p i t

4

a cherry seed
Change the vowel.

an animal that is taken care of by people
Change the first letter.

p e t

3

l e t

2

to allow
"The teacher ___ me lead the song."
Change the vowel.

a piece of land
"Dad parked the car in the parking ___."
Change the first letter.

l o t

1

h o t

Daily Word Ladders Grades 1–2 © 2008 by Timothy V. Rasinski, Scholastic Teaching Resources

Name _____

Read the clues, then write the words.
Start at the bottom and climb to the top.

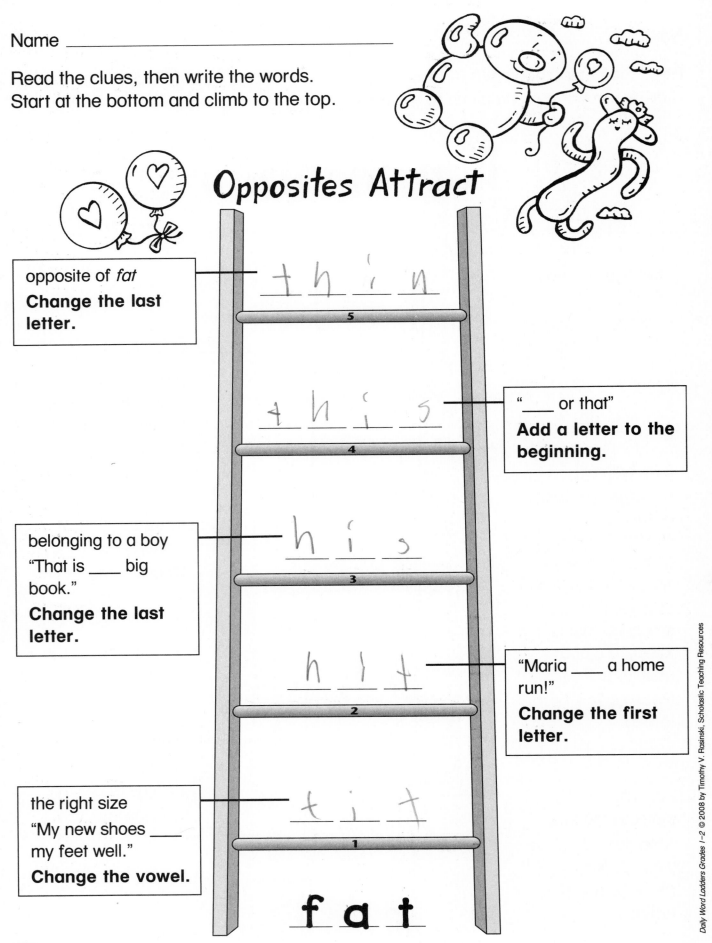

Opposites Attract

opposite of *fat*
Change the last letter.

t h i n

5

"___ or that"
Add a letter to the beginning.

t h i s

4

belonging to a boy
"That is ___ big book."
Change the last letter.

h i s

3

"Maria ___ a home run!"
Change the first letter.

h i t

2

the right size
"My new shoes ___ my feet well."
Change the vowel.

t i t

1

f a t

Daily Word Ladders Grades 1–2 © 2008 by Timothy V. Rasinski, Scholastic Teaching Resources

Name _____

Read the clues, then write the words.
Start at the bottom and climb to the top.

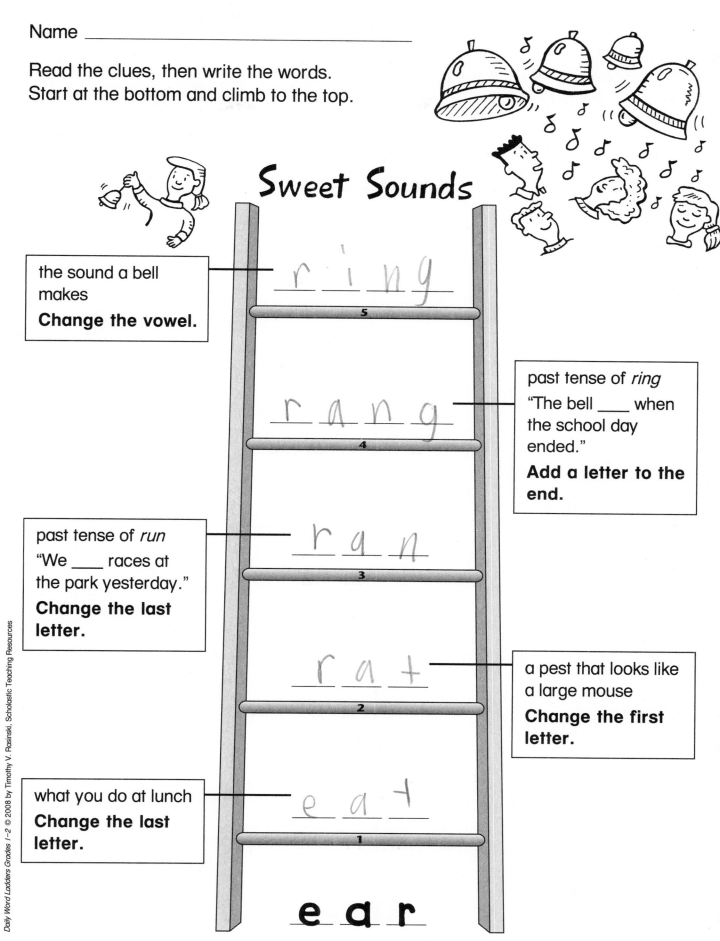

Sweet Sounds

the sound a bell makes
Change the vowel. → r i n g
5

r a n g ← past tense of *ring*
"The bell ___ when the school day ended."
Add a letter to the end.
4

past tense of *run*
"We ___ races at the park yesterday."
Change the last letter. → r a n
3

r a t ← a pest that looks like a large mouse
Change the first letter.
2

what you do at lunch
Change the last letter. → e a t
1

e a r

Name _____

Read the clues, then write the words.
Start at the bottom and climb to the top.

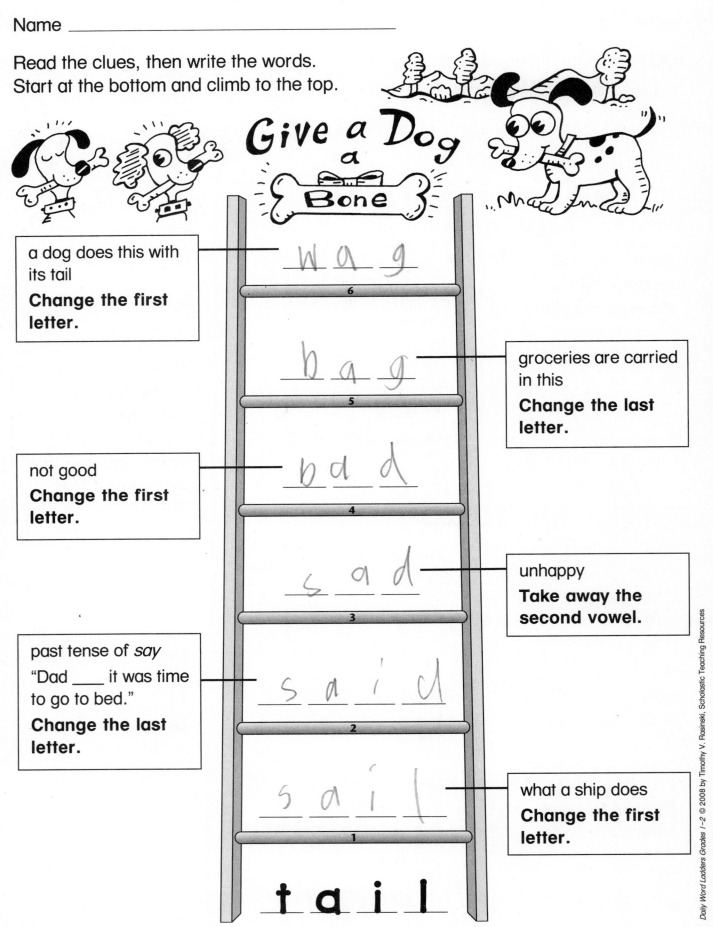

Give a Dog a Bone

a dog does this with its tail
Change the first letter.

w a g

6

b a g

5

groceries are carried in this
Change the last letter.

not good
Change the first letter.

b a d

4

s a d

3

unhappy
Take away the second vowel.

past tense of *say*
"Dad ____ it was time to go to bed."
Change the last letter.

s a i d

2

s a i l

1

what a ship does
Change the first letter.

t a i l

Daily Word Ladders Grades 1–2 © 2008 by Timothy V. Rasinski, Scholastic Teaching Resources

Name _____

Read the clues, then write the words.
Start at the bottom and climb to the top.

Here to There

moving much faster than a walk
Change the first letter.

r u n

5

enjoyment in doing something
"We have ___ dancing to the music."
Take away the last two letters, then add one.

t u n

4

to hold as much as possible
"The pot is ___ of water."
Change the vowel.

t u l l

3

to drop to the ground
"I saw him ___ off the chair."
Change the first letter.

t a l l

2

this stands between two rooms
Change the last letter.

w a l l

1

w a l k

Daily Word Ladders Grades 1–2 © 2008 by Timothy V. Rasinski, Scholastic Teaching Resources

Name _____

Read the clues, then write the words.
Start at the bottom and climb to the top.

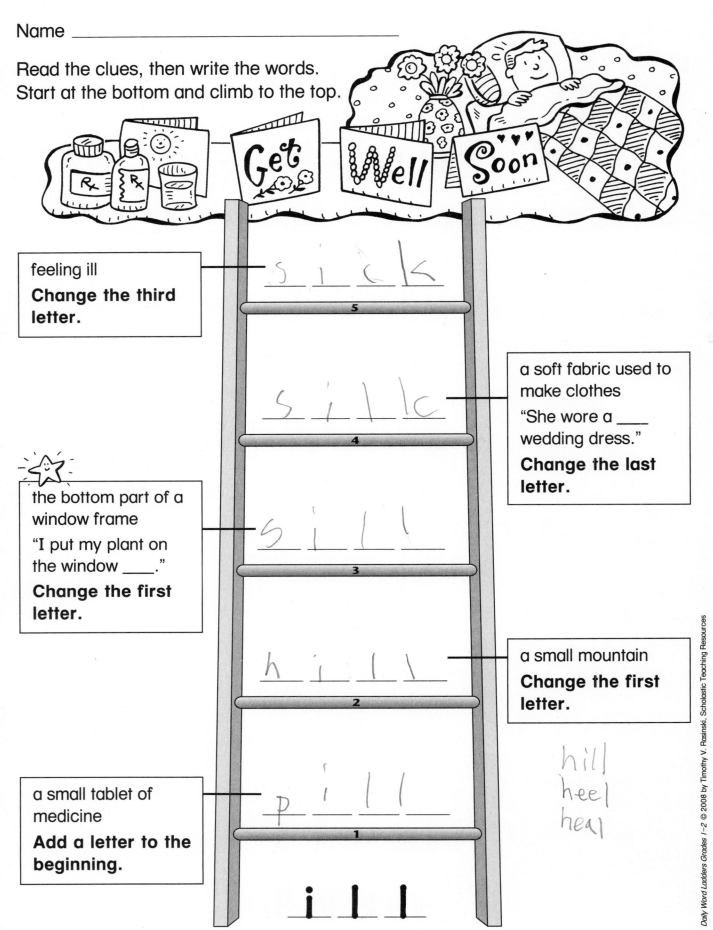

feeling ill
Change the third letter.

s i c k

5

s i l k

4

a soft fabric used to make clothes
"She wore a ___ wedding dress."
Change the last letter.

the bottom part of a window frame
"I put my plant on the window ___."
Change the first letter.

s i l l

3

h i l l

2

a small mountain
Change the first letter.

hill
heel
heal

a small tablet of medicine
Add a letter to the beginning.

p i l l

1

i l l

22

Daily Word Ladders Grades 1–2 © 2008 by Timothy V. Rasinski, Scholastic Teaching Resources

Name _____

Read the clues, then write the words.
Start at the bottom and climb to the top.

In the Can

to be able to
"I ____ ride a bike!"
Change the last letter.

c a n

5

a pet that purrs
Take away the third letter.

c a t

4

a doctor puts this on a broken arm or leg
Change the last letter.

c a s t

3

c a s h

2

another word for *money*
Take away the second letter.

this happens when two cars run into each other
Change the first letter.

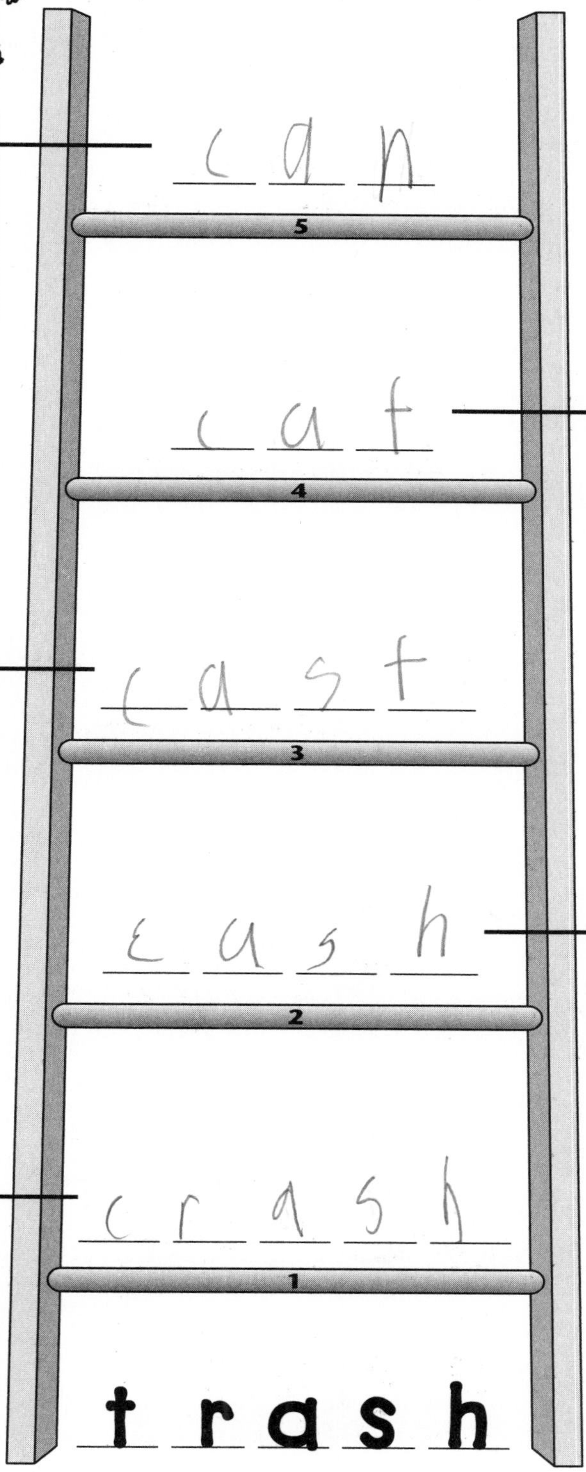

c r a s h

1

t r a s h

Name _____

Read the clues, then write the words.
Start at the bottom and climb to the top.

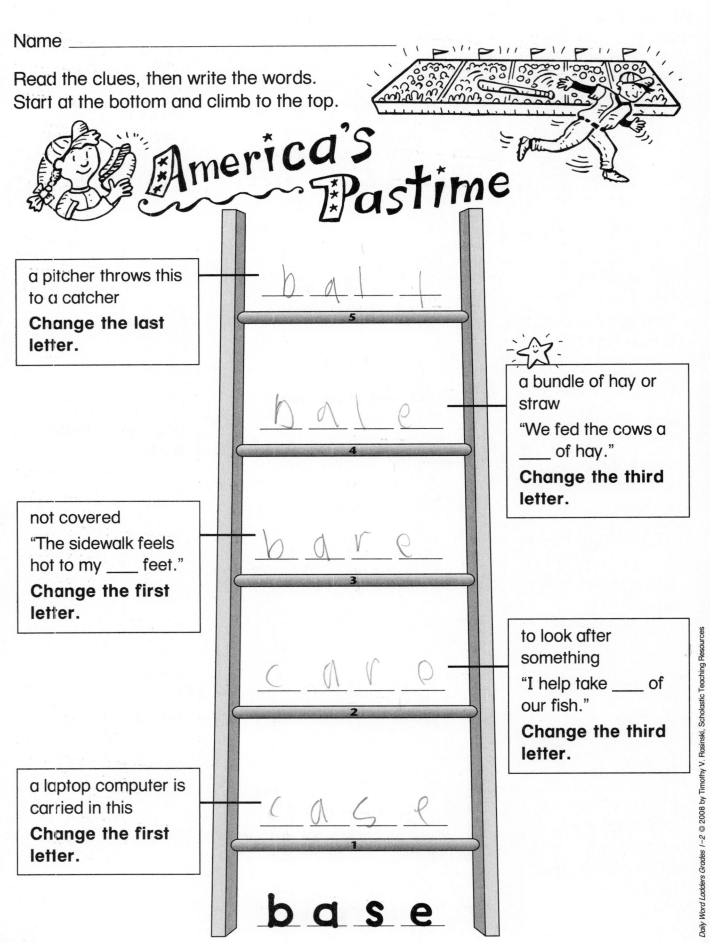

America's Pastime

a pitcher throws this to a catcher
Change the last letter.

b a l t

5

a bundle of hay or straw
"We fed the cows a ___ of hay."
Change the third letter.

b a l e

4

not covered
"The sidewalk feels hot to my ___ feet."
Change the first letter.

b a r e

3

to look after something
"I help take ___ of our fish."
Change the third letter.

c a r e

2

a laptop computer is carried in this
Change the first letter.

c a s e

1

b a s e

Daily Word Ladders Grades 1–2 © 2008 by Timothy V. Rasinski, Scholastic Teaching Resources

Name _____

Read the clues, then write the words.
Start at the bottom and climb to the top.

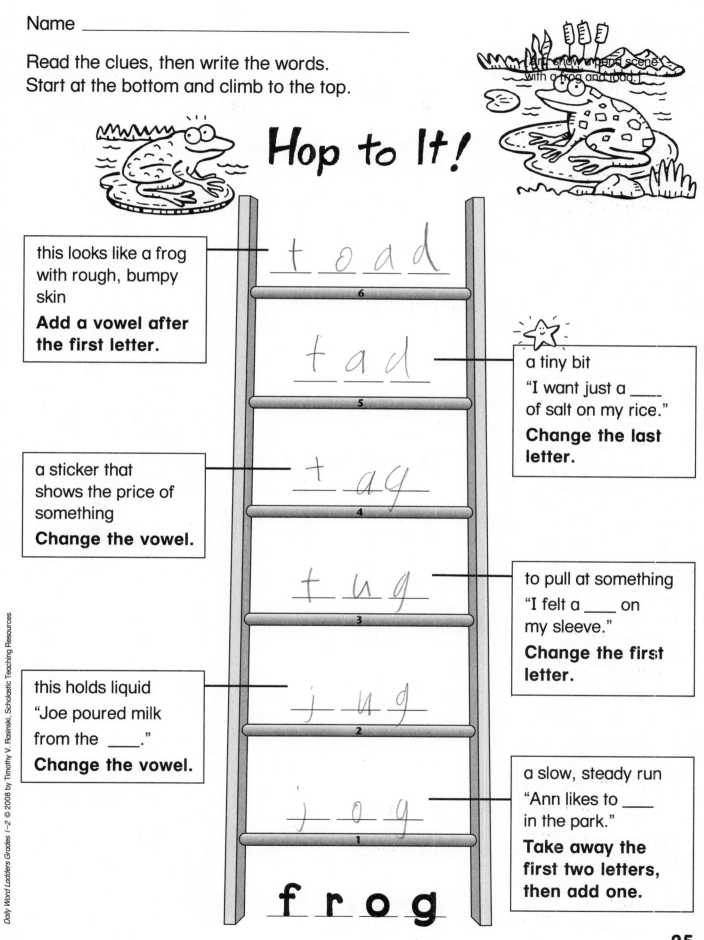

Hop to It!

this looks like a frog with rough, bumpy skin
Add a vowel after the first letter.

t o a d

6

a tiny bit
"I want just a ____ of salt on my rice."
Change the last letter.

t a d

5

a sticker that shows the price of something
Change the vowel.

t a g

4

to pull at something
"I felt a ____ on my sleeve."
Change the first letter.

t u g

3

this holds liquid
"Joe poured milk from the ____."
Change the vowel.

j u g

2

a slow, steady run
"Ann likes to ____ in the park."
Take away the first two letters, then add one.

j o g

1

f r o g

Daily Word Ladders Grades 1–2 © 2008 by Timothy V. Rasinski, Scholastic Teaching Resources

Name _____

Read the clues, then write the words.
Start at the bottom and climb to the top.

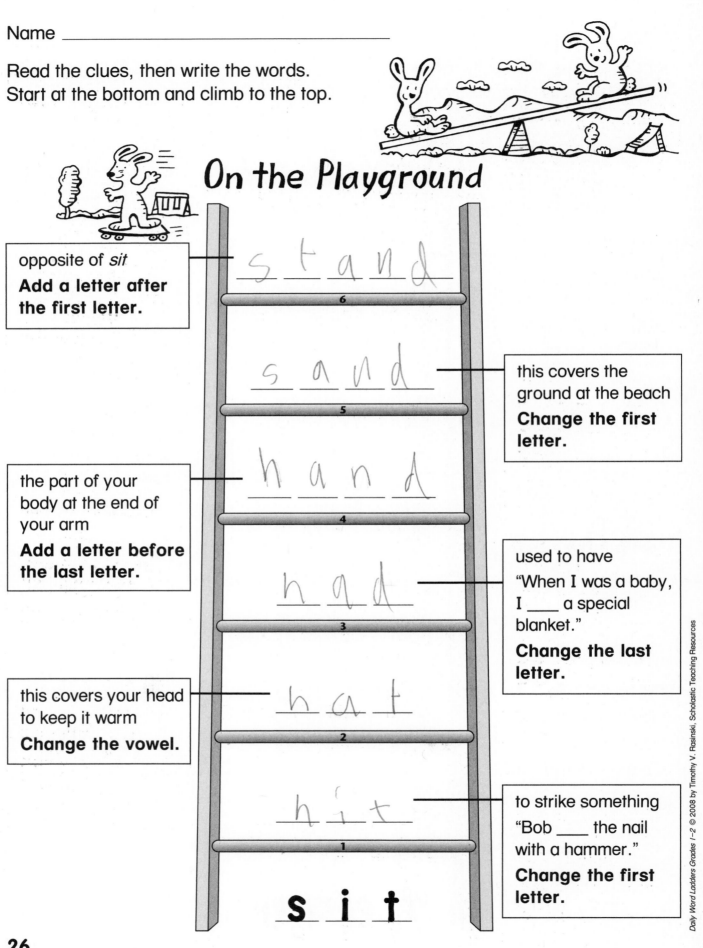

On the Playground

opposite of *sit*
Add a letter after the first letter.

s t a n d

6

s a n d

5

this covers the ground at the beach
Change the first letter.

the part of your body at the end of your arm
Add a letter before the last letter.

h a n d

4

h a d

3

used to have
"When I was a baby, I ____ a special blanket."
Change the last letter.

this covers your head to keep it warm
Change the vowel.

h a t

2

h i t

1

to strike something
"Bob ____ the nail with a hammer."
Change the first letter.

s i t

Daily Word Ladders Grades 1–2 © 2008 by Timothy V. Rasinski, Scholastic Teaching Resources

Name _____

Read the clues, then write the words.
Start at the bottom and climb to the top.

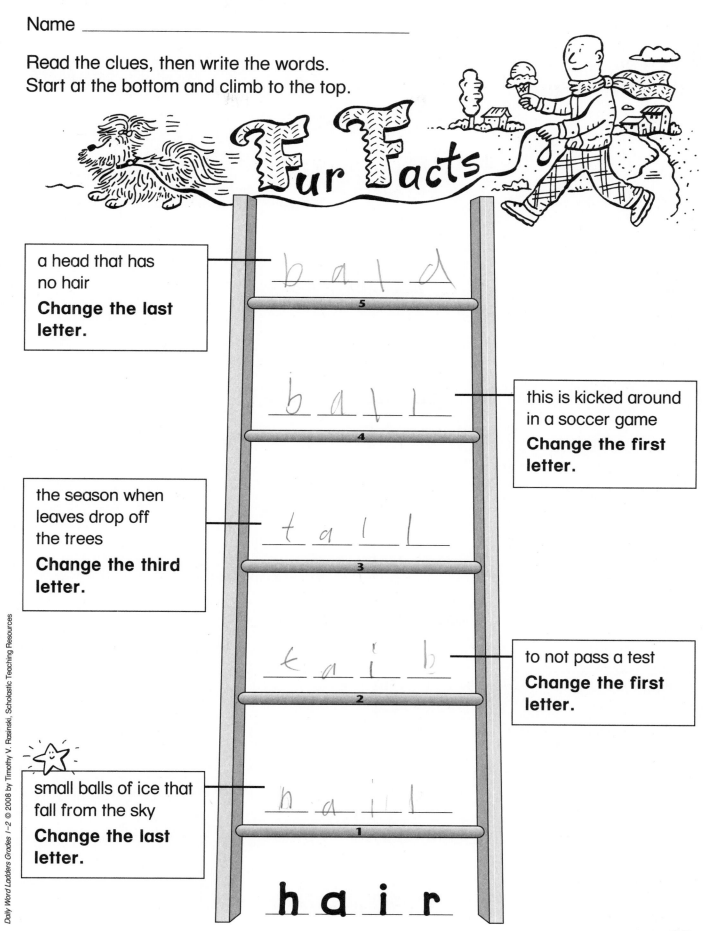

Fur Facts

a head that has no hair
Change the last letter.

b a l d

5

b a l l

4

this is kicked around in a soccer game
Change the first letter.

the season when leaves drop off the trees
Change the third letter.

t a l l

3

t a i l

2

to not pass a test
Change the first letter.

small balls of ice that fall from the sky
Change the last letter.

h a i l

1

h a i r

Name _____

Read the clues, then write the words.
Start at the bottom and climb to the top.

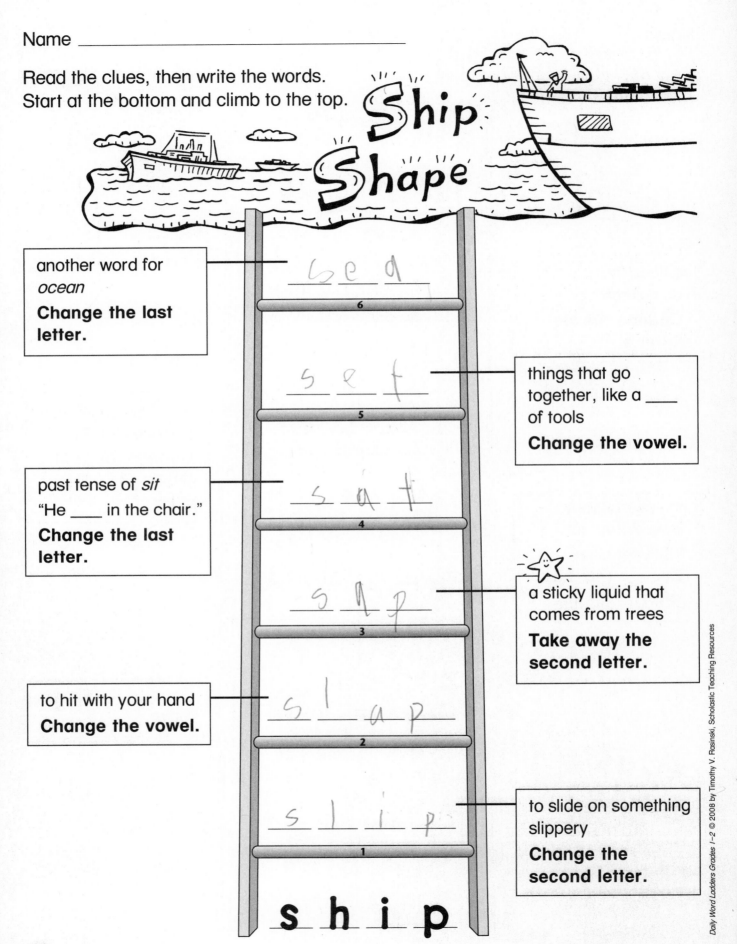

Ship Shape

another word for *ocean*
Change the last letter.

things that go together, like a ____ of tools
Change the vowel.

past tense of *sit*
"He ____ in the chair."
Change the last letter.

a sticky liquid that comes from trees
Take away the second letter.

to hit with your hand
Change the vowel.

to slide on something slippery
Change the second letter.

6 — sed
5 — set
4 — sat
3 — sap
2 — slap
1 — slip

s h i p

28

Daily Word Ladders Grades 1–2 © 2008 by Timothy V. Rasinski, Scholastic Teaching Resources

Name _____

Read the clues, then write the words.
Start at the bottom and climb to the top.

Pail Problem

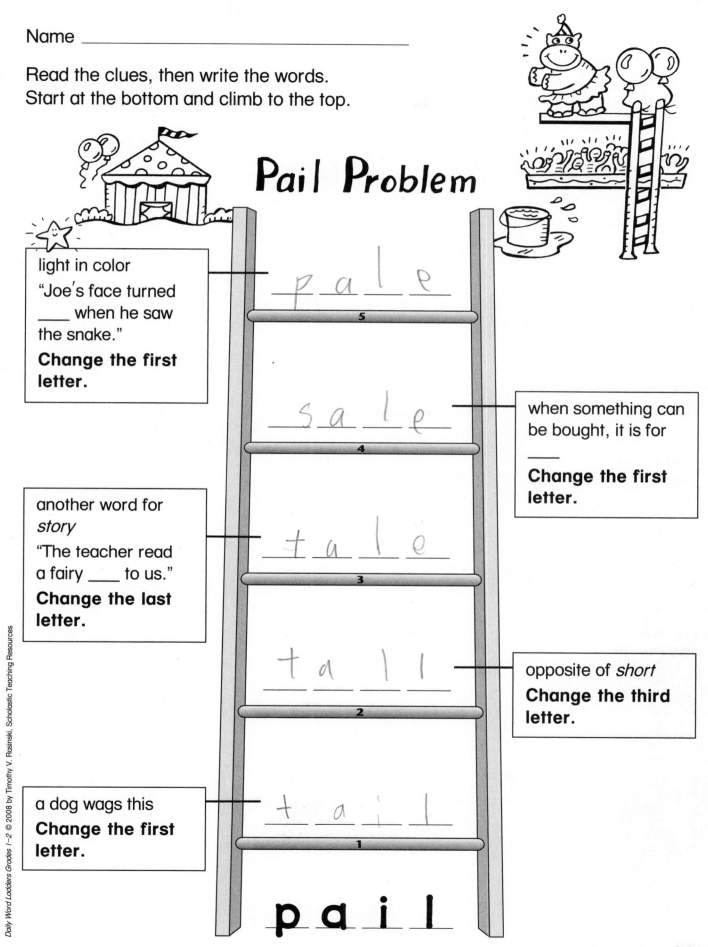

light in color
"Joe's face turned ___ when he saw the snake."
Change the first letter.

p a l e
5

s a l e
4

when something can be bought, it is for ___
Change the first letter.

another word for *story*
"The teacher read a fairy ___ to us."
Change the last letter.

t a l e
3

t a l l
2

opposite of *short*
Change the third letter.

a dog wags this
Change the first letter.

t a i l
1

p a i l

29

Name _____

Read the clues, then write the words.
Start at the bottom and climb to the top.

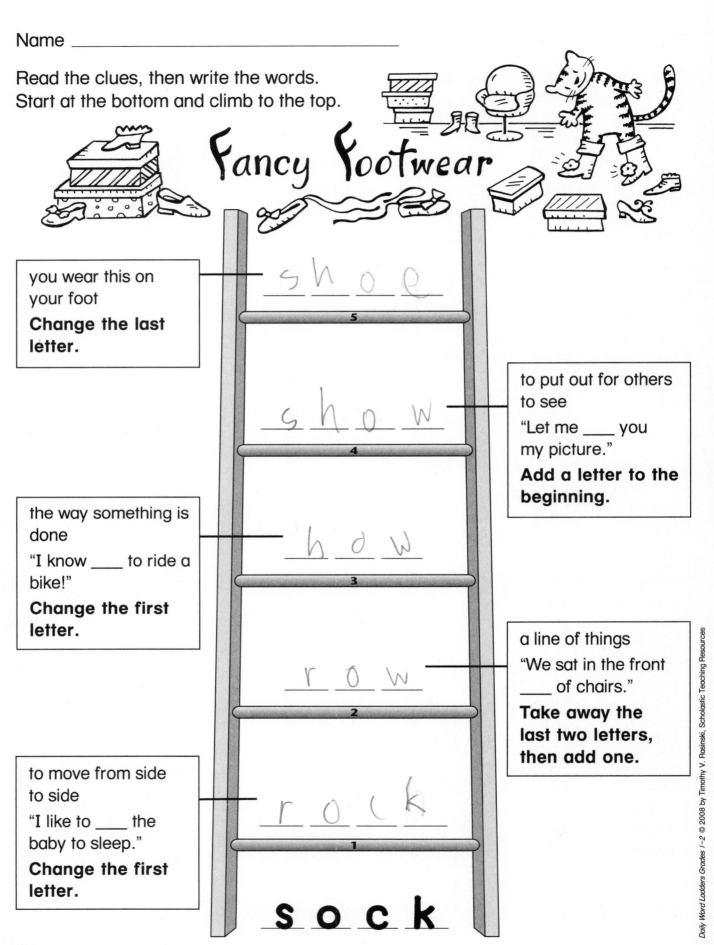

Fancy Footwear

you wear this on your foot
Change the last letter.

s h o e

5

to put out for others to see
"Let me ____ you my picture."
Add a letter to the beginning.

s h o w

4

the way something is done
"I know ____ to ride a bike!"
Change the first letter.

h o w

3

a line of things
"We sat in the front ____ of chairs."
Take away the last two letters, then add one.

r o w

2

to move from side to side
"I like to ____ the baby to sleep."
Change the first letter.

r o c k

1

s o c k

Daily Word Ladders Grades 1–2 © 2008 by Timothy V. Rasinski, Scholastic Teaching Resources

Name _____

Read the clues, then write the words.
Start at the bottom and climb to the top.

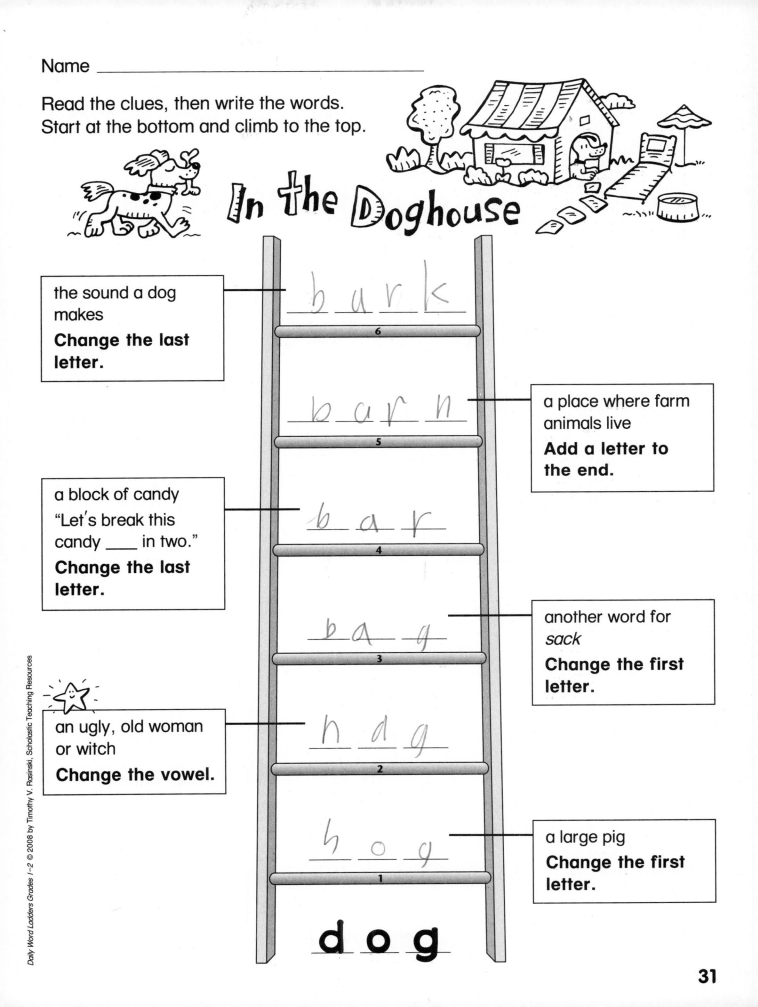

In the Doghouse

the sound a dog makes
Change the last letter.

b u r k
6

b a r n
5

a place where farm animals live
Add a letter to the end.

a block of candy
"Let's break this candy ___ in two."
Change the last letter.

b a r
4

b a g
3

another word for *sack*
Change the first letter.

an ugly, old woman or witch
Change the vowel.

h a g
2

h o g
1

a large pig
Change the first letter.

d o g

Name _____

Read the clues, then write the words.
Start at the bottom and climb to the top.

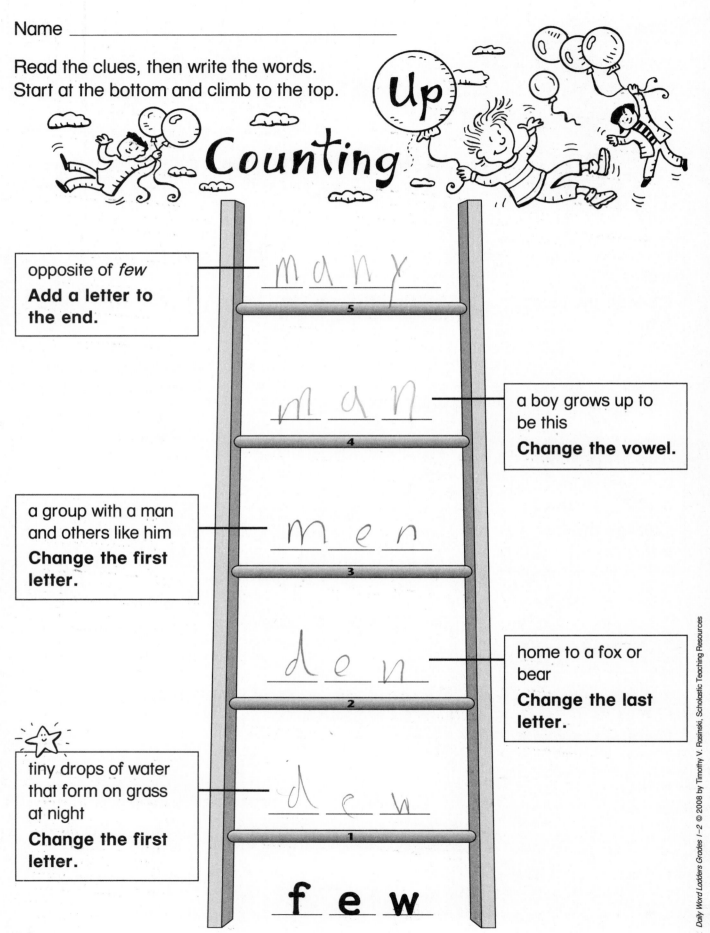

Counting **Up**

opposite of *few*
Add a letter to the end.

m a n y

5

m a n

4

a boy grows up to be this
Change the vowel.

a group with a man and others like him
Change the first letter.

m e n

3

d e n

2

home to a fox or bear
Change the last letter.

tiny drops of water that form on grass at night
Change the first letter.

d e w

1

f e w

Daily Word Ladders Grades 1–2 © 2008 by Timothy V. Rasinski, Scholastic Teaching Resources

Name _____

Read the clues, then write the words.
Start at the bottom and climb to the top.

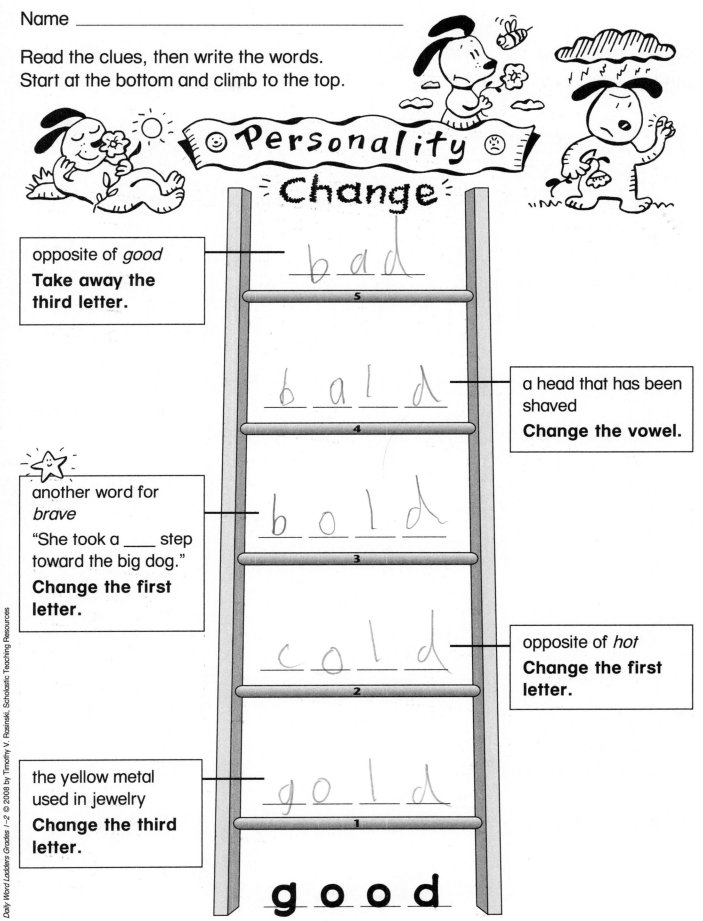

Personality Change

opposite of *good*
Take away the third letter.

b a d

5

b a l d

a head that has been shaved
Change the vowel.

4

another word for *brave*
"She took a ____ step toward the big dog."
Change the first letter.

b o l d

3

c o l d

opposite of *hot*
Change the first letter.

2

the yellow metal used in jewelry
Change the third letter.

g o l d

1

g o o d

Name _____

Read the clues, then write the words.
Start at the bottom and climb to the top.

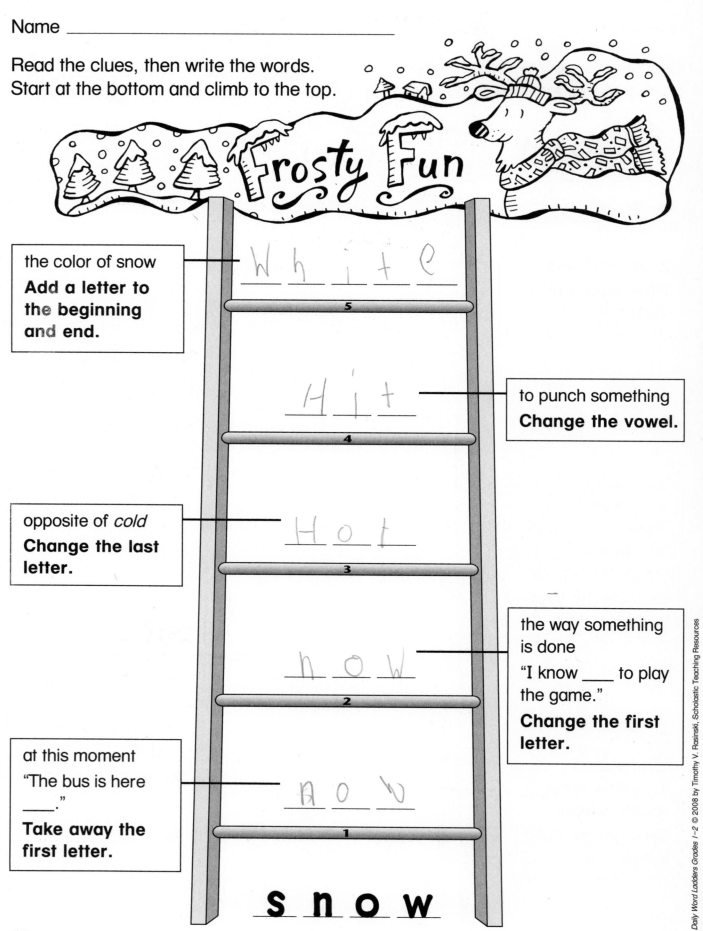

Frosty Fun

the color of snow
Add a letter to the beginning and end.

White

to punch something
Change the vowel.

Hit

opposite of *cold*
Change the last letter.

Hot

the way something is done
"I know ____ to play the game."
Change the first letter.

n o w

at this moment
"The bus is here ____."
Take away the first letter.

n o w

s n o w

Daily Word Ladders Grades 1–2 © 2008 by Timothy V. Rasinski, Scholastic Teaching Resources

Name _____

Read the clues, then write the words.
Start at the bottom and climb to the top.

Warm and Cozy

this burns wood
Change the first letter.

_f i r e_

5

a metal thread used to connect things
"The ___ to my earphones is very long."
Change the first vowel.

_w i r e_

4

past tense of *wear*
"Todd ___ new shoes yesterday."
Change the first letter.

_w o r e_

3

not exciting, dull
"This movie is a real ___."
Change the last letter.

_b o r e_

2

your birthday falls on the day you were ___
Change the vowel.

_b o r n_

1

b u r n

Name _____

Read the clues, then write the words.
Start at the bottom and climb to the top.

Under the Stars

a place with tents
Change the first letter.

people in wheelchairs use this instead of stairs
Add a letter to the end.

a male sheep
Change the last letter.

kept going
"The big truck ____ the red light."
Change the first letter.

a light brown color
Change the vowel.

5 + 5
Take away the last letter.

6

5

4

3

2

1

t e n t

Daily Word Ladders Grades 1–2 © 2008 by Timothy V. Rasinski, Scholastic Teaching Resources

Name _____

Read the clues, then write the words.
Start at the bottom and climb to the top.

a baby dog
Change the last letter.

to place something
"She ____ the dish on the table."
Change the vowel.

another word for *hole*
Change the first letter.

to have torn food with your teeth
"Pat ____ into the hot dog."
Take away the last letter.

to use your teeth to break off food
Change the first letter.

a toy that you fly in the wind
Take away one middle letter and the last letter.

6

5

4

3

2

1

k i t t e n

Name _____

Read the clues, then write the words.
Start at the bottom and climb to the top.

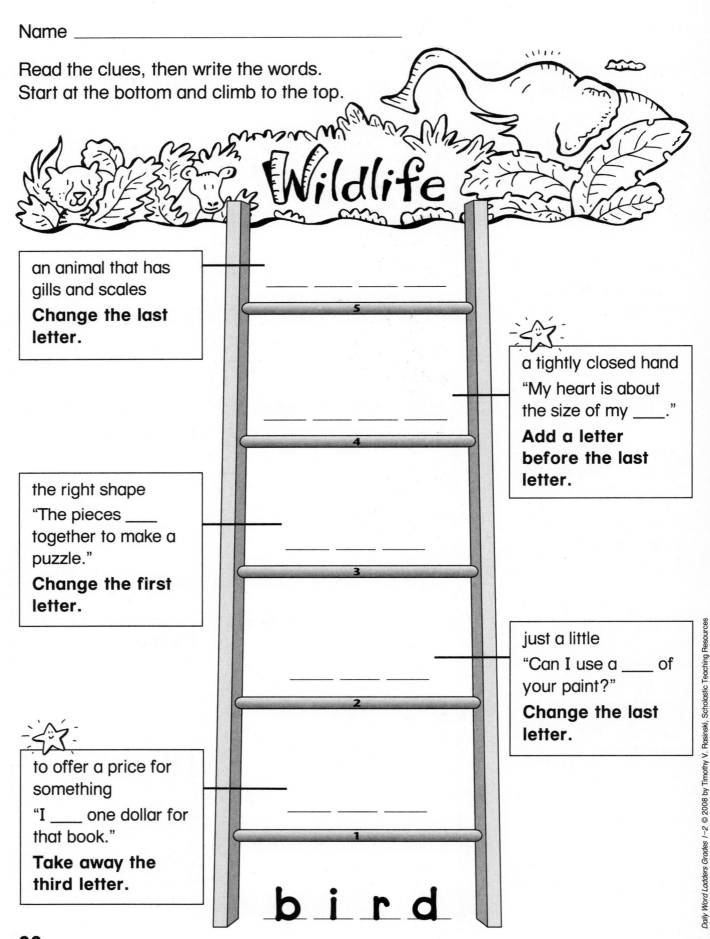

Wildlife

an animal that has gills and scales
Change the last letter.

5 _ _ _ _

a tightly closed hand
"My heart is about the size of my ___."
Add a letter before the last letter.

4 _ _ _ _

the right shape
"The pieces ___ together to make a puzzle."
Change the first letter.

3 _ _ _ _

just a little
"Can I use a ___ of your paint?"
Change the last letter.

2 _ _ _ _

to offer a price for something
"I ___ one dollar for that book."
Take away the third letter.

1

b i r d

Daily Word Ladders Grades 1–2 © 2008 by Timothy V. Rasinski, Scholastic Teaching Resources

Name _____

Read the clues, then write the words.
Start at the bottom and climb to the top.

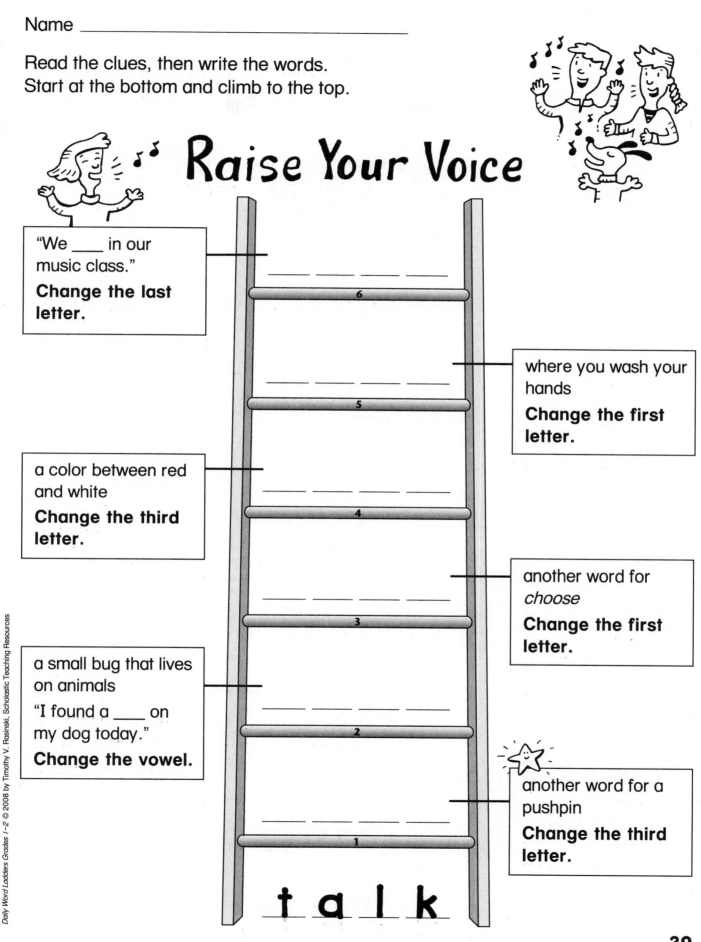

Raise Your Voice

"We ____ in our music class."
Change the last letter.

where you wash your hands
Change the first letter.

a color between red and white
Change the third letter.

another word for *choose*
Change the first letter.

a small bug that lives on animals
"I found a ____ on my dog today."
Change the vowel.

another word for a pushpin
Change the third letter.

6

5

4

3

2

1

t a l k

Daily Word Ladders Grades 1–2 © 2008 by Timothy V. Rasinski, Scholastic Teaching Resources

Name _____

Read the clues, then write the words.
Start at the bottom and climb to the top.

One More

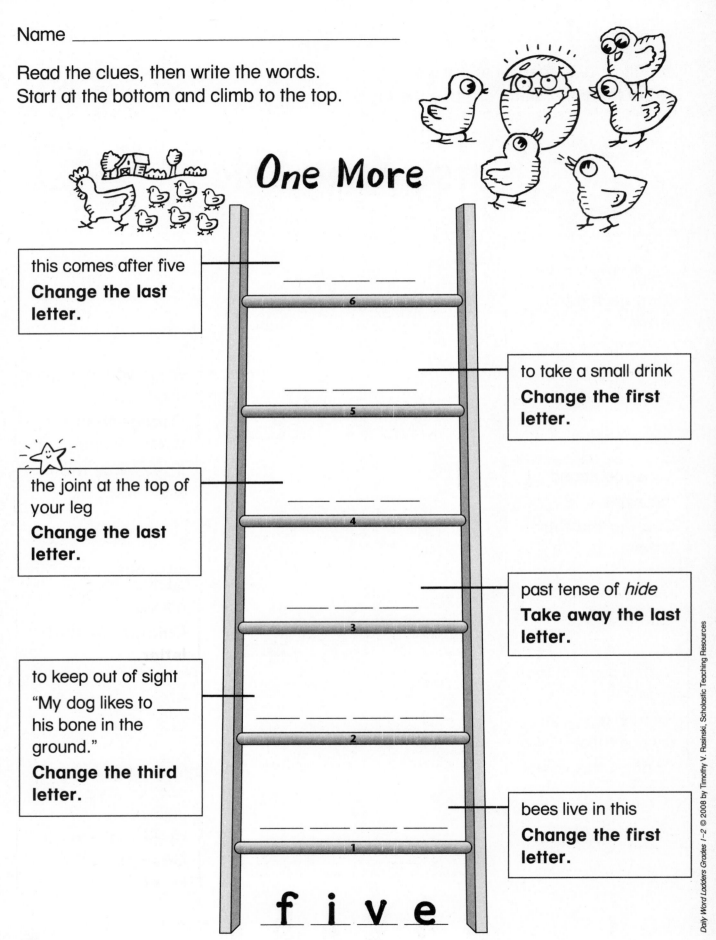

this comes after five
Change the last letter.

to take a small drink
Change the first letter.

the joint at the top of your leg
Change the last letter.

past tense of *hide*
Take away the last letter.

to keep out of sight
"My dog likes to ___ his bone in the ground."
Change the third letter.

bees live in this
Change the first letter.

6

5

4

3

2

1

f i v e

Daily Word Ladders Grades 1–2 © 2008 by Timothy V. Rasinski, Scholastic Teaching Resources

Name _____

Read the clues, then write the words.
Start at the bottom and climb to the top.

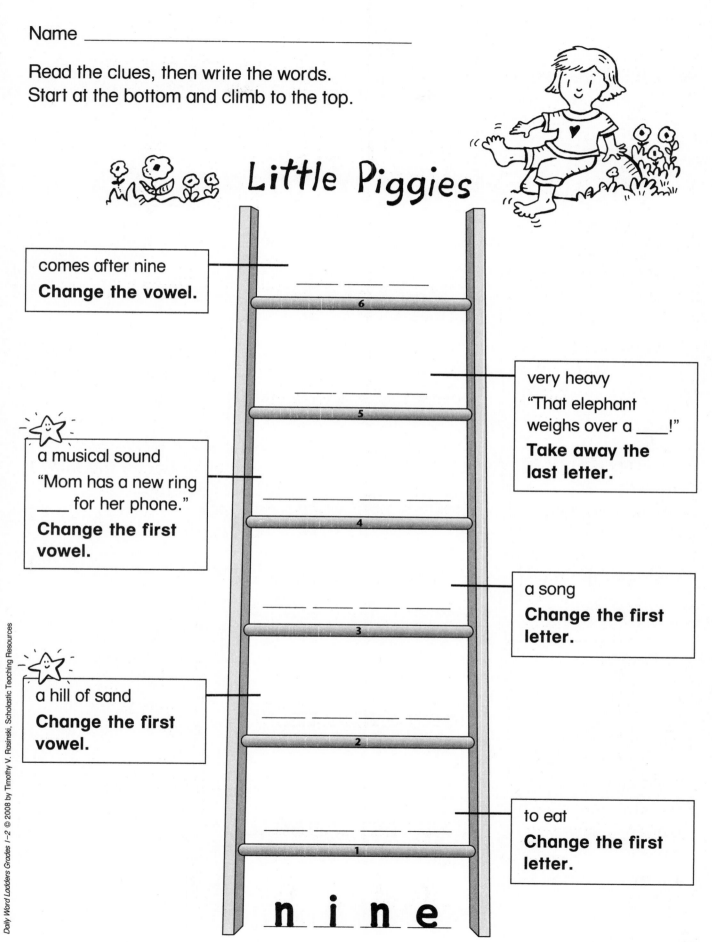

Little Piggies

comes after nine
Change the vowel. → 6 _ _ _ _ _

very heavy
"That elephant weighs over a ____!"
Take away the last letter. → 5 _ _ _ _ _

a musical sound
"Mom has a new ring ____ for her phone."
Change the first vowel. → 4 _ _ _ _ _

a song
Change the first letter. → 3 _ _ _ _

a hill of sand
Change the first vowel. → 2 _ _ _ _

to eat
Change the first letter. → 1 _ _ _ _

n i n e

Name _____

Read the clues, then write the words.
Start at the bottom and climb to the top.

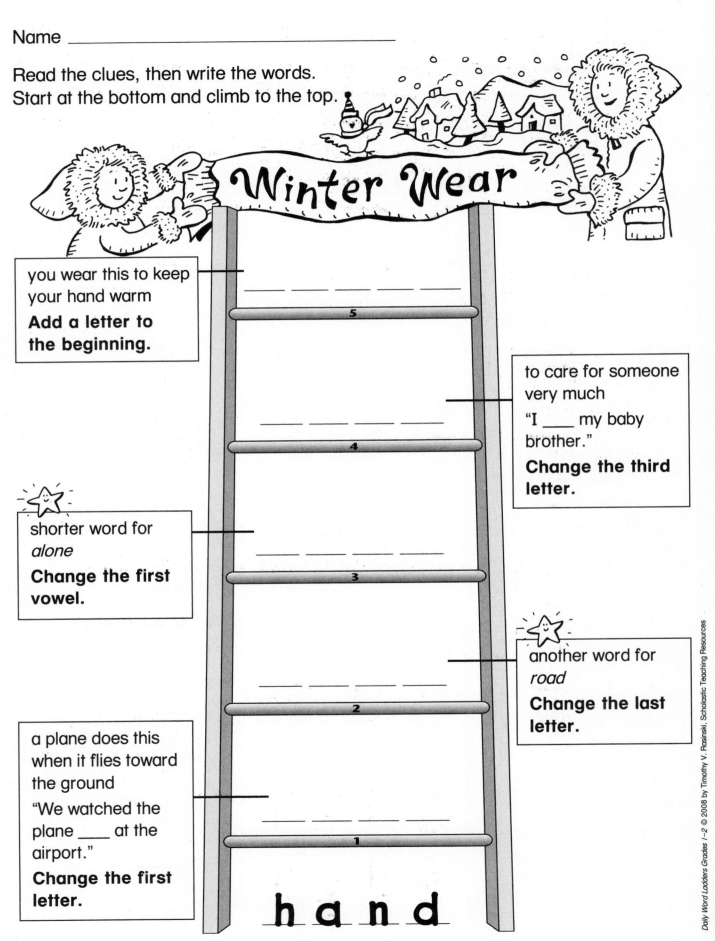

Winter Wear

you wear this to keep
your hand warm
**Add a letter to
the beginning.**

to care for someone
very much
"I ____ my baby
brother."
**Change the third
letter.**

shorter word for
alone
**Change the first
vowel.**

5

4

3

another word for
road
**Change the last
letter.**

a plane does this
when it flies toward
the ground
"We watched the
plane ____ at the
airport."
**Change the first
letter.**

2

1

h a n d

Daily Word Ladders Grades 1–2 © 2008 by Timothy V. Rasinski, Scholastic Teaching Resources

Name _____

Read the clues, then write the words.
Start at the bottom and climb to the top.

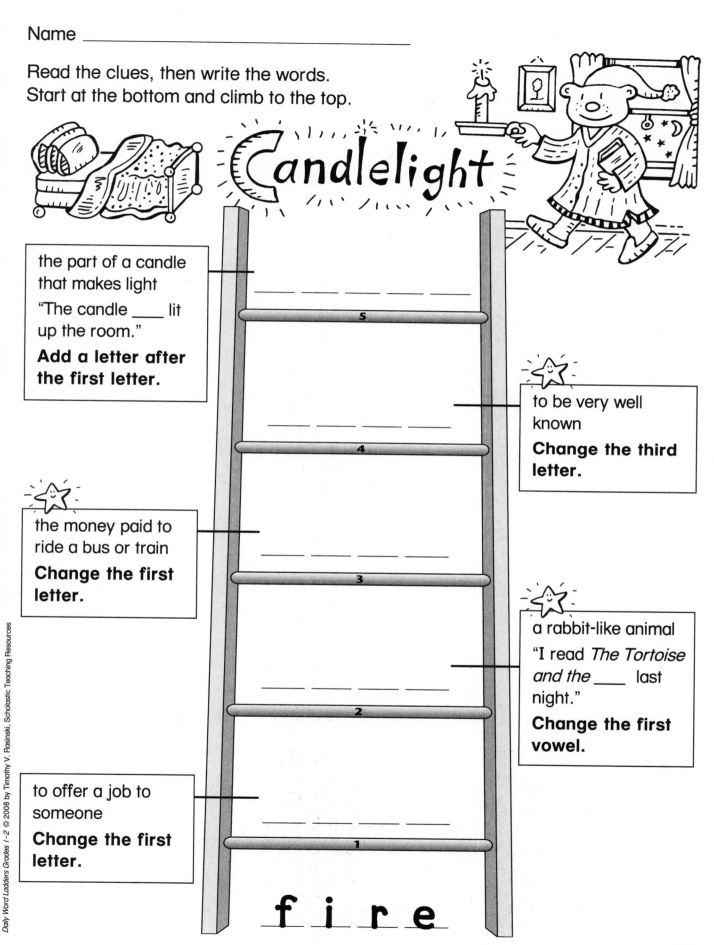

Candlelight

the part of a candle that makes light

"The candle ____ lit up the room."

Add a letter after the first letter.

to be very well known

Change the third letter.

the money paid to ride a bus or train

Change the first letter.

a rabbit-like animal

"I read *The Tortoise and the* ____ last night."

Change the first vowel.

to offer a job to someone

Change the first letter.

5

4

3

2

1

f i r e

Name _____

Read the clues, then write the words.
Start at the bottom and climb to the top.

Eyeglass Holders

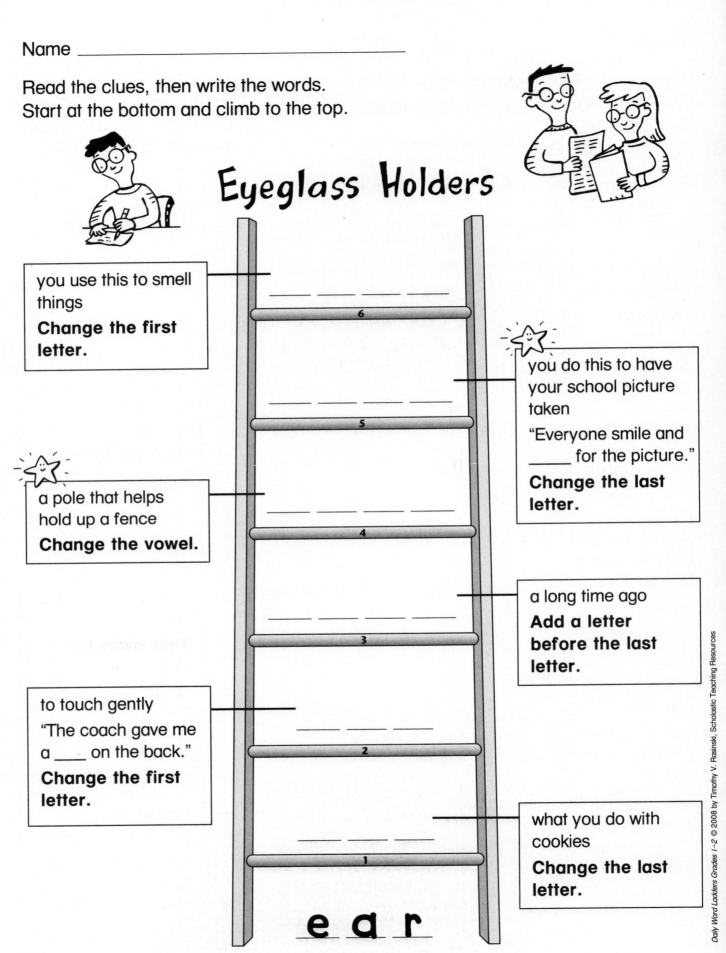

you use this to smell things
Change the first letter.

you do this to have your school picture taken
"Everyone smile and _____ for the picture."
Change the last letter.

a pole that helps hold up a fence
Change the vowel.

a long time ago
Add a letter before the last letter.

to touch gently
"The coach gave me a ___ on the back."
Change the first letter.

what you do with cookies
Change the last letter.

6

5

4

3

2

1

e a r

Daily Word Ladders Grades 1–2 © 2008 by Timothy V. Rasinski, Scholastic Teaching Resources

Name _____

Read the clues, then write the words.
Start at the bottom and climb to the top.

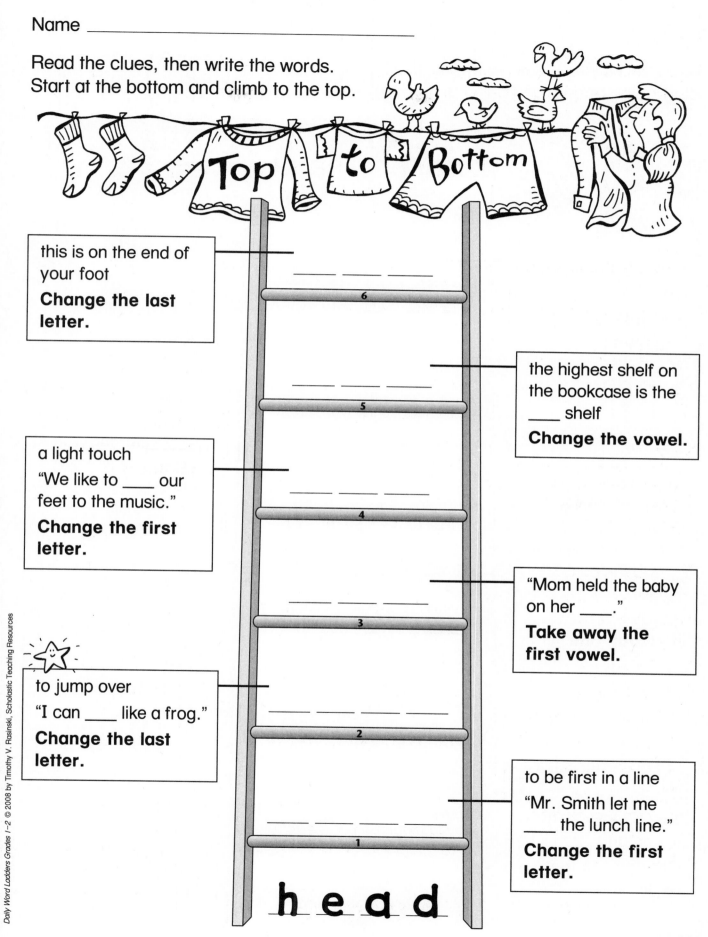

Top to Bottom

this is on the end of your foot
Change the last letter.

the highest shelf on the bookcase is the ___ shelf
Change the vowel.

a light touch
"We like to ___ our feet to the music."
Change the first letter.

"Mom held the baby on her ___."
Take away the first vowel.

to jump over
"I can ___ like a frog."
Change the last letter.

to be first in a line
"Mr. Smith let me ___ the lunch line."
Change the first letter.

6

5

4

3

2

1

h e a d

Name _____

Read the clues, then write the words.
Start at the bottom and climb to the top.

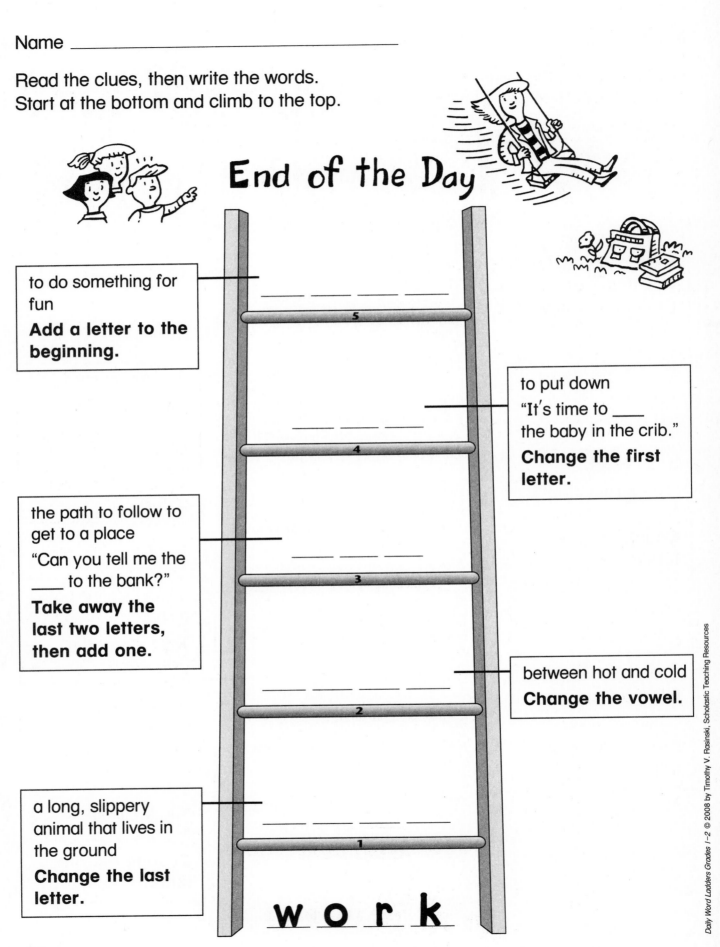

End of the Day

to do something for fun
Add a letter to the beginning.

_____ _____ _____ _____

5

to put down
"It's time to ____ the baby in the crib."
Change the first letter.

_____ _____ _____

4

the path to follow to get to a place
"Can you tell me the ____ to the bank?"
Take away the last two letters, then add one.

_____ _____ _____

3

between hot and cold
Change the vowel.

_____ _____ _____ _____

2

a long, slippery animal that lives in the ground
Change the last letter.

_____ _____ _____ _____

1

w o r k

Daily Word Ladders Grades 1–2 © 2008 by Timothy V. Rasinski, Scholastic Teaching Resources

Name _____

Read the clues, then write the words.
Start at the bottom and climb to the top.

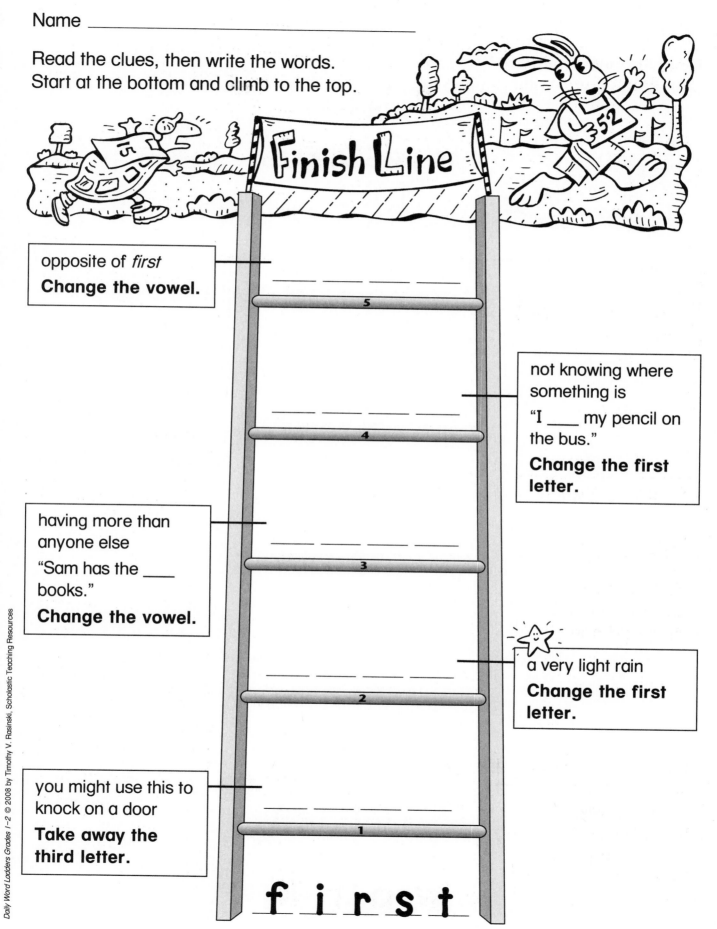

Finish Line

opposite of *first*
Change the vowel.

5 _ _ _ _ _

not knowing where something is
"I ____ my pencil on the bus."
Change the first letter.

4 _ _ _ _ _

having more than anyone else
"Sam has the ____ books."
Change the vowel.

3 _ _ _ _ _

a very light rain
Change the first letter.

2 _ _ _ _ _

you might use this to knock on a door
Take away the third letter.

1 _ _ _ _ _

f i r s t

Daily Word Ladders Grades 1–2 © 2008 by Timothy V. Rasinski, Scholastic Teaching Resources

Name _____

Read the clues, then write the words.
Start at the bottom and climb to the top.

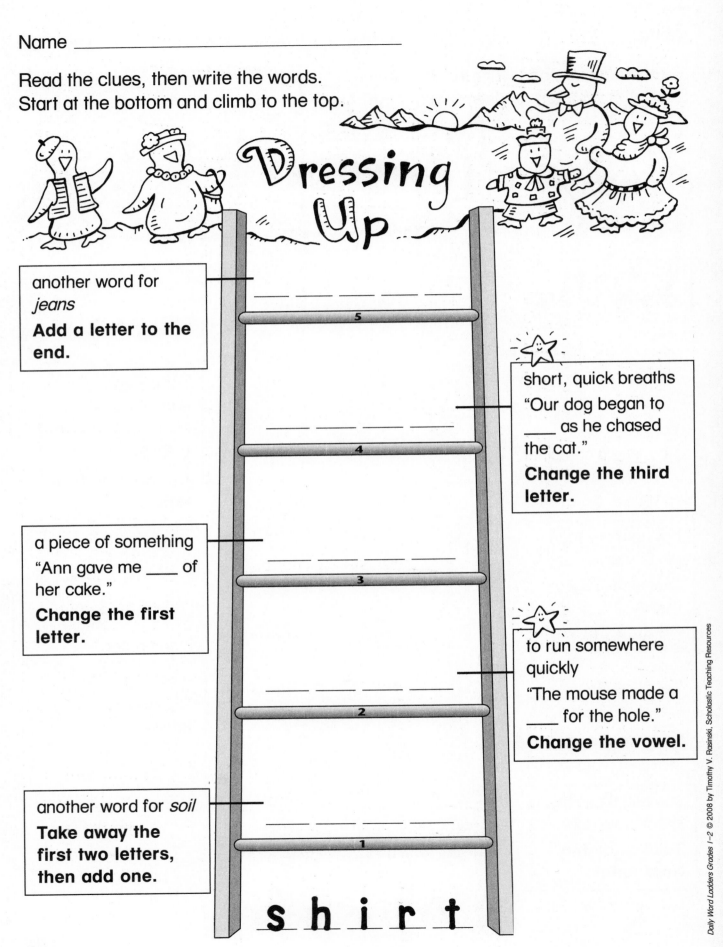

Dressing Up

another word for *jeans*
Add a letter to the end.

short, quick breaths
"Our dog began to ___ as he chased the cat."
Change the third letter.

a piece of something
"Ann gave me ___ of her cake."
Change the first letter.

to run somewhere quickly
"The mouse made a ___ for the hole."
Change the vowel.

another word for *soil*
Take away the first two letters, then add one.

5

4

3

2

1

s h i r t

Daily Word Ladders Grades 1–2 © 2008 by Timothy V. Rasinski, Scholastic Teaching Resources

Name _____

Read the clues, then write the words.
Start at the bottom and climb to the top.

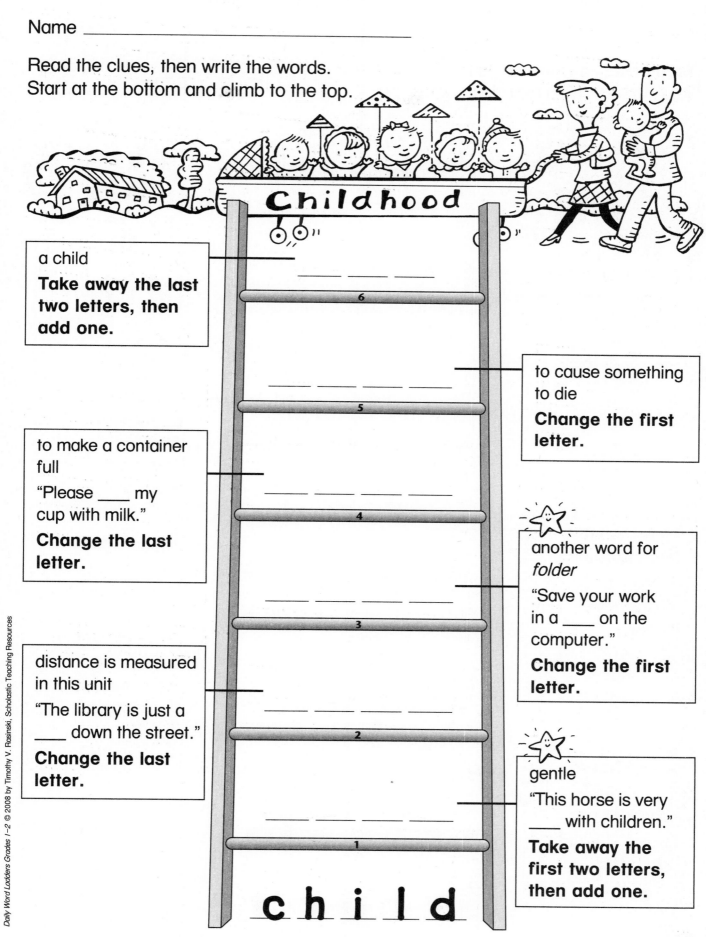

Childhood

a child
Take away the last two letters, then add one.

_ _ _ _ _ _
6

to cause something to die
Change the first letter.

_ _ _ _ _
5

to make a container full
"Please ____ my cup with milk."
Change the last letter.

_ _ _ _
4

another word for *folder*
"Save your work in a ____ on the computer."
Change the first letter.

_ _ _ _ _
3

distance is measured in this unit
"The library is just a ____ down the street."
Change the last letter.

_ _ _ _
2

gentle
"This horse is very ____ with children."
Take away the first two letters, then add one.

_ _ _ _ _
1

c h i l d

Daily Word Ladders Grades 1–2 © 2008 by Timothy V. Rasinski, Scholastic Teaching Resources

Name _____

Read the clues, then write the words.
Start at the bottom and climb to the top.

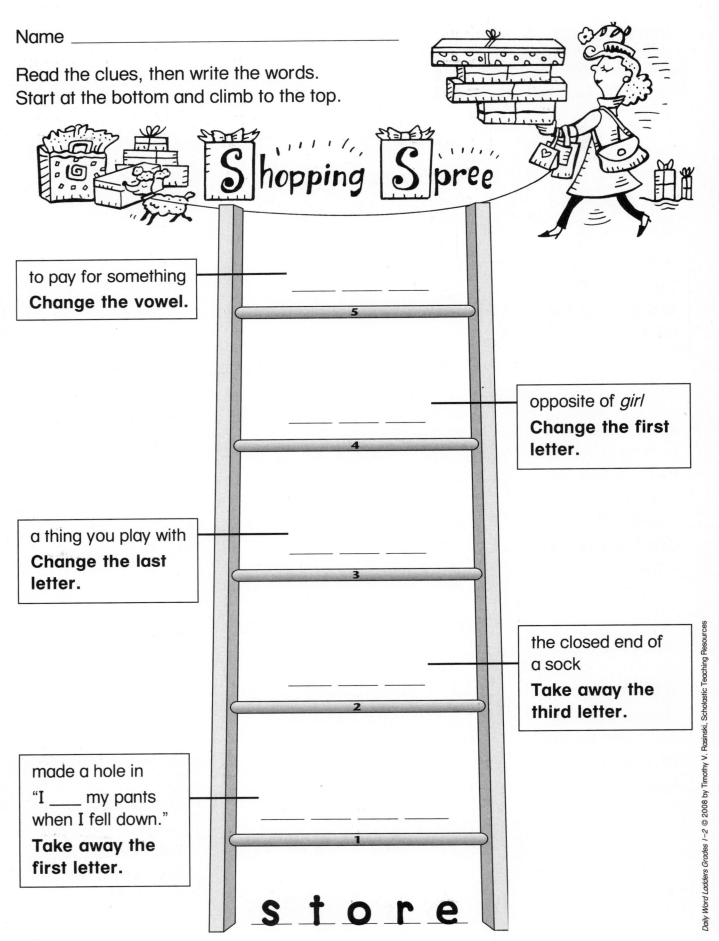

Shopping Spree

to pay for something
Change the vowel.

_ _ _ _ _   5

opposite of *girl*
Change the first letter.

_ _ _ _ _   4

a thing you play with
Change the last letter.

_ _ _ _   3

the closed end of a sock
Take away the third letter.

_ _ _   2

made a hole in
"I ____ my pants when I fell down."
Take away the first letter.

_ _ _ _ _   1

s t o r e

Daily Word Ladders Grades 1–2 © 2008 by Timothy V. Rasinski, Scholastic Teaching Resources

Name _____

Read the clues, then write the words.
Start at the bottom and climb to the top.

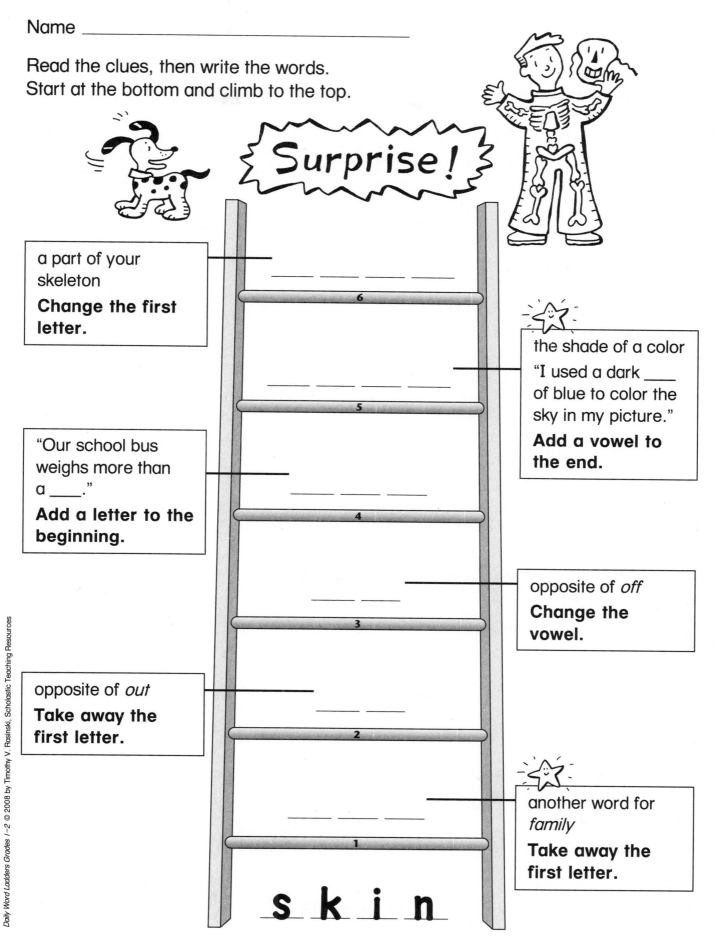

Surprise!

a part of your skeleton
Change the first letter.

— 6 — _ _ _ _

— 5 — _ _ _ _ _

the shade of a color
"I used a dark ____ of blue to color the sky in my picture."
Add a vowel to the end.

"Our school bus weighs more than a ____."
Add a letter to the beginning.

— 4 — _ _ _ _ _

— 3 — _ _ _ _

opposite of *off*
Change the vowel.

opposite of *out*
Take away the first letter.

— 2 — _ _ _

another word for *family*
Take away the first letter.

— 1 — _ _ _ _ _

s k i n

Daily Word Ladders Grades 1–2 © 2008 by Timothy V. Rasinski, Scholastic Teaching Resources

Name _____

Read the clues, then write the words.
Start at the bottom and climb to the top.

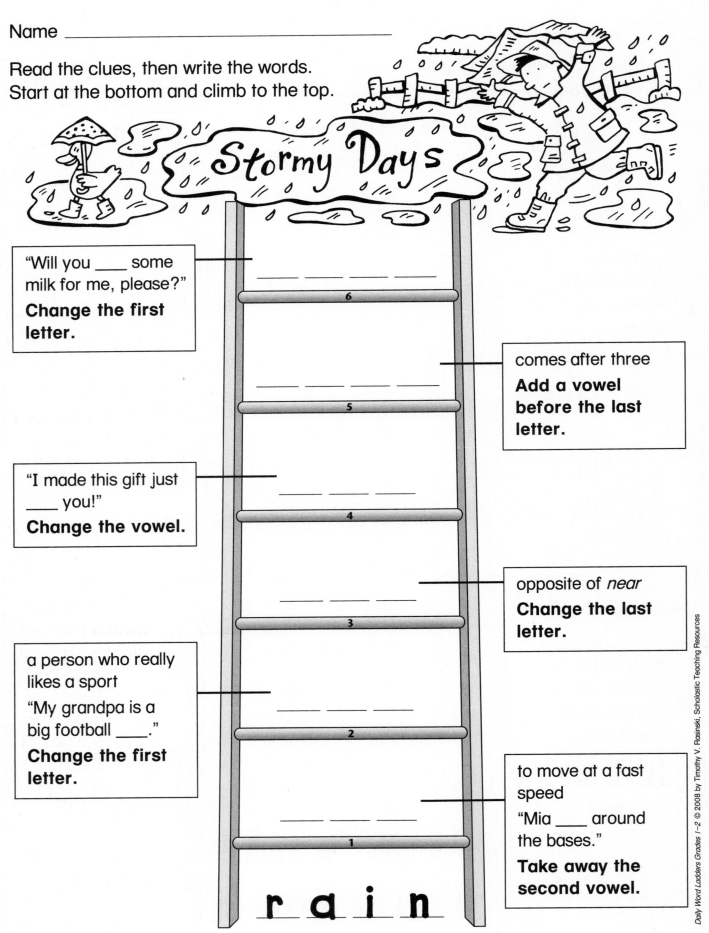

Stormy Days

"Will you ____ some milk for me, please?"
Change the first letter.

6 _____

comes after three
Add a vowel before the last letter.

5 _____

"I made this gift just ____ you!"
Change the vowel.

4 _____

opposite of *near*
Change the last letter.

3 _____

a person who really likes a sport
"My grandpa is a big football ____."
Change the first letter.

2 _____

to move at a fast speed
"Mia ____ around the bases."
Take away the second vowel.

1 _____

r a i n

Daily Word Ladders Grades 1–2 © 2008 by Timothy V. Rasinski, Scholastic Teaching Resources

Name _____

Read the clues, then write the words.
Start at the bottom and climb to the top.

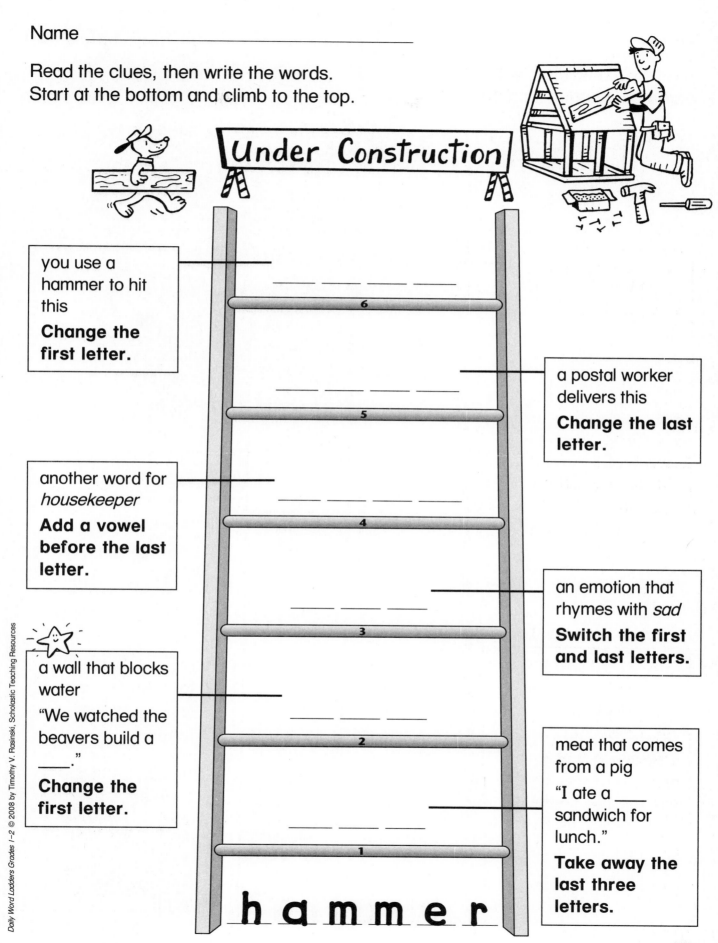

Under Construction

you use a hammer to hit this
Change the first letter.

_ _ _ _ _ _   6

a postal worker delivers this
Change the last letter.

_ _ _ _ _   5

another word for *housekeeper*
Add a vowel before the last letter.

_ _ _ _   4

an emotion that rhymes with *sad*
Switch the first and last letters.

_ _ _   3

a wall that blocks water
"We watched the beavers build a _____."
Change the first letter.

_ _ _   2

meat that comes from a pig
"I ate a ____ sandwich for lunch."
Take away the last three letters.

_ _ _   1

h a m m e r

Daily Word Ladders Grades 1–2 © 2008 by Timothy V. Rasinski, Scholastic Teaching Resources

Name _____

Read the clues, then write the words.
Start at the bottom and climb to the top.

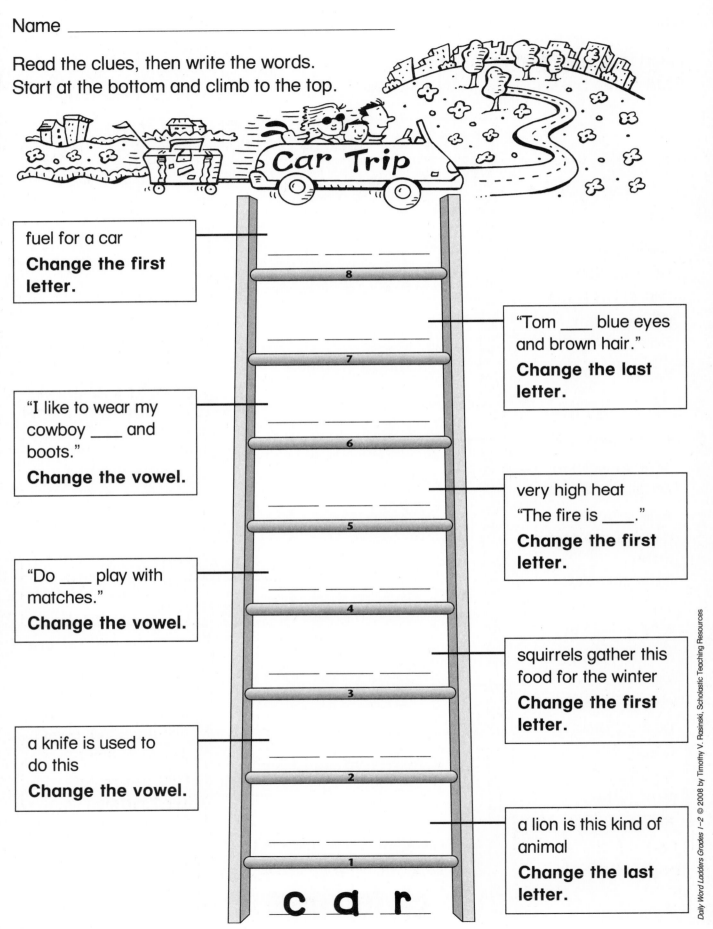

fuel for a car
Change the first letter.

"Tom ____ blue eyes and brown hair."
Change the last letter.

"I like to wear my cowboy ____ and boots."
Change the vowel.

very high heat
"The fire is ____."
Change the first letter.

"Do ____ play with matches."
Change the vowel.

squirrels gather this food for the winter
Change the first letter.

a knife is used to do this
Change the vowel.

a lion is this kind of animal
Change the last letter.

c a r

Name _____

Read the clues, then write the words.
Start at the bottom and climb to the top.

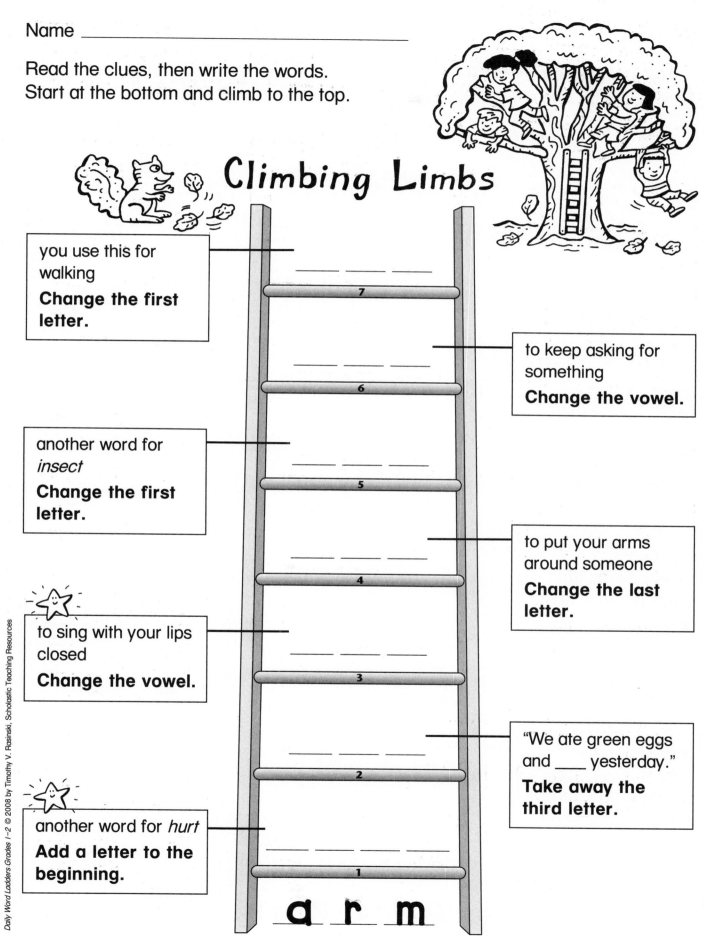

Climbing Limbs

you use this for walking
Change the first letter.

7 _____ _____ _____

to keep asking for something
Change the vowel.

6 _____ _____ _____

another word for *insect*
Change the first letter.

5 _____ _____ _____

to put your arms around someone
Change the last letter.

4 _____ _____ _____

to sing with your lips closed
Change the vowel.

3 _____ _____ _____

"We ate green eggs and ____ yesterday."
Take away the third letter.

2 _____ _____ _____

another word for *hurt*
Add a letter to the beginning.

1 _____ _____ _____

a   r   m

Daily Word Ladders Grades 1–2 © 2008 by Timothy V. Rasinski, Scholastic Teaching Resources

Name _____

Read the clues, then write the words.
Start at the bottom and climb to the top.

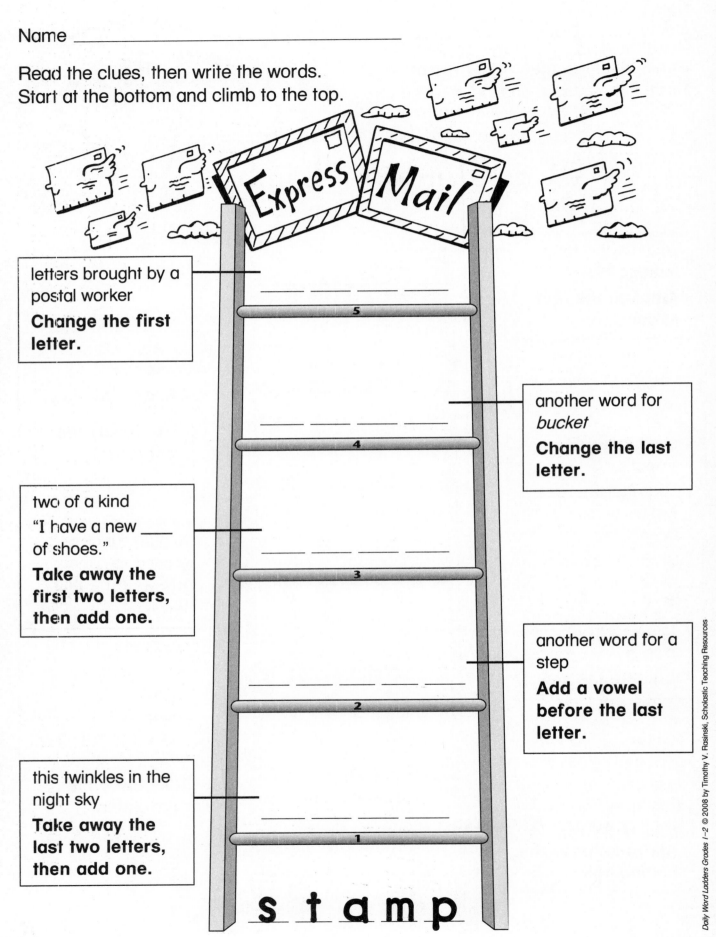

letters brought by a postal worker
Change the first letter.

another word for *bucket*
Change the last letter.

two of a kind
"I have a new ____ of shoes."
Take away the first two letters, then add one.

another word for a step
Add a vowel before the last letter.

this twinkles in the night sky
Take away the last two letters, then add one.

5

4

3

2

1

s t a m p

Name _____

Read the clues, then write the words.
Start at the bottom and climb to the top.

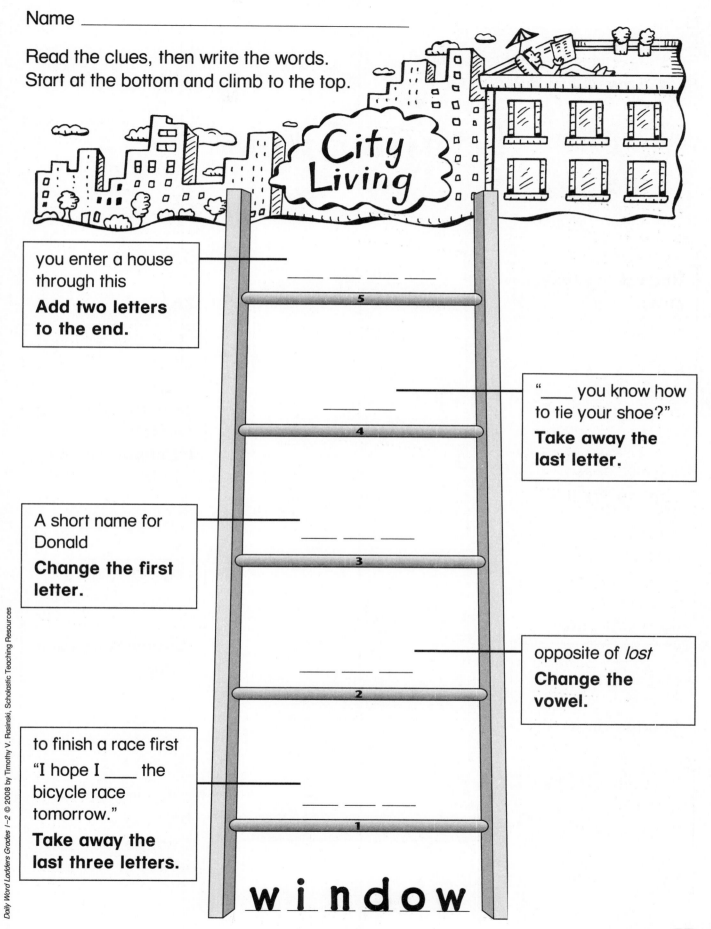

City Living

you enter a house through this
Add two letters to the end.

_ _ _ _ _ 5

" ____ you know how to tie your shoe?"
Take away the last letter.

_ _ _ 4

A short name for Donald
Change the first letter.

_ _ _ _ 3

opposite of *lost*
Change the vowel.

_ _ _ 2

to finish a race first
"I hope I ____ the bicycle race tomorrow."
Take away the last three letters.

_ _ _ _ 1

w i n d o w

Name _____

Read the clues, then write the words.
Start at the bottom and climb to the top.

Let's Go Fishing

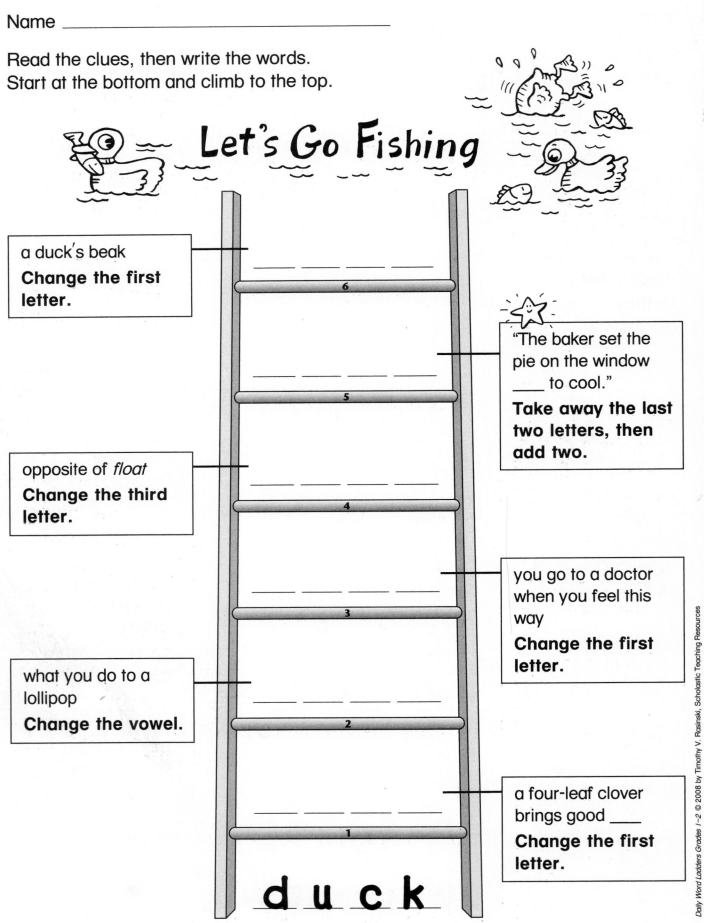

a duck's beak
Change the first letter.

"The baker set the pie on the window ____ to cool."
Take away the last two letters, then add two.

opposite of *float*
Change the third letter.

you go to a doctor when you feel this way
Change the first letter.

what you do to a lollipop
Change the vowel.

a four-leaf clover brings good ____
Change the first letter.

6

5

4

3

2

1

d u c k

Daily Word Ladders Grades 1–2 © 2008 by Timothy V. Rasinski, Scholastic Teaching Resources

Name _____

Read the clues, then write the words.
Start at the bottom and climb to the top.

Blastoff!

opposite of *now*
Add a letter to the end.

6

opposite of *early*
Change the first letter.

5

to dislike something a lot
"I ____ to swim in a cold pool."
Add a vowel to the end.

4

"I wore a sun ____ on my head at the beach."
Change the vowel.

3

the weather gets this way in the summer
Change the first letter.

2

"A penguin does ____ fly."
Change the last letter.

1

n o w

Daily Word Ladders Grades 1–2 © 2008 by Timothy V. Rasinski, Scholastic Teaching Resources

Name _____

Read the clues, then write the words.
Start at the bottom and climb to the top.

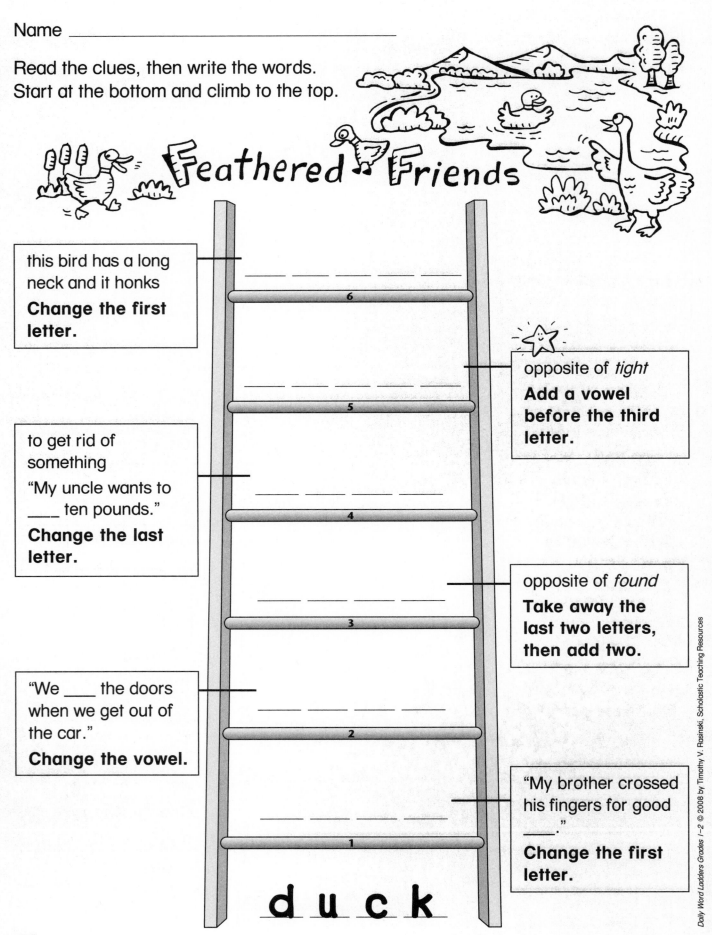

Feathered Friends

this bird has a long neck and it honks
Change the first letter.

opposite of *tight*
Add a vowel before the third letter.

to get rid of something
"My uncle wants to ___ ten pounds."
Change the last letter.

opposite of *found*
Take away the last two letters, then add two.

"We ___ the doors when we get out of the car."
Change the vowel.

"My brother crossed his fingers for good ___."
Change the first letter.

d u c k

6
5
4
3
2
1

Daily Word Ladders Grades 1–2 © 2008 by Timothy V. Rasinski, Scholastic Teaching Resources

Name _____

Read the clues, then write the words.
Start at the bottom and climb to the top.

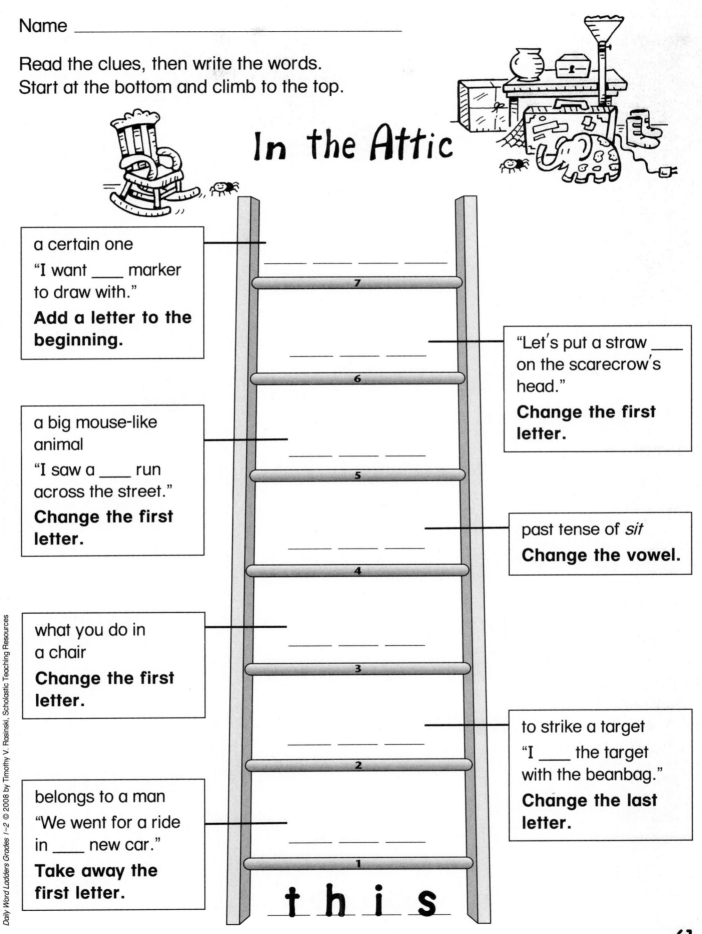

In the Attic

a certain one

"I want ____ marker to draw with."

Add a letter to the beginning.

_ _ _ _

7

"Let's put a straw ____ on the scarecrow's head."

Change the first letter.

_ _ _ _

6

a big mouse-like animal

"I saw a ____ run across the street."

Change the first letter.

_ _ _

5

past tense of *sit*
Change the vowel.

_ _ _

4

what you do in a chair

Change the first letter.

_ _ _

3

to strike a target

"I ____ the target with the beanbag."

Change the last letter.

_ _ _

2

belongs to a man

"We went for a ride in ____ new car."

Take away the first letter.

_ _ _

1

t h i s

Name _____

Read the clues, then write the words.
Start at the bottom and climb to the top.

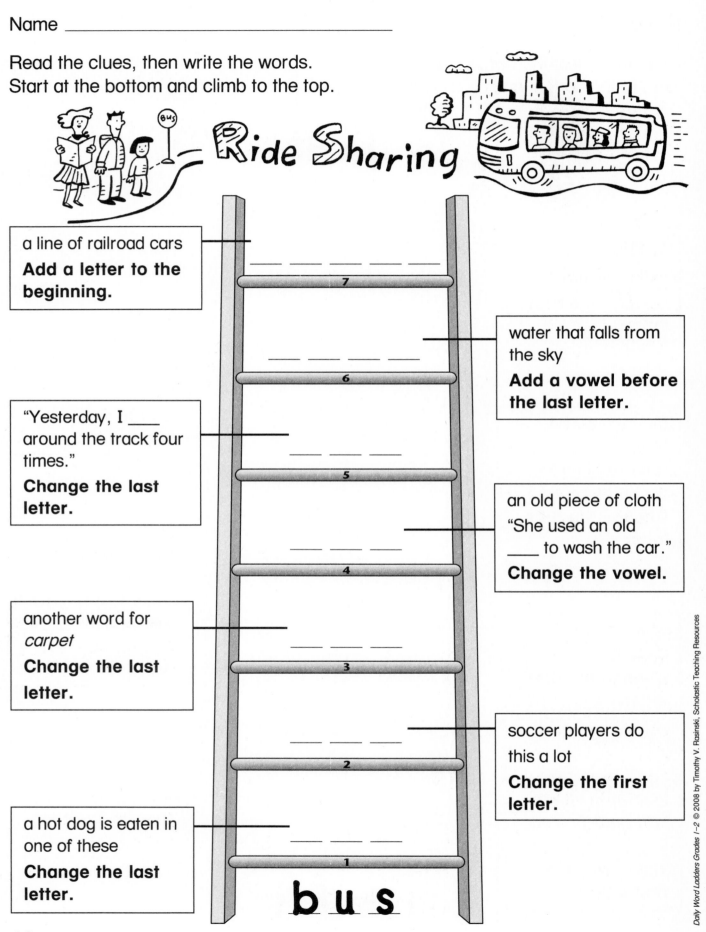

Ride Sharing

a line of railroad cars
Add a letter to the beginning.

water that falls from the sky
Add a vowel before the last letter.

"Yesterday, I ____ around the track four times."
Change the last letter.

an old piece of cloth
"She used an old ____ to wash the car."
Change the vowel.

another word for *carpet*
Change the last letter.

soccer players do this a lot
Change the first letter.

a hot dog is eaten in one of these
Change the last letter.

7

6

5

4

3

2

1

b u s

Daily Word Ladders Grades 1–2 © 2008 by Timothy V. Rasinski, Scholastic Teaching Resources

Name _____

Read the clues, then write the words.
Start at the bottom and climb to the top.

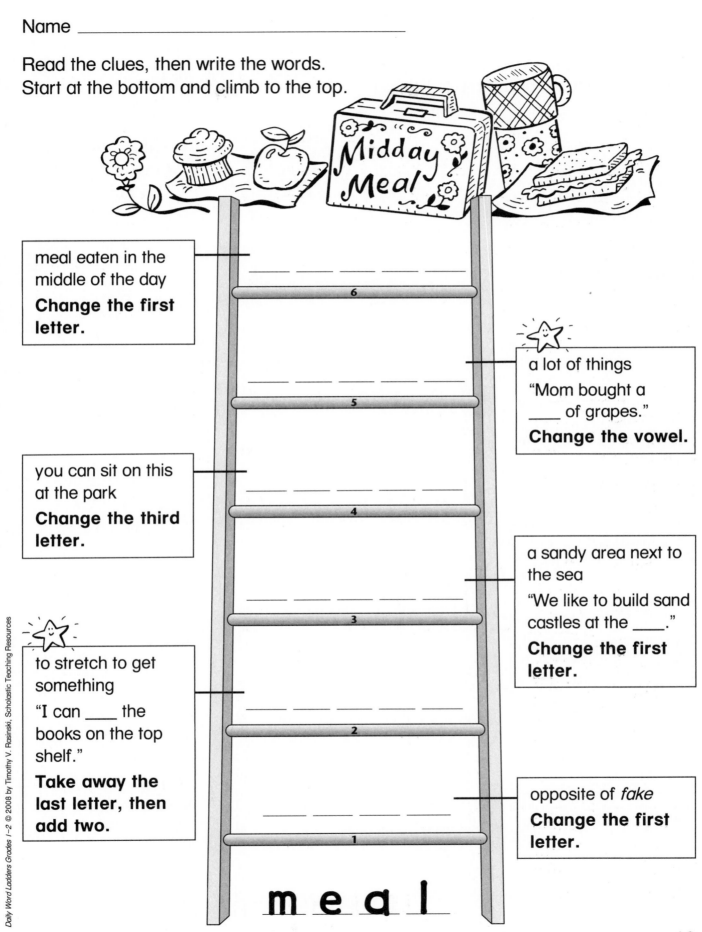

meal eaten in the middle of the day
Change the first letter.

a lot of things
"Mom bought a ___ of grapes."
Change the vowel.

you can sit on this at the park
Change the third letter.

a sandy area next to the sea
"We like to build sand castles at the ___."
Change the first letter.

to stretch to get something
"I can ___ the books on the top shelf."
Take away the last letter, then add two.

opposite of *fake*
Change the first letter.

6

5

4

3

2

1

m e a l

Name _____

Read the clues, then write the words.
Start at the bottom and climb to the top.

Different Tastes

when you really dislike something, you ____ it
Add a vowel to the end.

6 _ _ _ _

you wear this on your head at a birthday party
Change the vowel.

5 _ _ _ _

a pot of boiling water is very ____
Take away the third letter.

4 _ _ _ _

a person who gives a party
Change the first letter.

3 _ _ _ _ _

when you don't know where you are
"We got ____ in the woods."
Change the last letter.

2 _ _ _ _

opposite of *win*
Change the third letter.

1 _ _ _ _

l o v e

Daily Word Ladders Grades 1–2 © 2008 by Timothy V. Rasinski, Scholastic Teaching Resources

Name _____

Read the clues, then write the words.
Start at the bottom and climb to the top.

The Whole Story

opposite of *start*
Change the vowel.

_ _ _ _ _   6

"We learn how to read ___ write at school."
Change the last letter.

_ _ _ _ _   5

you might see this insect at a picnic
Take away the first letter.

_ _ _ _ _   4

how a dog breathes when it gets hot
Change the third letter.

_ _ _ _ _   3

a long time ago
"In the ___, people did not have phones."
Change the third letter.

_ _ _ _ _   2

a role in a play
"Joe played the ___ of the king in our class play."
Take away the first two letters, then add one.

_ _ _ _ _   1

s t a r t

Name _____

Read the clues, then write the words.
Start at the bottom and climb to the top.

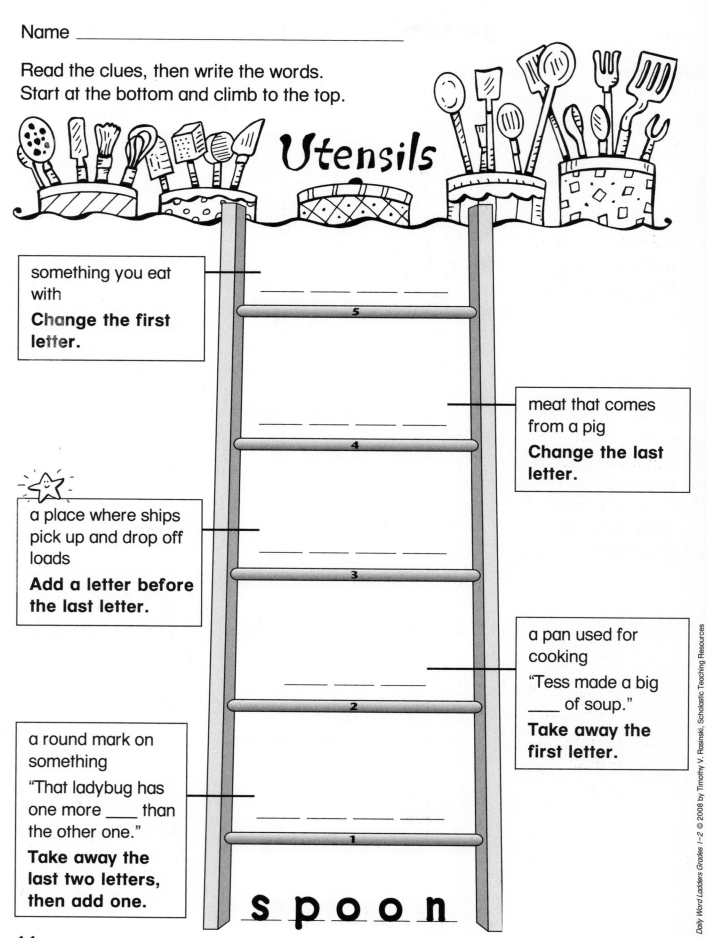

Utensils

something you eat with
Change the first letter.

_ _ _ _ _ (5)

meat that comes from a pig
Change the last letter.

_ _ _ _ (4)

a place where ships pick up and drop off loads
Add a letter before the last letter.

_ _ _ _ (3)

a pan used for cooking
"Tess made a big ___ of soup."
Take away the first letter.

_ _ _ (2)

a round mark on something
"That ladybug has one more ___ than the other one."
Take away the last two letters, then add one.

_ _ _ _ (1)

s p o o n

66

Daily Word Ladders Grades 1–2 © 2008 by Timothy V. Rasinski, Scholastic Teaching Resources

Name _____

Read the clues, then write the words.
Start at the bottom and climb to the top.

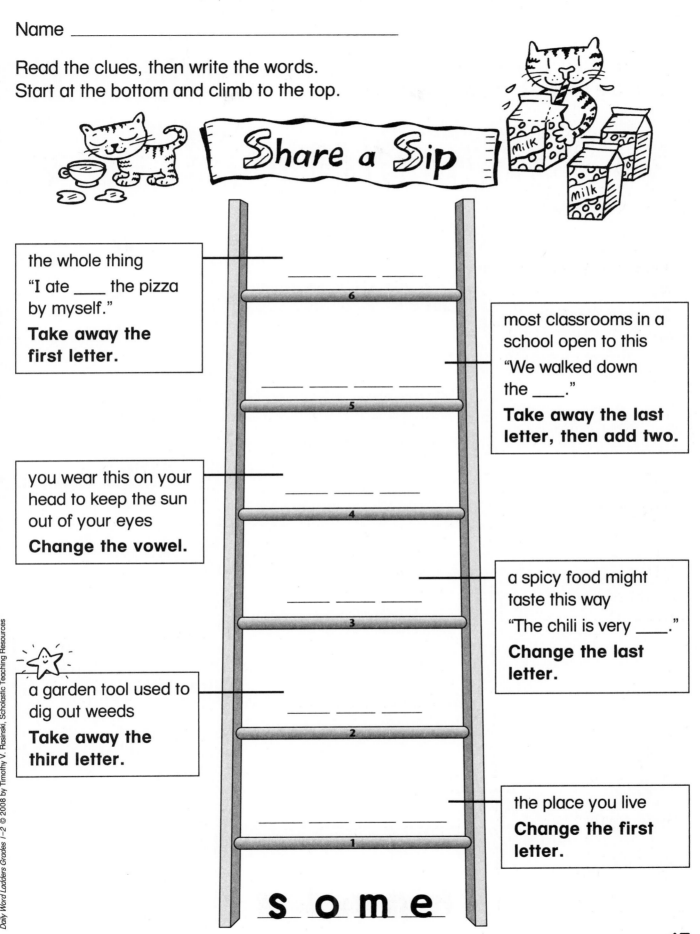

Share a Sip

the whole thing

"I ate ____ the pizza by myself."

Take away the first letter.

most classrooms in a school open to this

"We walked down the ____."

Take away the last letter, then add two.

you wear this on your head to keep the sun out of your eyes

Change the vowel.

a spicy food might taste this way

"The chili is very ____."

Change the last letter.

a garden tool used to dig out weeds

Take away the third letter.

the place you live

Change the first letter.

6

5

4

3

2

1

s o m e

Daily Word Ladders Grades 1–2 © 2008 by Timothy V. Rasinski, Scholastic Teaching Resources

Name _____

Read the clues, then write the words.
Start at the bottom and climb to the top.

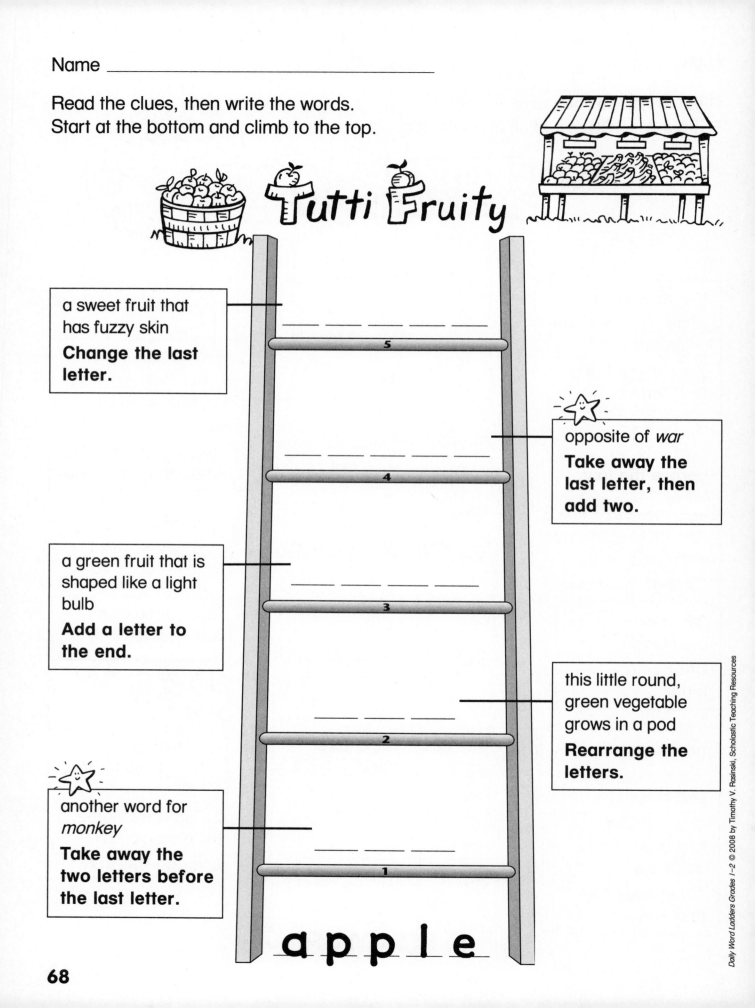

Tutti Fruity

a sweet fruit that has fuzzy skin
Change the last letter.

_ _ _ _ _   5

opposite of *war*
Take away the last letter, then add two.

_ _ _ _   4

a green fruit that is shaped like a light bulb
Add a letter to the end.

_ _ _ _   3

this little round, green vegetable grows in a pod
Rearrange the letters.

_ _ _   2

another word for *monkey*
Take away the two letters before the last letter.

_ _ _   1

a p p l e

Daily Word Ladders Grades 1–2 © 2008 by Timothy V. Rasinski, Scholastic Teaching Resources

Name _____

Read the clues, then write the words.
Start at the bottom and climb to the top.

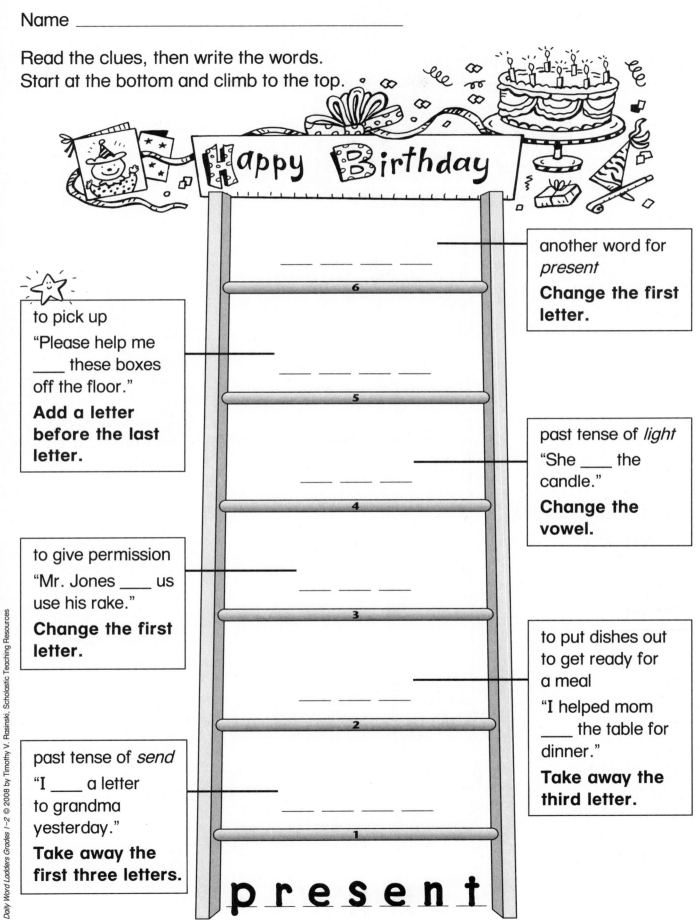

Happy Birthday

another word for *present*
Change the first letter.

to pick up
"Please help me ___ these boxes off the floor."
Add a letter before the last letter.

past tense of *light*
"She ___ the candle."
Change the vowel.

to give permission
"Mr. Jones ___ us use his rake."
Change the first letter.

to put dishes out to get ready for a meal
"I helped mom ___ the table for dinner."
Take away the third letter.

past tense of *send*
"I ___ a letter to grandma yesterday."
Take away the first three letters.

_ _ _ _ _   6

_ _ _ _   5

_ _ _   4

_ _ _   3

_ _ _ _   2

_ _ _ _   1

p r e s e n t

Name _____

Read the clues, then write the words.
Start at the bottom and climb to the top.

New and **Not-So-New**

opposite of *new*
Take away the first letter.

6 _ _ _ _

to carry
"Kay asked me to ___ her books."
Change the last letter.

5 _ _ _ _

you use a shovel to dig this in the ground
Add a letter before the last letter.

4 _ _ _ _

a tool used to dig weeds out of a garden
Change the last letter.

3 _ _ _

a word used to ask something
"___ much does that shirt cost?"
Change the first letter.

2 _ _ _

at this time
"Let's go eat lunch ___."
Change the vowel.

1 _ _ _ _

n e w

70

Daily Word Ladders Grades 1–2 © 2008 by Timothy V. Rasinski, Scholastic Teaching Resources

Name _____

Read the clues, then write the words.
Start at the bottom and climb to the top.

Growing Things

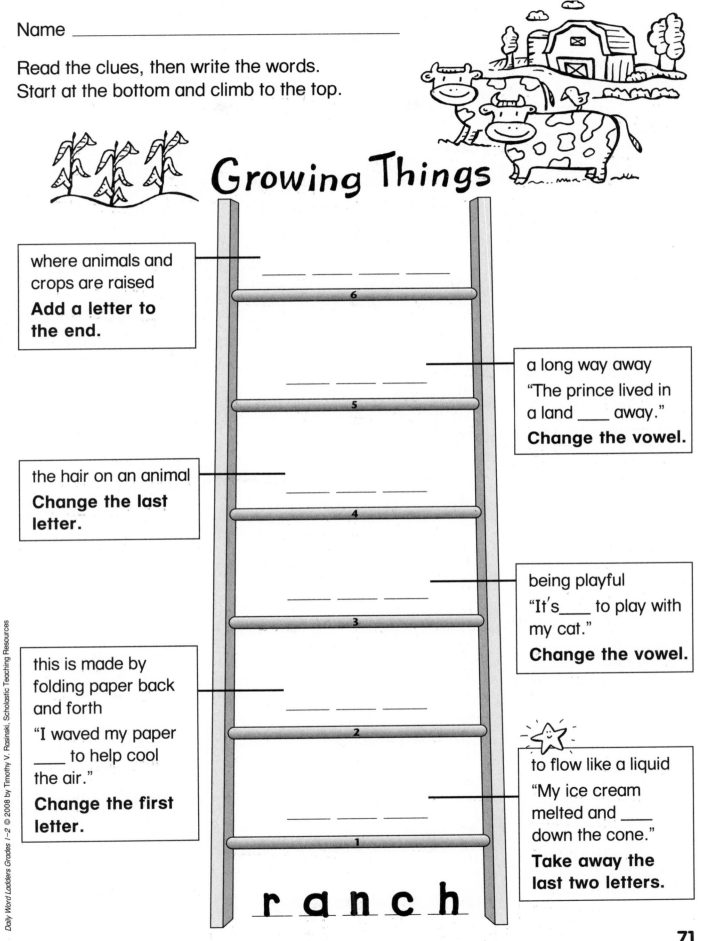

where animals and crops are raised
Add a letter to the end.

a long way away
"The prince lived in a land ____ away."
Change the vowel.

the hair on an animal
Change the last letter.

being playful
"It's ____ to play with my cat."
Change the vowel.

this is made by folding paper back and forth
"I waved my paper ____ to help cool the air."
Change the first letter.

to flow like a liquid
"My ice cream melted and ____ down the cone."
Take away the last two letters.

6

5

4

3

2

1

r a n c h

Name _____

Read the clues, then write the words.
Start at the bottom and climb to the top.

Lesson Learned

a baby chicken
Change the vowel.

you do this to see if
your answer is correct
"Please ____ your
answers on the
answer key."
**Take away the first
letter, then add two.**

a wooden porch
"We sat outside on
the ____."
**Take away the
last letter, then
add two.**

where a fox lives
**Take away the last
letter.**

"When the car hit the
post, it left a ____
in the door."
**Change the first
letter.**

"My family sleeps in a
____ when we go
camping."
**Add a letter to the
end.**

7 + 3
**Change the first
letter.**

h e n

Daily Word Ladders Grades 1–2 © 2008 by Timothy V. Rasinski, Scholastic Teaching Resources

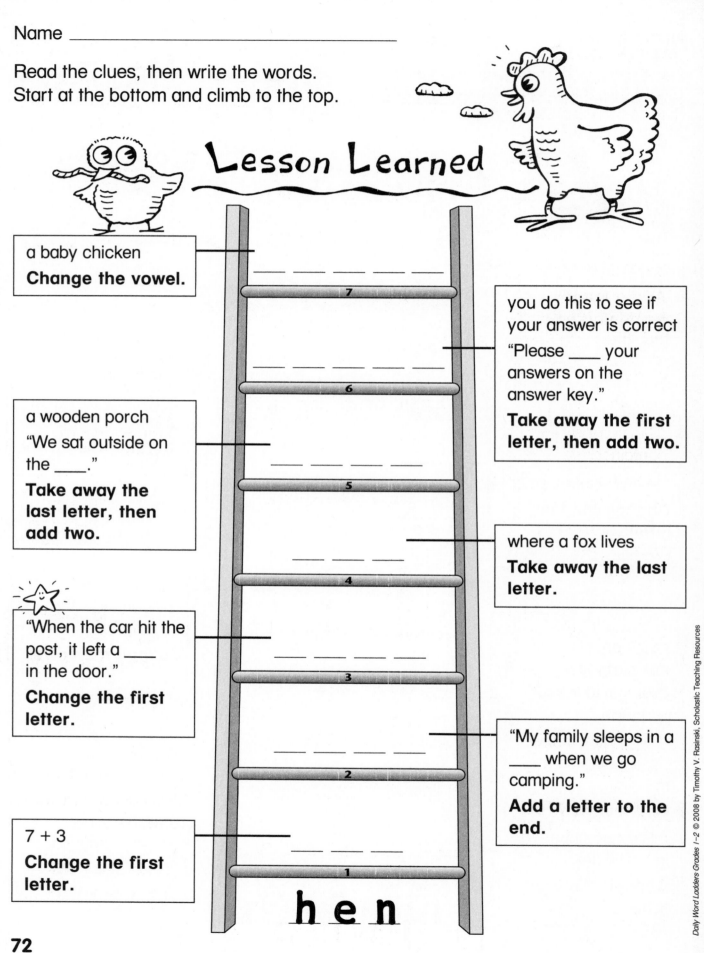

Name _____

Read the clues, then write the words.
Start at the bottom and climb to the top.

Simon Says

opposite of *sit*
Add a letter to the beginning and end.

7

"Her skin turned ___ after she sat in the sun."
Change the first letter.

6

a kind of food container
"Mom bought a ___ of beans at the store."
Change the last letter.

5

the lid of a toothpaste tube
"Please put the ___ back on the toothpaste."
Change the vowel.

4

many people drink coffee in this
Change the first letter.

3

a dog is called this after it's born
Take away the third letter.

2

this is used to put air in a bike tire
Change the first letter.

1

j u m p

Name _____

Read the clues, then write the words.
Start at the bottom and climb to the top.

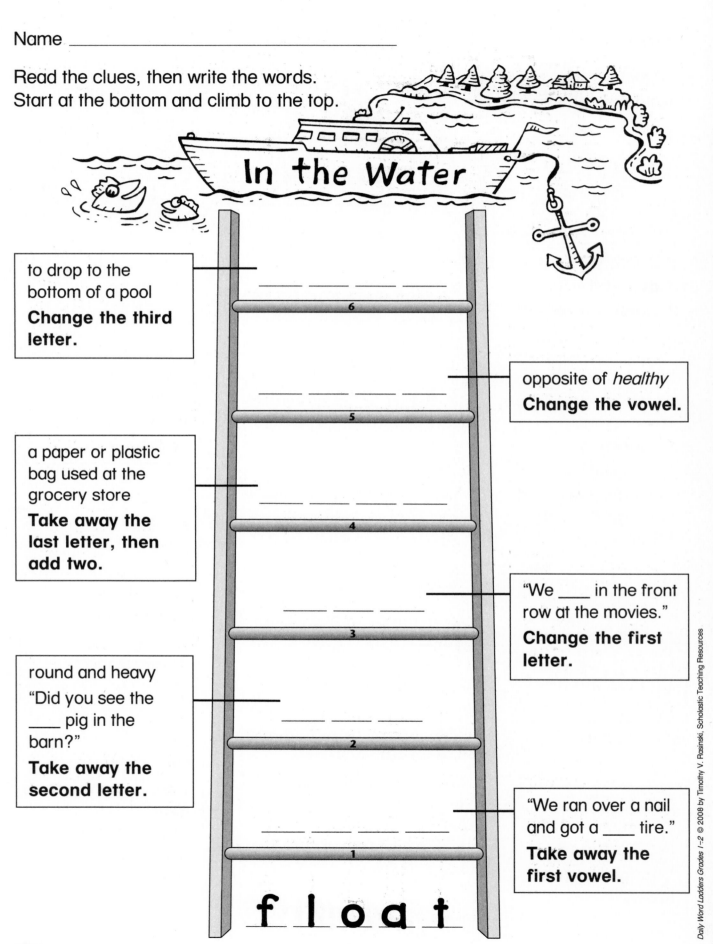

In the Water

to drop to the bottom of a pool
Change the third letter.

— — — — — 6

opposite of *healthy*
Change the vowel.

— — — — — 5

a paper or plastic bag used at the grocery store
Take away the last letter, then add two.

— — — — — 4

"We ___ in the front row at the movies."
Change the first letter.

— — — — — 3

round and heavy
"Did you see the ___ pig in the barn?"
Take away the second letter.

— — — 2

"We ran over a nail and got a ___ tire."
Take away the first vowel.

— — — — 1

f l o a t

Daily Word Ladders Grades 1–2 © 2008 by Timothy V. Rasinski, Scholastic Teaching Resources

Name _____

Read the clues, then write the words.
Start at the bottom and climb to the top.

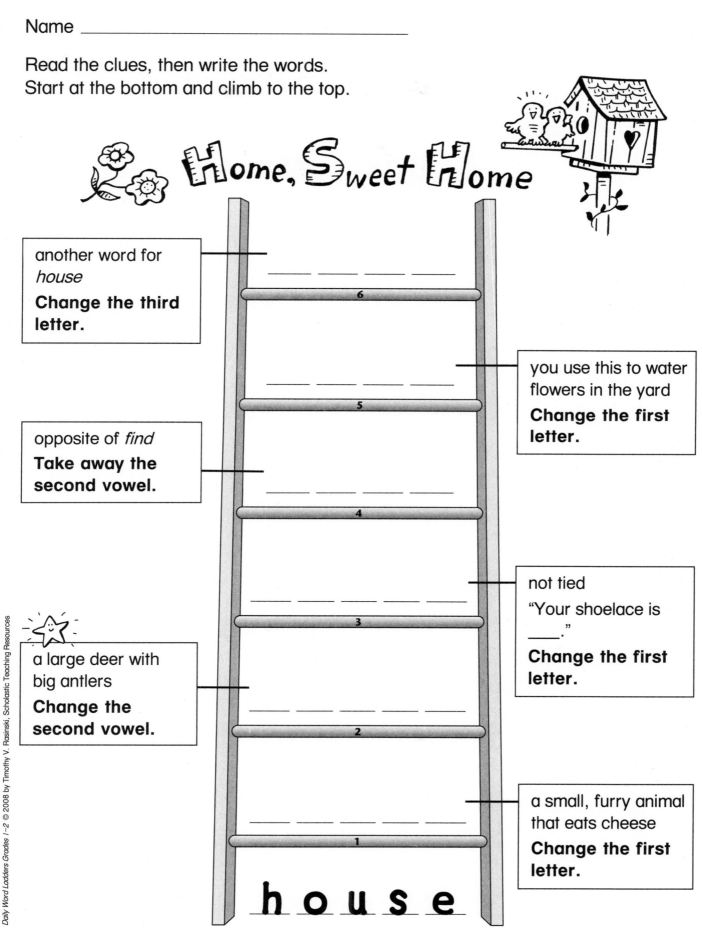

Home, Sweet Home

another word for *house*
Change the third letter.

you use this to water flowers in the yard
Change the first letter.

opposite of *find*
Take away the second vowel.

not tied
"Your shoelace is ___."
Change the first letter.

a large deer with big antlers
Change the second vowel.

a small, furry animal that eats cheese
Change the first letter.

h o u s e

Name _____

Read the clues, then write the words.
Start at the bottom and climb to the top.

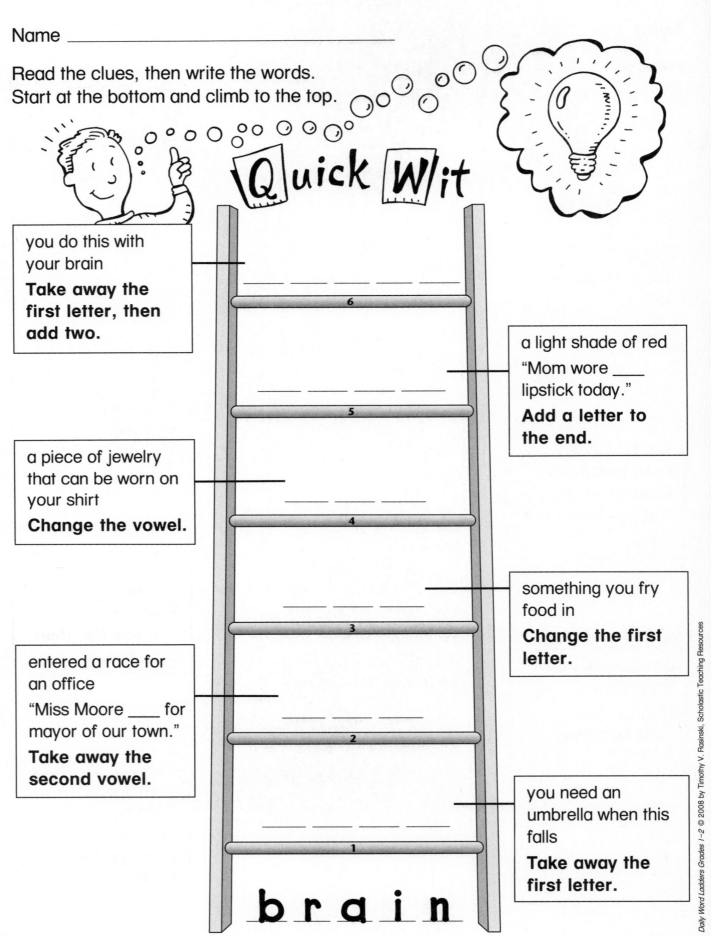

Quick Wit

you do this with your brain
Take away the first letter, then add two.

a light shade of red
"Mom wore ____ lipstick today."
Add a letter to the end.

a piece of jewelry that can be worn on your shirt
Change the vowel.

something you fry food in
Change the first letter.

entered a race for an office
"Miss Moore ____ for mayor of our town."
Take away the second vowel.

you need an umbrella when this falls
Take away the first letter.

6
5
4
3
2
1

b r a i n

Daily Word Ladders Grades 1–2 © 2008 by Timothy V. Rasinski, Scholastic Teaching Resources

Name _____

Read the clues, then write the words.
Start at the bottom and climb to the top.

Sky Scrapers

the color of the sky
Change the first letter.

6 _____

this is used to stick things together
Take away the first letter, then add two.

5 _____

a short name for Susan
Change the last letter.

4 _____

this lights up the day
Take away the two vowels, then add one.

3 _____

"Have you ___ my coat?"
Change the first letter.

2 _____

a short word for *teenager*
Take away the first two letters, then add one.

1 _____

g r e e n

Daily Word Ladders Grades 1–2 © 2008 by Timothy V. Rasinski, Scholastic Teaching Resources

Name _____

Read the clues, then write the words.
Start at the bottom and climb to the top.

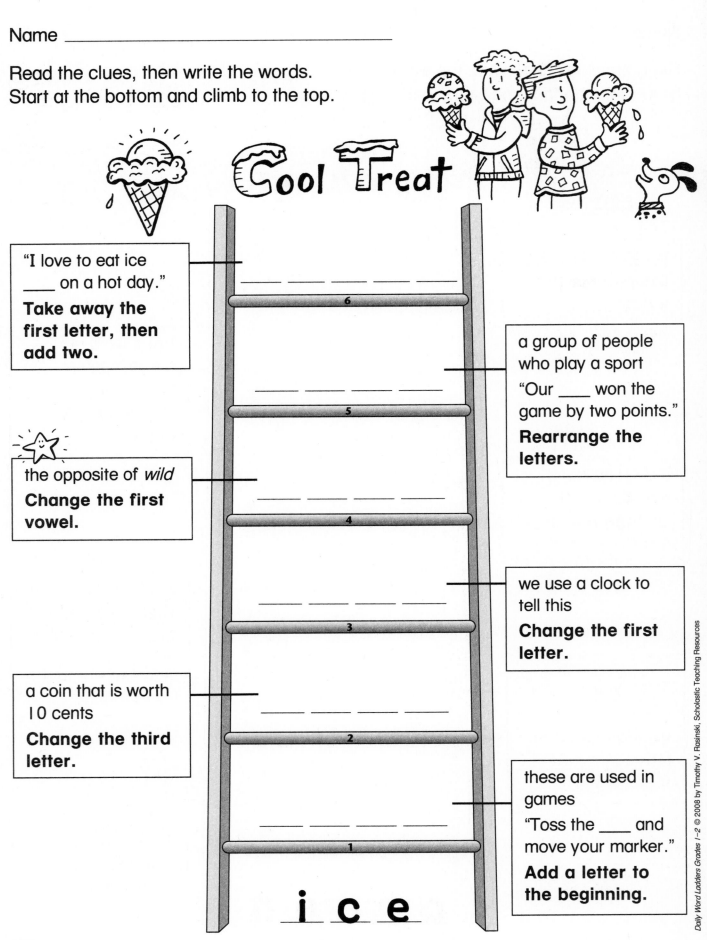

Cool Treat

"I love to eat ice
___ on a hot day."
**Take away the
first letter, then
add two.**

a group of people
who play a sport
"Our ___ won the
game by two points."
**Rearrange the
letters.**

the opposite of *wild*
**Change the first
vowel.**

we use a clock to
tell this
**Change the first
letter.**

a coin that is worth
10 cents
**Change the third
letter.**

these are used in
games
"Toss the ___ and
move your marker."
**Add a letter to
the beginning.**

i c e

6

5

4

3

2

1

Daily Word Ladders Grades 1–2 © 2008 by Timothy V. Rasinski, Scholastic Teaching Resources

Name _____

Read the clues, then write the words.
Start at the bottom and climb to the top.

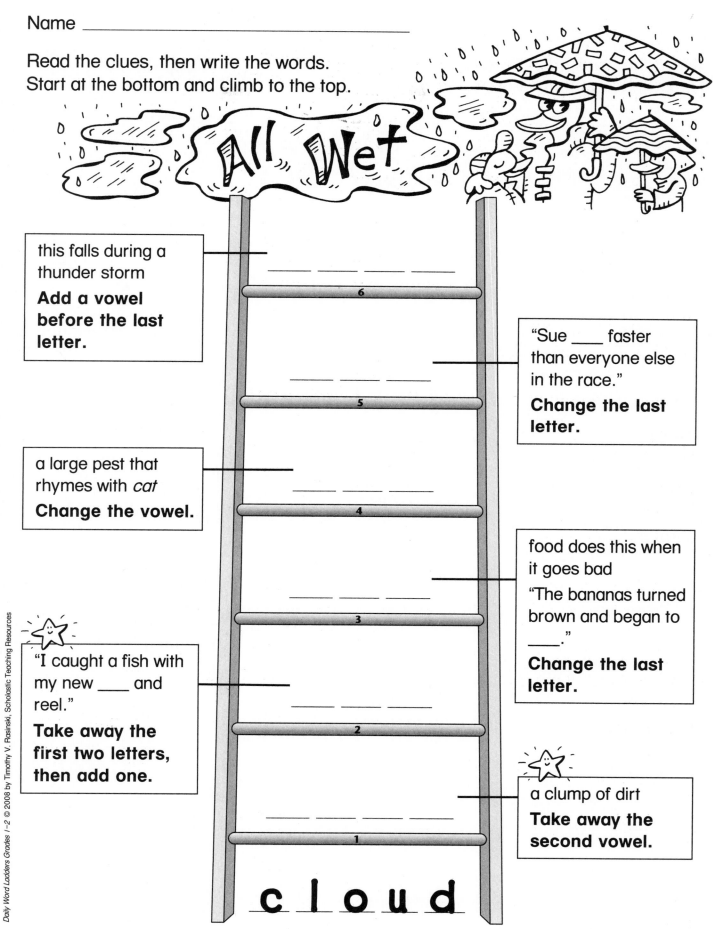

All Wet

this falls during a thunder storm
Add a vowel before the last letter.

6 ____ ____ ____ ____

"Sue ____ faster than everyone else in the race."
Change the last letter.

5 ____ ____ ____ ____

a large pest that rhymes with *cat*
Change the vowel.

4 ____ ____ ____

food does this when it goes bad
"The bananas turned brown and began to ____."
Change the last letter.

3 ____ ____ ____ ____

"I caught a fish with my new ____ and reel."
Take away the first two letters, then add one.

2 ____ ____ ____

a clump of dirt
Take away the second vowel.

1 ____ ____ ____ ____

c l o u d

Name _____

Read the clues, then write the words.
Start at the bottom and climb to the top.

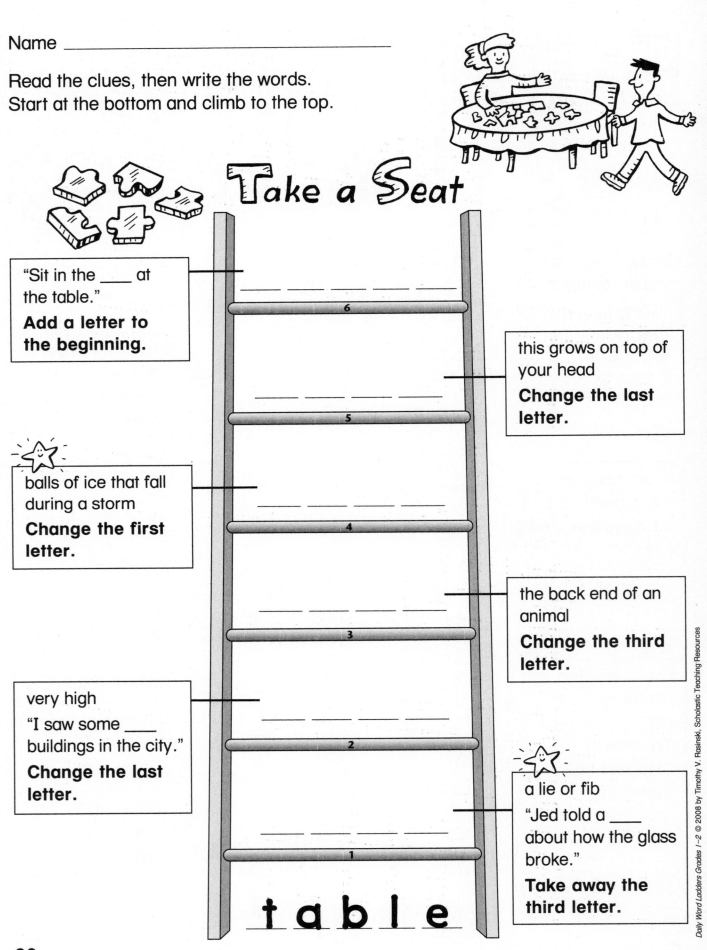

Take a Seat

"Sit in the ___ at the table."
Add a letter to the beginning.

this grows on top of your head
Change the last letter.

balls of ice that fall during a storm
Change the first letter.

the back end of an animal
Change the third letter.

very high
"I saw some ___ buildings in the city."
Change the last letter.

a lie or fib
"Jed told a ___ about how the glass broke."
Take away the third letter.

t a b l e

6
5
4
3
2
1

Name _____

Read the clues, then write the words.
Start at the bottom and climb to the top.

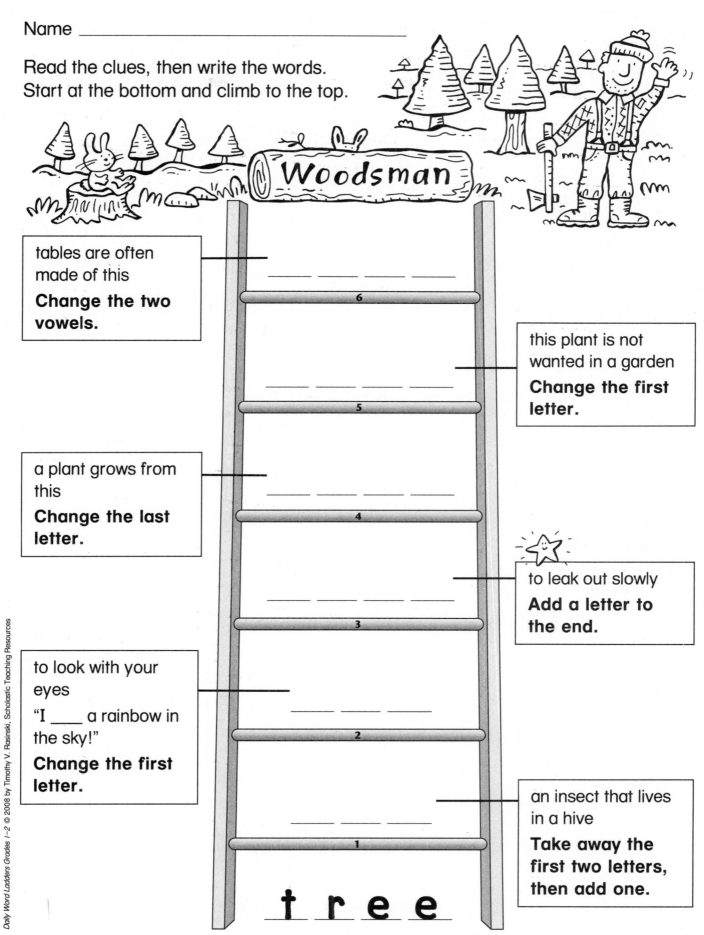

Woodsman

tables are often made of this
Change the two vowels.

_ _ _ _

6

this plant is not wanted in a garden
Change the first letter.

_ _ _ _

5

a plant grows from this
Change the last letter.

_ _ _ _

4

to leak out slowly
Add a letter to the end.

_ _ _ _

3

to look with your eyes
"I ____ a rainbow in the sky!"
Change the first letter.

_ _ _

2

an insect that lives in a hive
Take away the first two letters, then add one.

_ _ _

1

t r e e

Daily Word Ladders Grades 1–2 © 2008 by Timothy V. Rasinski, Scholastic Teaching Resources

Name _____

Read the clues, then write the words.
Start at the bottom and climb to the top.

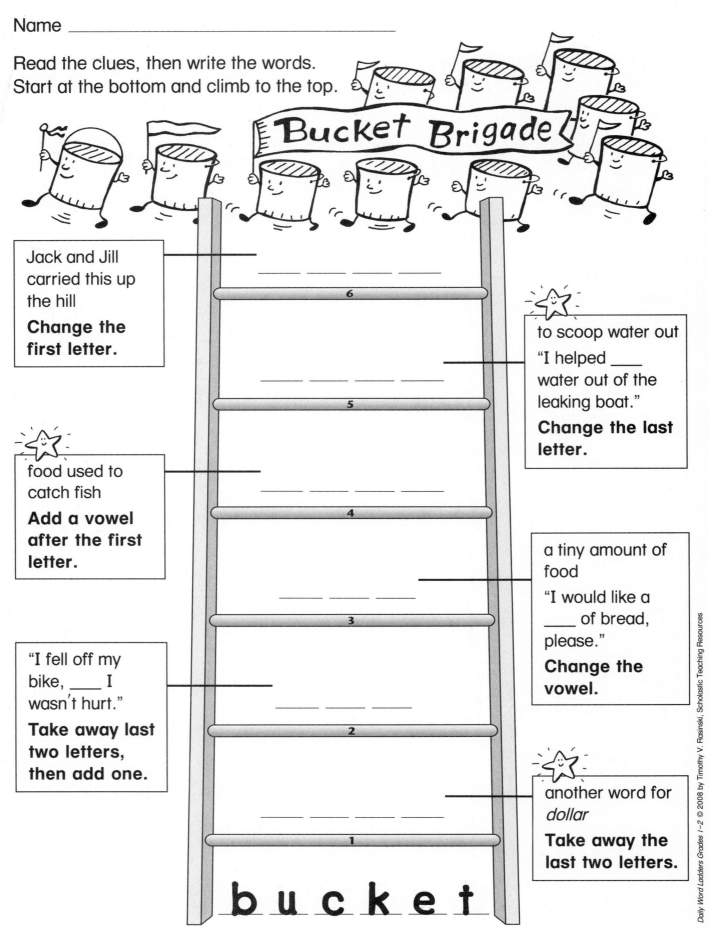

Bucket Brigade

Jack and Jill carried this up the hill
Change the first letter.

6 _ _ _ _ _ _

to scoop water out
"I helped ___ water out of the leaking boat."
Change the last letter.

5 _ _ _ _ _ _

food used to catch fish
Add a vowel after the first letter.

4 _ _ _ _ _

a tiny amount of food
"I would like a ___ of bread, please."
Change the vowel.

3 _ _ _ _ _

"I fell off my bike, ___ I wasn't hurt."
Take away last two letters, then add one.

2 _ _ _ _

another word for *dollar*
Take away the last two letters.

1 _ _ _ _

b u c k e t

Daily Word Ladders Grades 1–2 © 2008 by Timothy V. Rasinski, Scholastic Teaching Resources

Name _____

Read the clues, then write the words.
Start at the bottom and climb to the top.

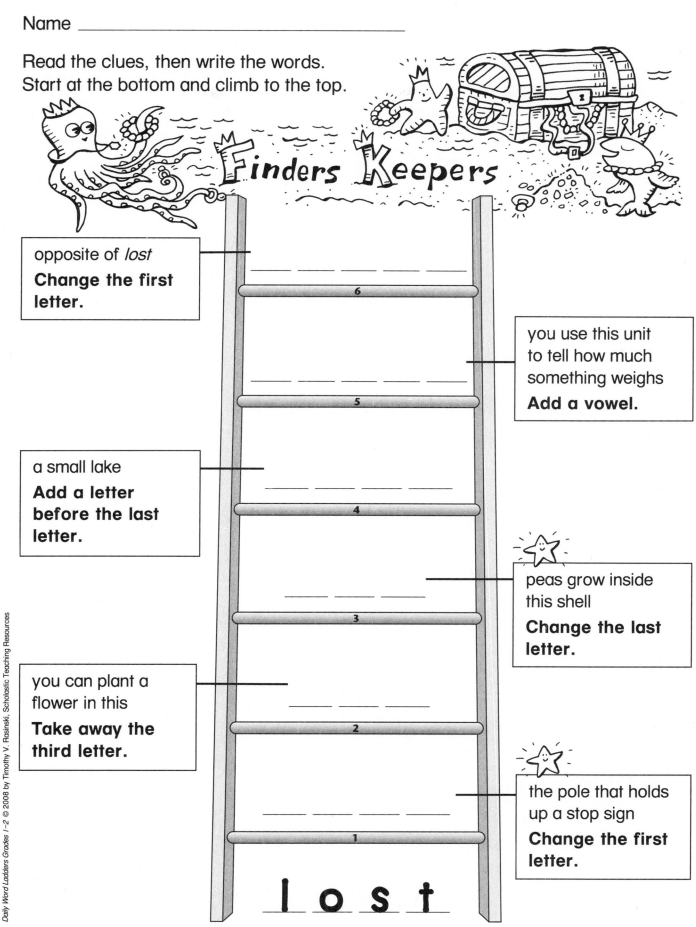

Finders Keepers

opposite of *lost*
Change the first letter.

you use this unit to tell how much something weighs
Add a vowel.

a small lake
Add a letter before the last letter.

peas grow inside this shell
Change the last letter.

you can plant a flower in this
Take away the third letter.

the pole that holds up a stop sign
Change the first letter.

6

5

4

3

2

1

l o s t

Daily Word Ladders Grades 1–2 © 2008 by Timothy V. Rasinski, Scholastic Teaching Resources

Name _____

Read the clues, then write the words.
Start at the bottom and climb to the top.

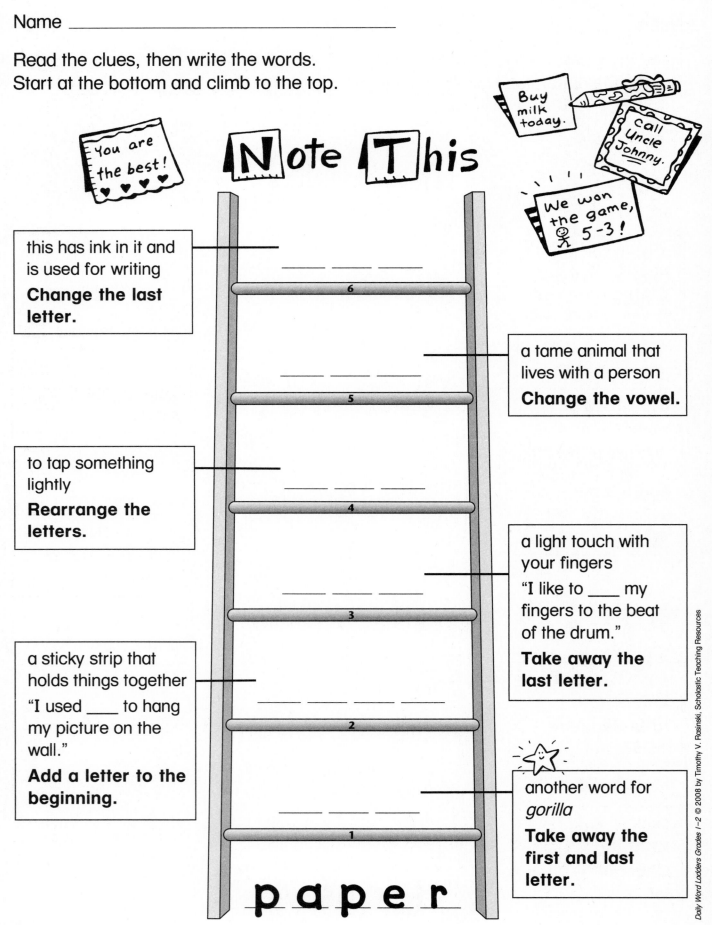

You are the best!

Note This

Buy milk today.

Call Uncle Johnny.

We won the game, 5-3!

this has ink in it and is used for writing
Change the last letter.

6 _____

a tame animal that lives with a person
Change the vowel.

5 _____

to tap something lightly
Rearrange the letters.

4 _____

a light touch with your fingers
"I like to ___ my fingers to the beat of the drum."
Take away the last letter.

3 _____

a sticky strip that holds things together
"I used ___ to hang my picture on the wall."
Add a letter to the beginning.

2 _____

another word for *gorilla*
Take away the first and last letter.

1 _____

p a p e r

Daily Word Ladders Grades 1–2 © 2008 by Timothy V. Rasinski, Scholastic Teaching Resources

Name _____

Read the clues, then write the words.
Start at the bottom and climb to the top.

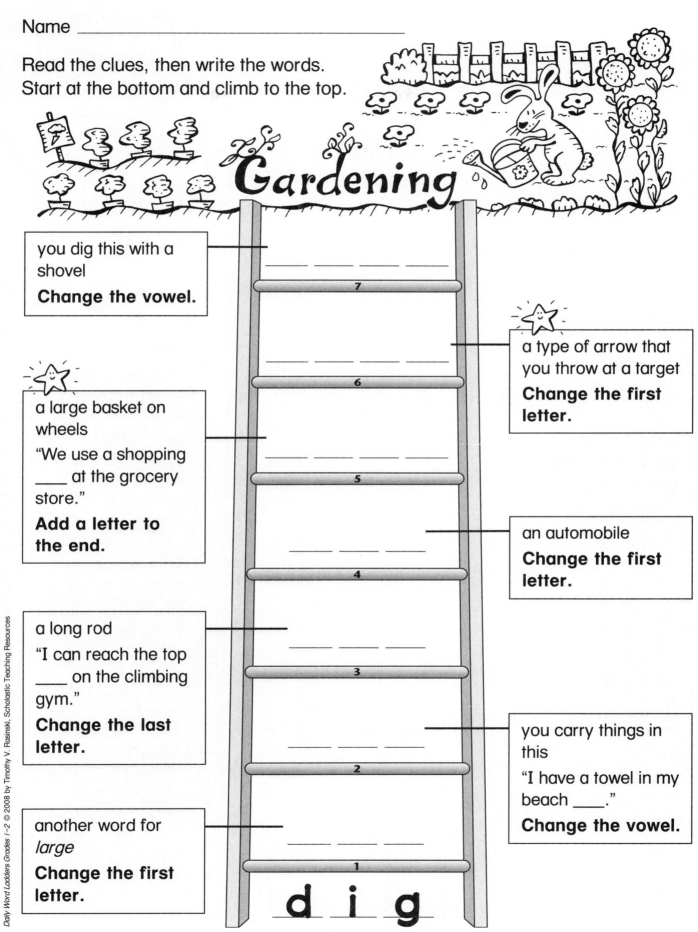

Gardening

you dig this with a shovel
Change the vowel.

a type of arrow that you throw at a target
Change the first letter.

a large basket on wheels
"We use a shopping ___ at the grocery store."
Add a letter to the end.

an automobile
Change the first letter.

a long rod
"I can reach the top ___ on the climbing gym."
Change the last letter.

you carry things in this
"I have a towel in my beach ___."
Change the vowel.

another word for *large*
Change the first letter.

7
6
5
4
3
2
1

d i g

Daily Word Ladders Grades 1–2 © 2008 by Timothy V. Rasinski, Scholastic Teaching Resources

Name _____

Read the clues, then write the words.
Start at the bottom and climb to the top.

Up We Go!

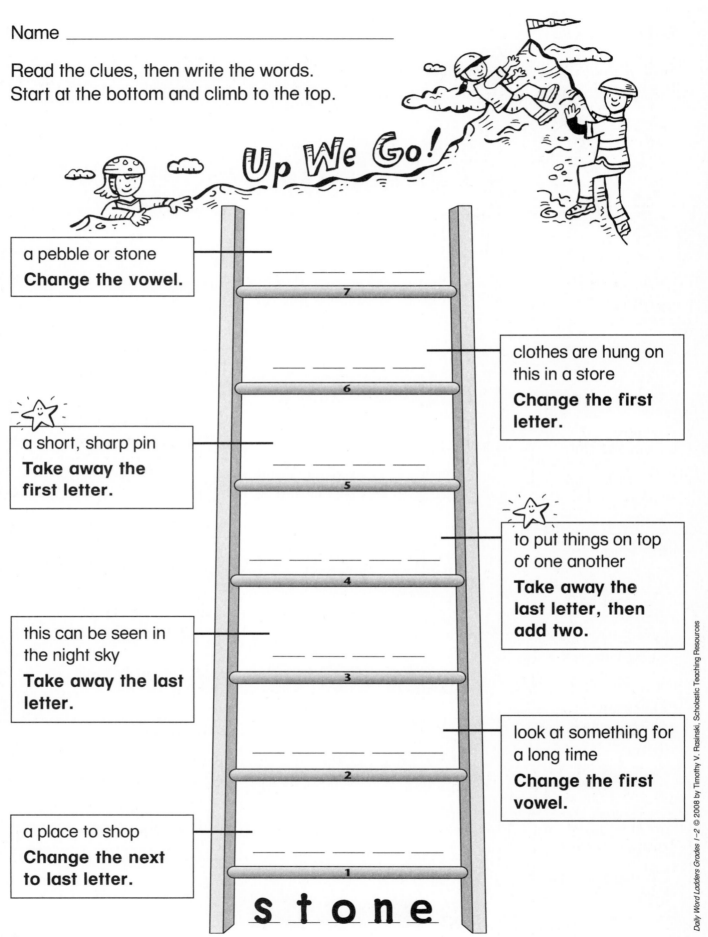

a pebble or stone
Change the vowel.

7 _ _ _ _ _

clothes are hung on this in a store
Change the first letter.

6 _ _ _ _ _

a short, sharp pin
Take away the first letter.

5 _ _ _ _ _

to put things on top of one another
Take away the last letter, then add two.

4 _ _ _ _ _

this can be seen in the night sky
Take away the last letter.

3 _ _ _ _ _

look at something for a long time
Change the first vowel.

2 _ _ _ _ _

a place to shop
Change the next to last letter.

1 _ _ _ _ _

s t o n e

Daily Word Ladders Grades 1–2 © 2008 by Timothy V. Rasinski, Scholastic Teaching Resources

Name _____

Read the clues, then write the words.
Start at the bottom and climb to the top.

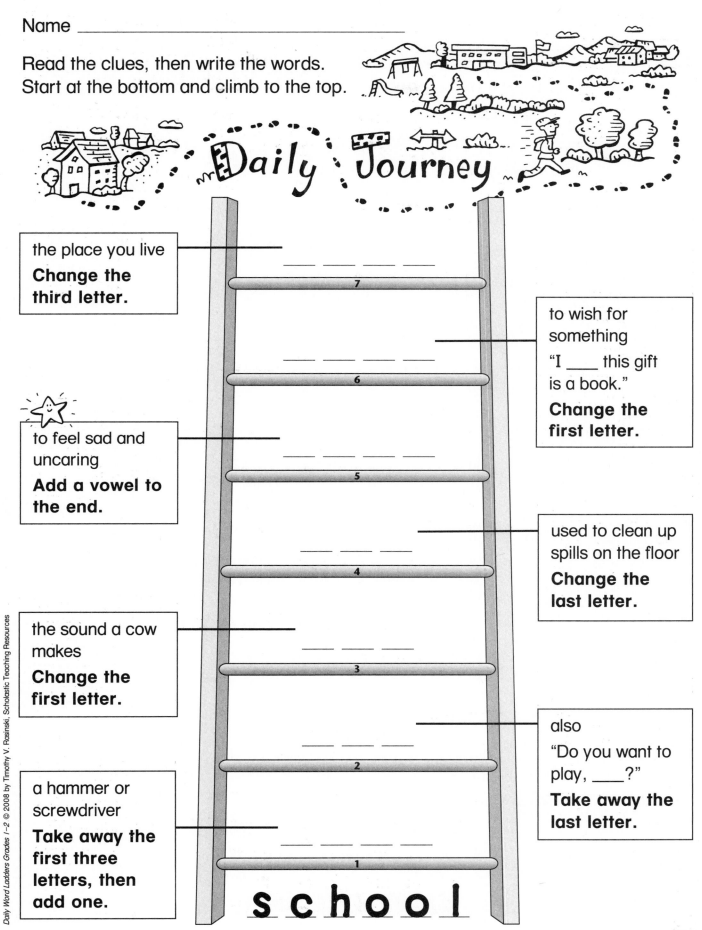

Daily Journey

the place you live
Change the third letter.

to wish for something
"I ___ this gift is a book."
Change the first letter.

to feel sad and uncaring
Add a vowel to the end.

used to clean up spills on the floor
Change the last letter.

the sound a cow makes
Change the first letter.

also
"Do you want to play, ___?"
Take away the last letter.

a hammer or screwdriver
Take away the first three letters, then add one.

7

6

5

4

3

2

1

s c h o o l

Daily Word Ladders Grades 1–2 © 2008 by Timothy V. Rasinski, Scholastic Teaching Resources

Name _____

Read the clues, then write the words.
Start at the bottom and climb to the top.

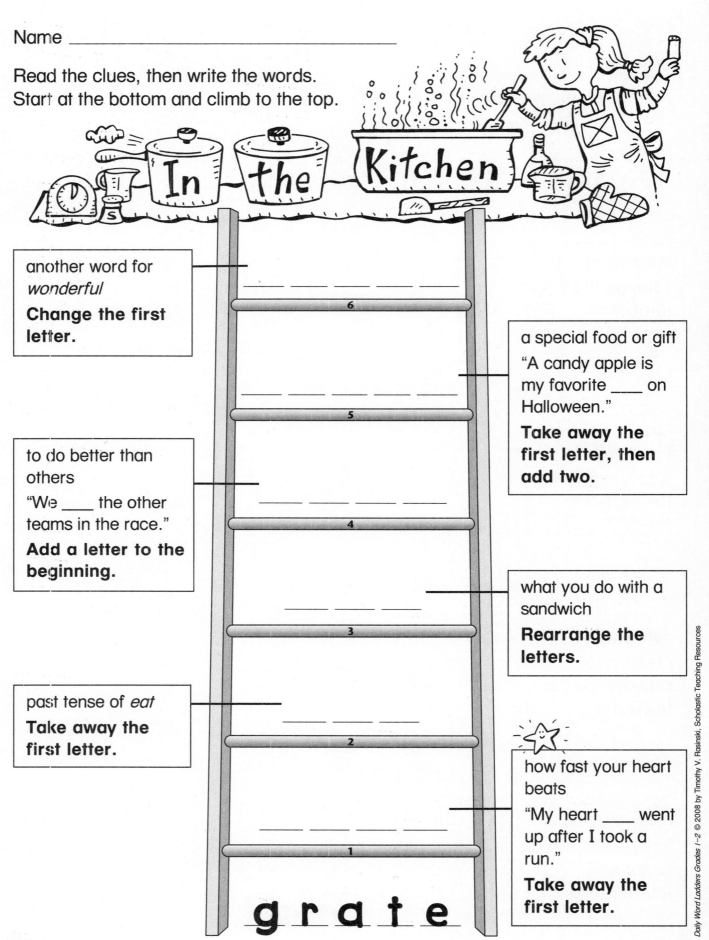

another word for *wonderful*
Change the first letter.

6 ___ ___ ___ ___ ___

a special food or gift
"A candy apple is my favorite ___ on Halloween."
Take away the first letter, then add two.

5 ___ ___ ___ ___ ___

to do better than others
"We ___ the other teams in the race."
Add a letter to the beginning.

4 ___ ___ ___ ___ ___

what you do with a sandwich
Rearrange the letters.

3 ___ ___ ___ ___

past tense of *eat*
Take away the first letter.

2 ___ ___ ___ ___

how fast your heart beats
"My heart ___ went up after I took a run."
Take away the first letter.

1 ___ ___ ___ ___ ___

g r a t e

Daily Word Ladders Grades 1–2 © 2008 by Timothy V. Rasinski, Scholastic Teaching Resources

Name _____

Read the clues, then write the words.
Start at the bottom and climb to the top.

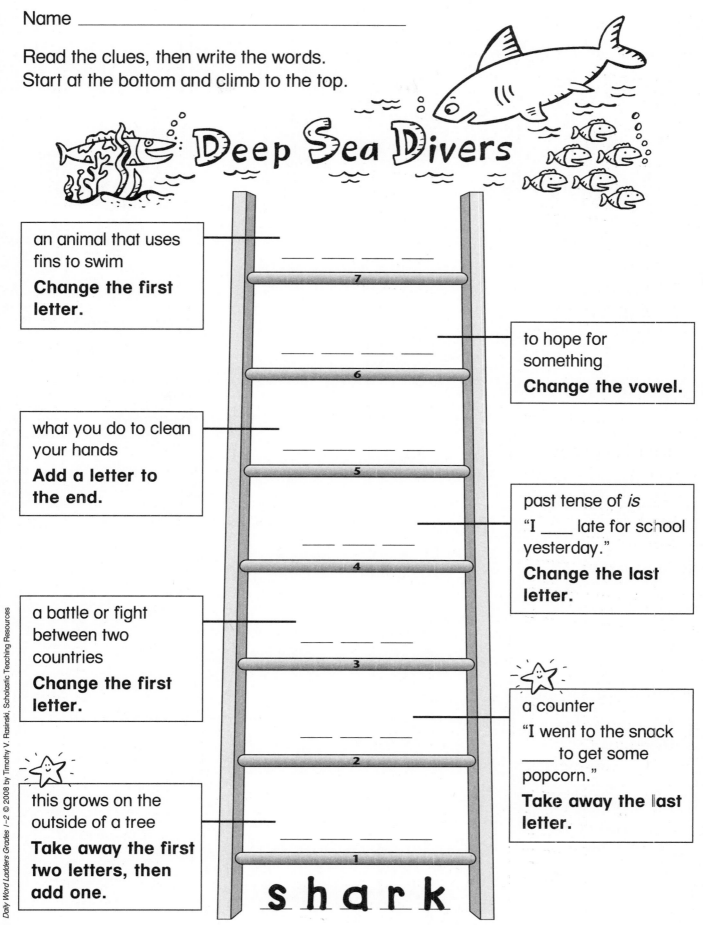

Deep Sea Divers

an animal that uses fins to swim
Change the first letter.

to hope for something
Change the vowel.

what you do to clean your hands
Add a letter to the end.

past tense of *is*
"I ____ late for school yesterday."
Change the last letter.

a battle or fight between two countries
Change the first letter.

a counter
"I went to the snack ____ to get some popcorn."
Take away the last letter.

this grows on the outside of a tree
Take away the first two letters, then add one.

7

6

5

4

3

2

1

s h a r k

Name _____

Read the clues, then write the words.
Start at the bottom and climb to the top.

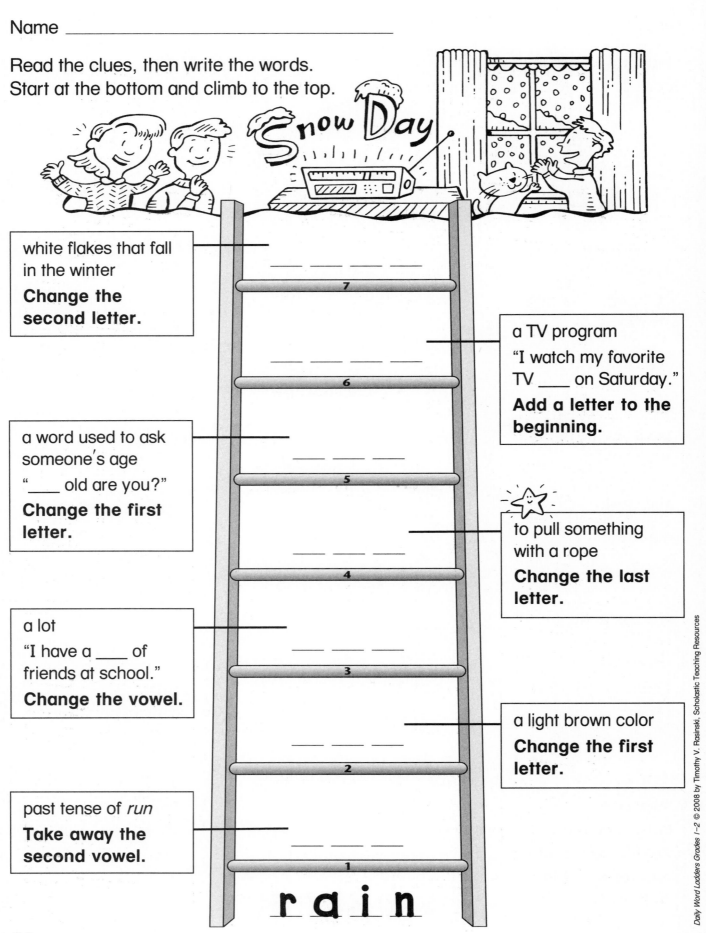

white flakes that fall
in the winter
**Change the
second letter.**

7 _ _ _ _

a TV program
"I watch my favorite
TV ___ on Saturday."
**Add a letter to the
beginning.**

6 _ _ _ _

a word used to ask
someone's age
"___ old are you?"
**Change the first
letter.**

5 _ _ _

to pull something
with a rope
**Change the last
letter.**

4 _ _ _

a lot
"I have a ___ of
friends at school."
Change the vowel.

3 _ _ _

a light brown color
**Change the first
letter.**

2 _ _ _

past tense of *run*
**Take away the
second vowel.**

1 _ _ _

r a i n

Daily Word Ladders Grades 1–2 © 2008 by Timothy V. Rasinski, Scholastic Teaching Resources

Name _____

Read the clues, then write the words.
Start at the bottom and climb to the top.

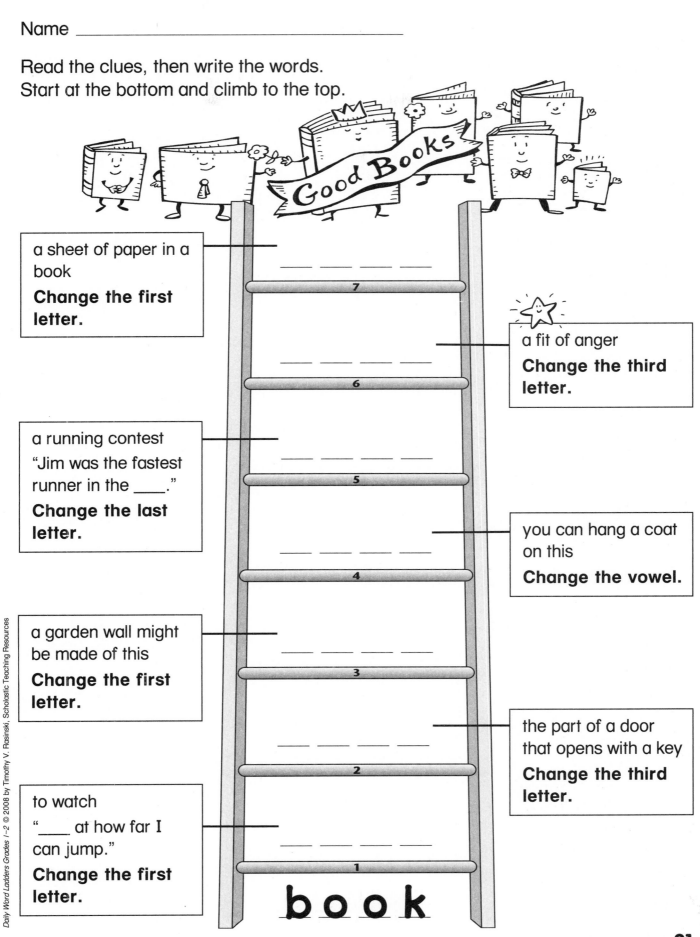

Good Books

a sheet of paper in a book
Change the first letter.

7 _ _ _ _

a fit of anger
Change the third letter.

6 _ _ _ _

a running contest
"Jim was the fastest runner in the ___."
Change the last letter.

5 _ _ _ _

you can hang a coat on this
Change the vowel.

4 _ _ _ _

a garden wall might be made of this
Change the first letter.

3 _ _ _ _

the part of a door that opens with a key
Change the third letter.

2 _ _ _ _

to watch
"___ at how far I can jump."
Change the first letter.

1 _ _ _ _

b o o k

Daily Word Ladders Grades 1–2 © 2008 by Timothy V. Rasinski, Scholastic Teaching Resources

91

Name _____

Read the clues, then write the words.
Start at the bottom and climb to the top.

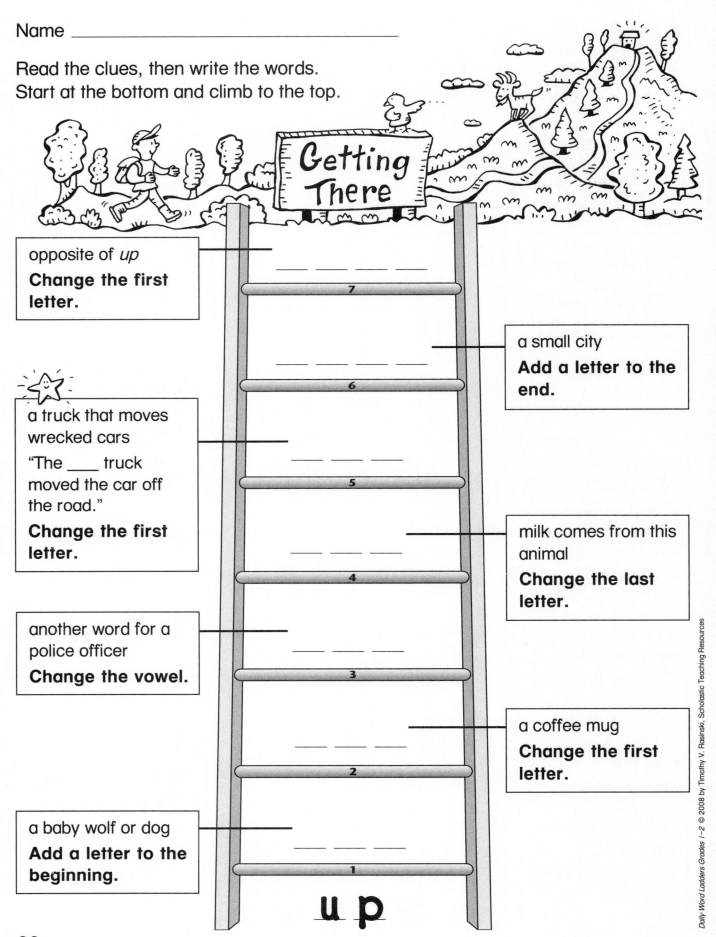

Getting There

opposite of *up*
Change the first letter.

— — — — — — 7

a small city
Add a letter to the end.

— — — — — 6

a truck that moves wrecked cars
"The ____ truck moved the car off the road."
Change the first letter.

— — — — 5

milk comes from this animal
Change the last letter.

— — — 4

another word for a police officer
Change the vowel.

— — — — 3

a coffee mug
Change the first letter.

— — — 2

a baby wolf or dog
Add a letter to the beginning.

— — — 1

u p

Daily Word Ladders Grades 1–2 © 2008 by Timothy V. Rasinski, Scholastic Teaching Resources

Name _____

Read the clues, then write the words.
Start at the bottom and climb to the top.

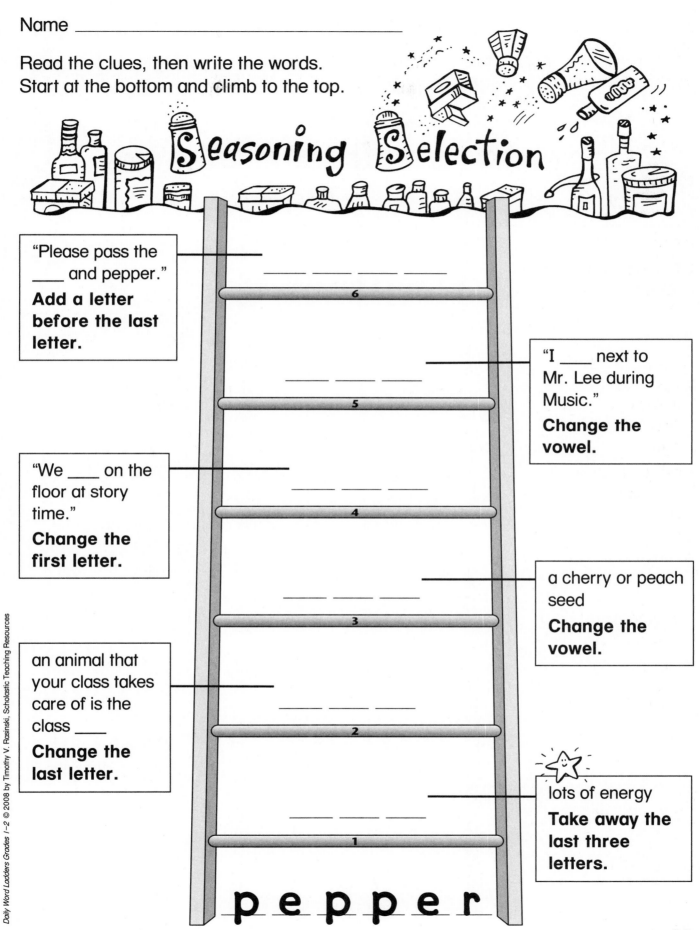

Seasoning Selection

"Please pass the
____ and pepper."
**Add a letter
before the last
letter.**

6 _ _ _ _ _ _

"I ____ next to
Mr. Lee during
Music."
**Change the
vowel.**

5 _ _ _ _ _

"We ____ on the
floor at story
time."
**Change the
first letter.**

4 _ _ _ _ _

a cherry or peach
seed
**Change the
vowel.**

3 _ _ _ _

an animal that
your class takes
care of is the
class ____
**Change the
last letter.**

2 _ _ _ _

lots of energy
**Take away the
last three
letters.**

1 _ _ _ _

p e p p e r

Daily Word Ladders Grades 1–2 © 2008 by Timothy V. Rasinski, Scholastic Teaching Resources

Name _____

Read the clues, then write the words.
Start at the bottom and climb to the top.

Stars and Stripes

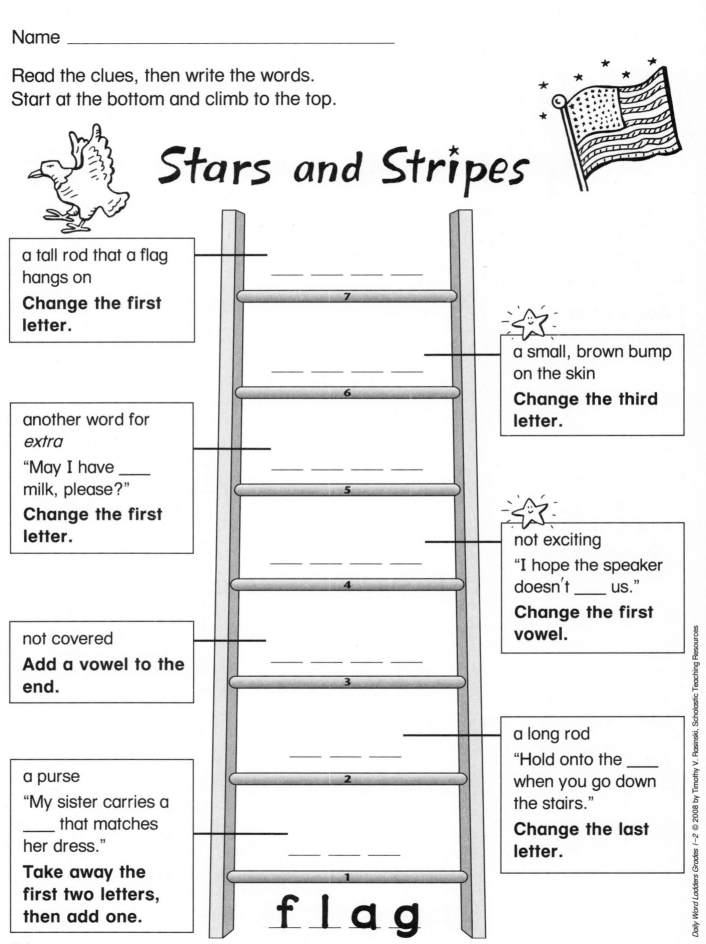

a tall rod that a flag hangs on
Change the first letter.

a small, brown bump on the skin
Change the third letter.

another word for *extra*
"May I have ___ milk, please?"
Change the first letter.

not exciting
"I hope the speaker doesn't ___ us."
Change the first vowel.

not covered
Add a vowel to the end.

a long rod
"Hold onto the ___ when you go down the stairs."
Change the last letter.

a purse
"My sister carries a ___ that matches her dress."
Take away the first two letters, then add one.

7

6

5

4

3

2

1

f l a g

Daily Word Ladders Grades 1–2 © 2008 by Timothy V. Rasinski, Scholastic Teaching Resources

Name _____

Read the clues, then write the words.
Start at the bottom and climb to the top.

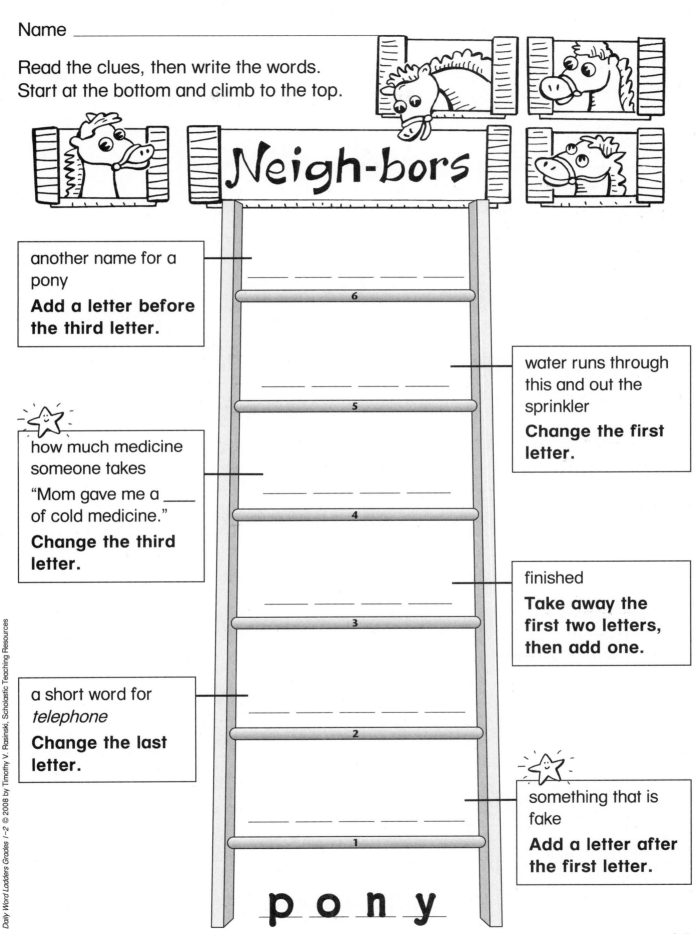

Neigh-bors

another name for a pony
Add a letter before the third letter.

water runs through this and out the sprinkler
Change the first letter.

how much medicine someone takes
"Mom gave me a ____ of cold medicine."
Change the third letter.

finished
Take away the first two letters, then add one.

a short word for *telephone*
Change the last letter.

something that is fake
Add a letter after the first letter.

6

5

4

3

2

1

p o n y

Name _____

Read the clues, then write the words.
Start at the bottom and climb to the top.

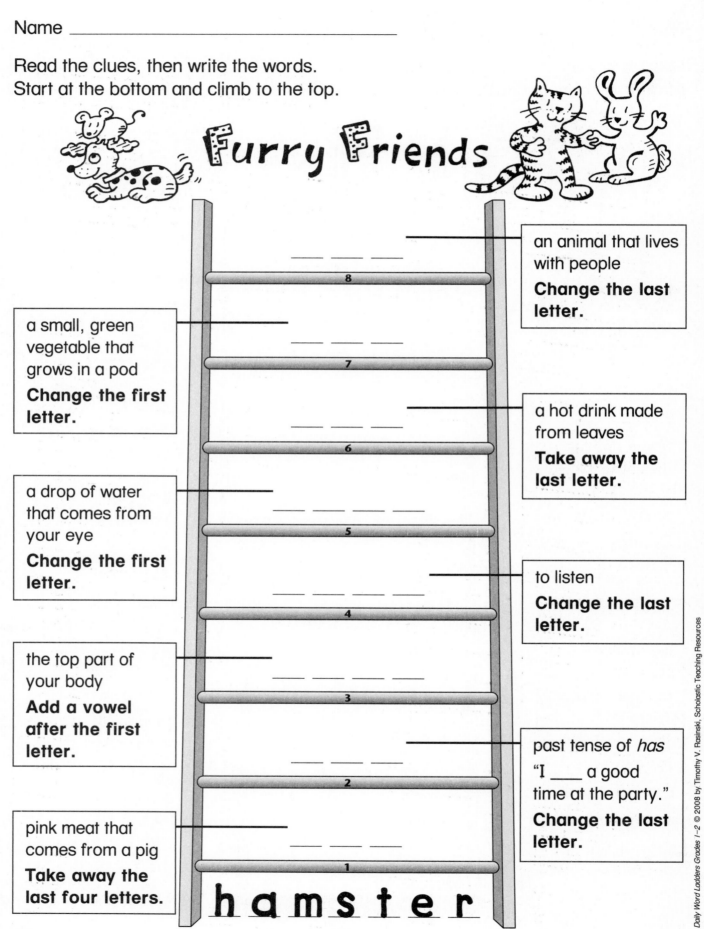

Furry Friends

an animal that lives with people
Change the last letter.

a small, green vegetable that grows in a pod
Change the first letter.

a hot drink made from leaves
Take away the last letter.

a drop of water that comes from your eye
Change the first letter.

to listen
Change the last letter.

the top part of your body
Add a vowel after the first letter.

past tense of *has*
"I ____ a good time at the party."
Change the last letter.

pink meat that comes from a pig
Take away the last four letters.

8

7

6

5

4

3

2

1

h a m s t e r

Daily Word Ladders Grades 1–2 © 2008 by Timothy V. Rasinski, Scholastic Teaching Resources

Name _____

Read the clues, then write the words.
Start at the bottom and climb to the top.

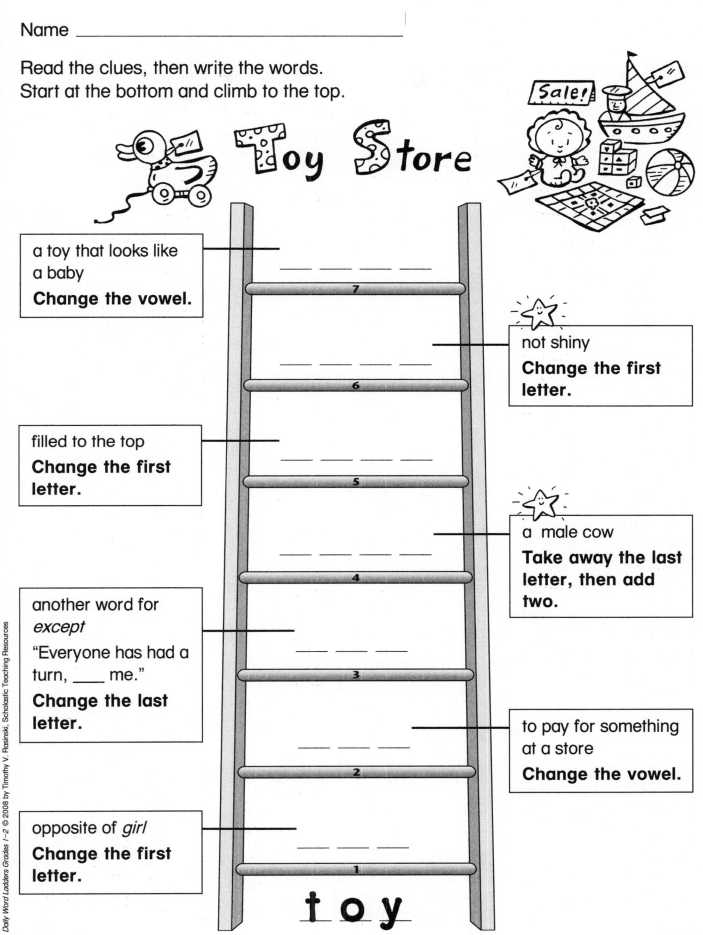

Toy Store

a toy that looks like a baby
Change the vowel.

_ _ _ _ (7)

not shiny
Change the first letter.

_ _ _ _ (6)

filled to the top
Change the first letter.

_ _ _ _ (5)

a male cow
Take away the last letter, then add two.

_ _ _ _ (4)

another word for *except*
"Everyone has had a turn, ___ me."
Change the last letter.

_ _ _ (3)

to pay for something at a store
Change the vowel.

_ _ _ _ (2)

opposite of *girl*
Change the first letter.

_ _ _ (1)

t o y

Name _____

Read the clues, then write the words.
Start at the bottom and climb to the top.

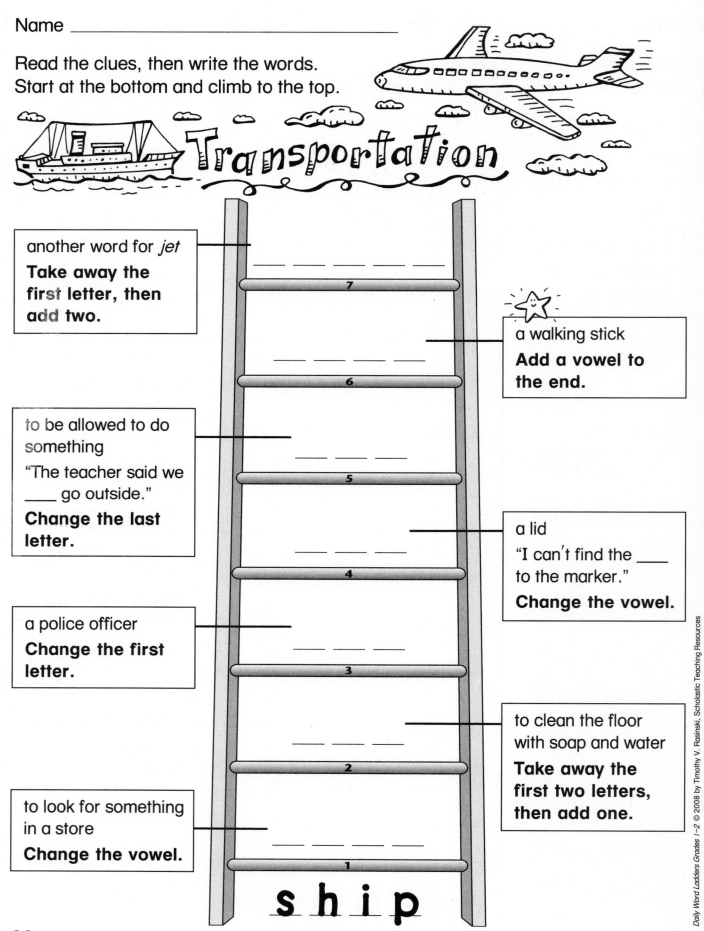

Transportation

another word for *jet*
Take away the first letter, then add two.

a walking stick
Add a vowel to the end.

to be allowed to do something
"The teacher said we ___ go outside."
Change the last letter.

a lid
"I can't find the ___ to the marker."
Change the vowel.

a police officer
Change the first letter.

to clean the floor with soap and water
Take away the first two letters, then add one.

to look for something in a store
Change the vowel.

7

6

5

4

3

2

1

s h i p

Daily Word Ladders Grades 1–2 © 2008 by Timothy V. Rasinski, Scholastic Teaching Resources

Name _____

Read the clues, then write the words.
Start at the bottom and climb to the top.

Score!

this is kicked over a goal post
Change the first letter.

___ ___ ___ ___ ___   7

___ ___ ___ ___ ___   6

a place with many stores in it
Take away the last letter, then add two.

a small rug
"Please wipe your feet on the door ___."
Change the first letter.

___ ___ ___   5

___ ___ ___ ___   4

a soft touch
"Dad gave me a ___ on the back."
Change the vowel.

a pan used for making soup
Take away the last two letters, then add one.

___ ___ ___   3

___ ___ ___ ___   2

a place to swim
Change the first letter.

to trick
"You tried to ___ me with that magic act."
Change the last letter.

___ ___ ___ ___   1

f o o t

Name _____

Read the clues, then write the words.
Start at the bottom and climb to the top.

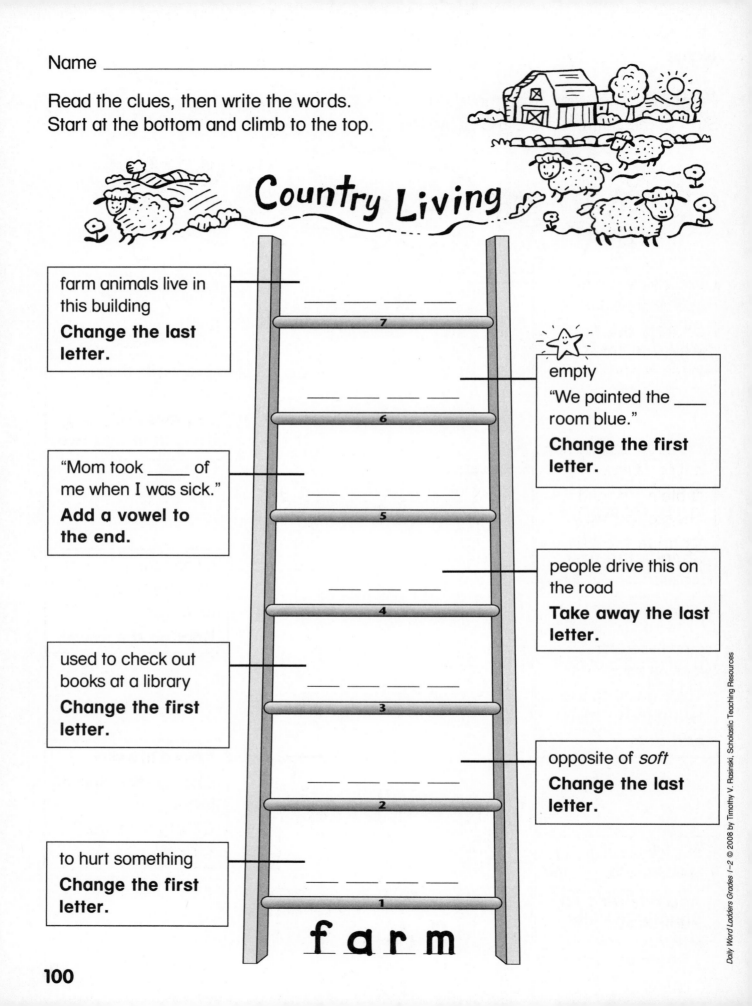

Country Living

farm animals live in this building
Change the last letter.

7 _ _ _ _

6 _ _ _ _

empty
"We painted the ____ room blue."
Change the first letter.

"Mom took _____ of me when I was sick."
Add a vowel to the end.

5 _ _ _ _

people drive this on the road
Take away the last letter.

used to check out books at a library
Change the first letter.

4 _ _ _ _ _

3 _ _ _ _

opposite of *soft*
Change the last letter.

2 _ _ _ _

to hurt something
Change the first letter.

1 _ _ _ _

f a r m

Daily Word Ladders Grades 1–2 © 2008 by Timothy V. Rasinski, Scholastic Teaching Resources

Name _____

Read the clues, then write the words.
Start at the bottom and climb to the top.

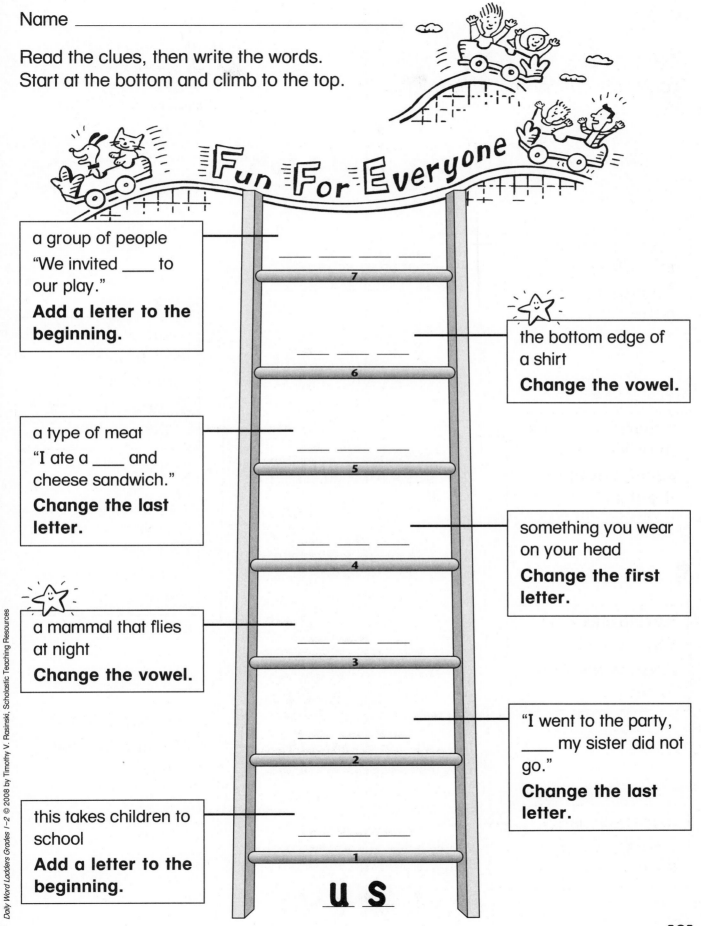

Fun For Everyone

a group of people
"We invited ____ to our play."
Add a letter to the beginning.

the bottom edge of a shirt
Change the vowel.

a type of meat
"I ate a ____ and cheese sandwich."
Change the last letter.

something you wear on your head
Change the first letter.

a mammal that flies at night
Change the vowel.

"I went to the party, ____ my sister did not go."
Change the last letter.

this takes children to school
Add a letter to the beginning.

U S

7

6

5

4

3

2

1

Name _____

Read the clues, then write the words.
Start at the bottom and climb to the top.

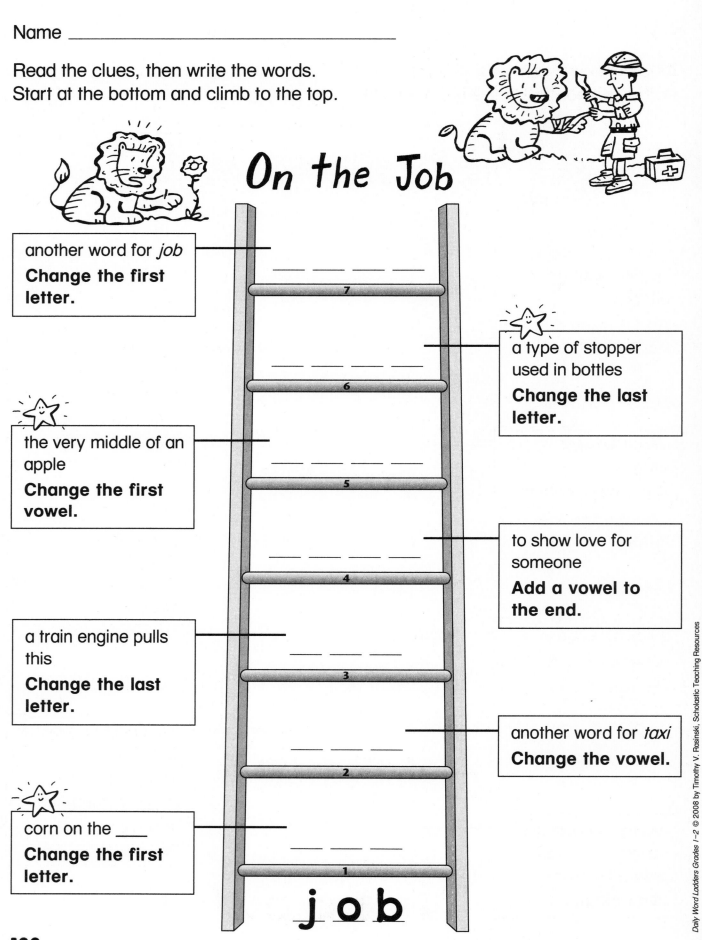

On the Job

another word for *job*
Change the first letter.

7 ___ ___ ___

a type of stopper used in bottles
Change the last letter.

6 ___ ___ ___ ___

the very middle of an apple
Change the first vowel.

5 ___ ___ ___ ___

to show love for someone
Add a vowel to the end.

4 ___ ___ ___ ___

a train engine pulls this
Change the last letter.

3 ___ ___ ___

another word for *taxi*
Change the vowel.

2 ___ ___ ___

corn on the ___
Change the first letter.

1 ___ ___ ___

j o b

102

Daily Word Ladders Grades 1–2 © 2008 by Timothy V. Rasinski, Scholastic Teaching Resources

Name _____

Read the clues, then write the words.
Start at the bottom and climb to the top.

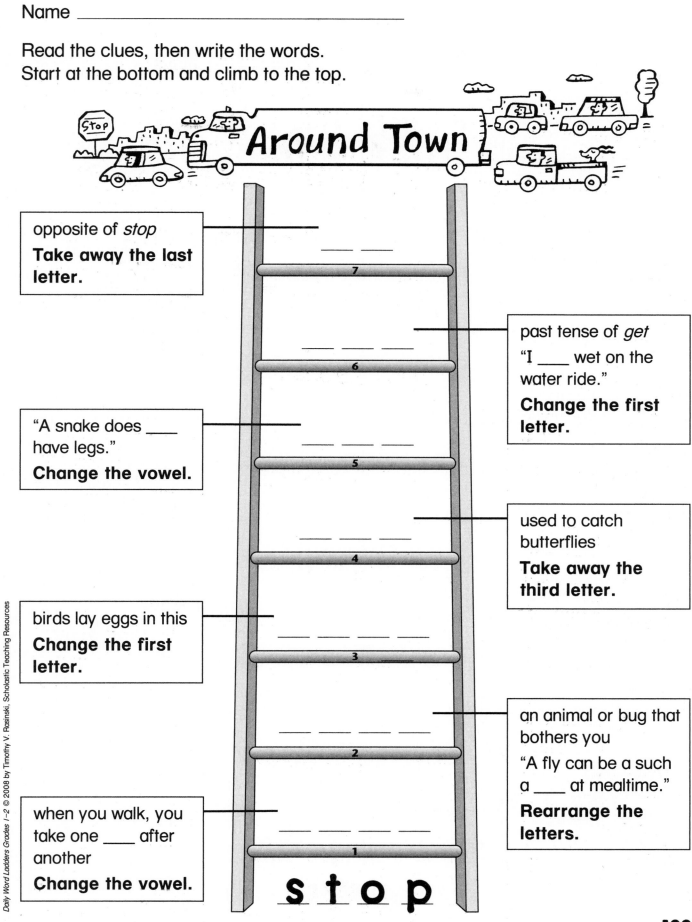

Around Town

opposite of *stop*
Take away the last letter.

7

past tense of *get*
"I ___ wet on the water ride."
Change the first letter.

6

"A snake does ___ have legs."
Change the vowel.

5

used to catch butterflies
Take away the third letter.

4

birds lay eggs in this
Change the first letter.

3

an animal or bug that bothers you
"A fly can be a such a ___ at mealtime."
Rearrange the letters.

2

when you walk, you take one ___ after another
Change the vowel.

1

s t o p

Name _____

Read the clues, then write the words.
Start at the bottom and climb to the top.

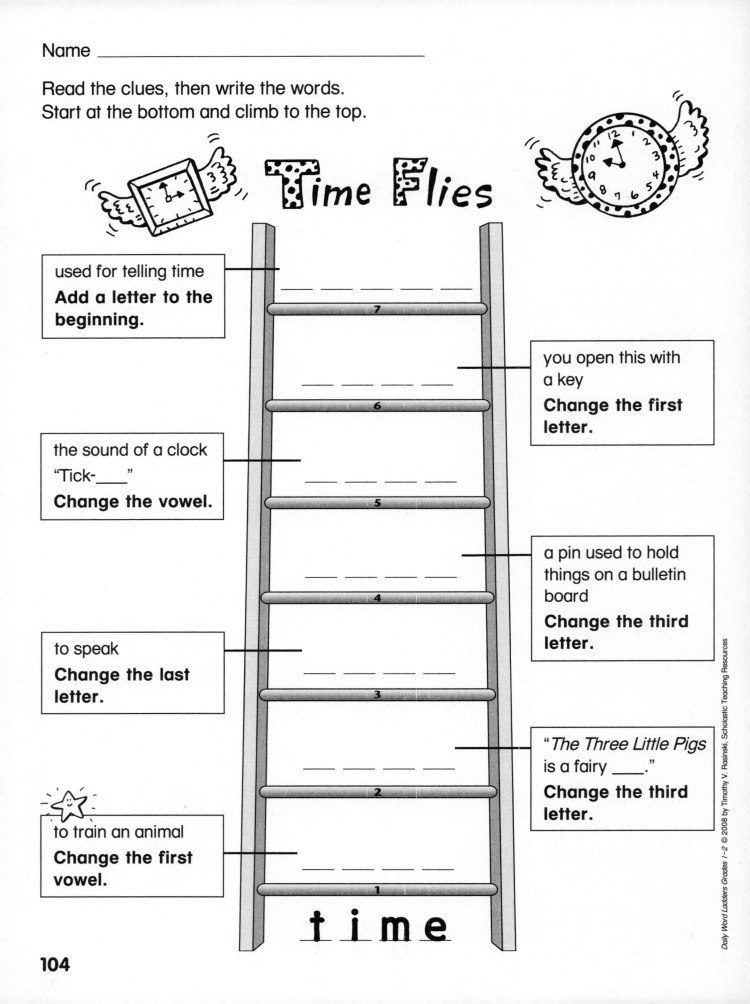

Time Flies

used for telling time
Add a letter to the beginning.

you open this with a key
Change the first letter.

the sound of a clock
"Tick-___"
Change the vowel.

a pin used to hold things on a bulletin board
Change the third letter.

to speak
Change the last letter.

"*The Three Little Pigs* is a fairy ___."
Change the third letter.

to train an animal
Change the first vowel.

7

6

5

4

3

2

1

t i m e

Daily Word Ladders Grades 1–2 © 2008 by Timothy V. Rasinski, Scholastic Teaching Resources

Name _____

Read the clues, then write the words.
Start at the bottom and climb to the top.

And the Winner Is...

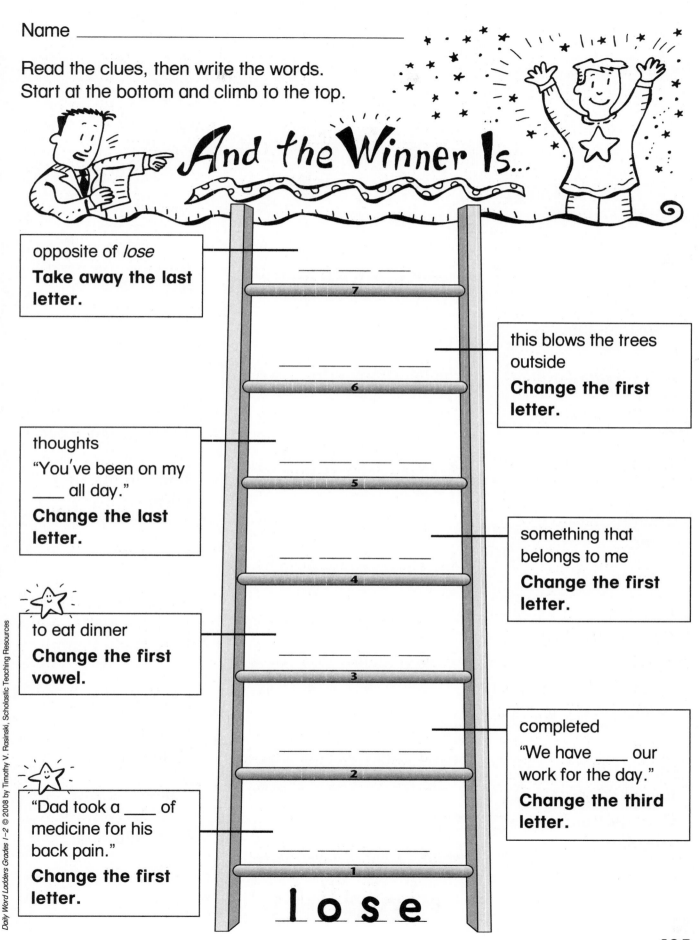

opposite of *lose*
Take away the last letter.

this blows the trees outside
Change the first letter.

thoughts
"You've been on my ____ all day."
Change the last letter.

something that belongs to me
Change the first letter.

to eat dinner
Change the first vowel.

completed
"We have ____ our work for the day."
Change the third letter.

"Dad took a ____ of medicine for his back pain."
Change the first letter.

7
6
5
4
3
2
1

l o s e

Name _____

Read the clues, then write the words.
Start at the bottom and climb to the top.

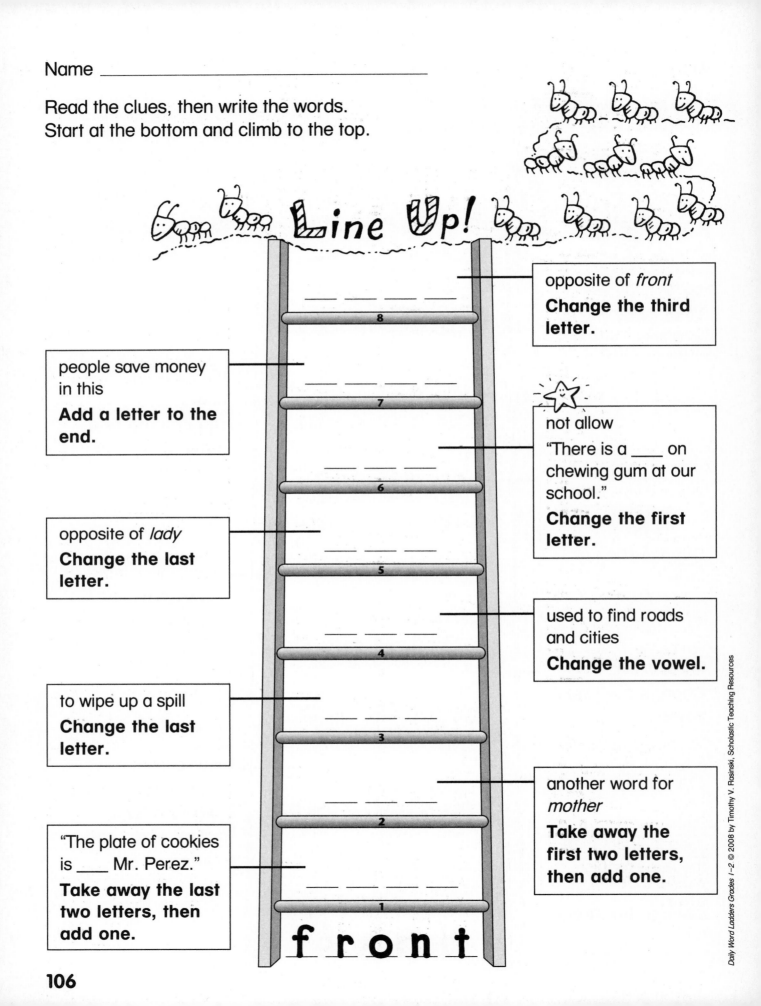

Line Up!

opposite of *front*
Change the third letter.

people save money in this
Add a letter to the end.

not allow
"There is a ____ on chewing gum at our school."
Change the first letter.

opposite of *lady*
Change the last letter.

used to find roads and cities
Change the vowel.

to wipe up a spill
Change the last letter.

another word for *mother*
Take away the first two letters, then add one.

"The plate of cookies is ____ Mr. Perez."
Take away the last two letters, then add one.

f r o n t

Daily Word Ladders Grades 1–2 © 2008 by Timothy V. Rosinski, Scholastic Teaching Resources

Name _____

Read the clues, then write the words.
Start at the bottom and climb to the top.

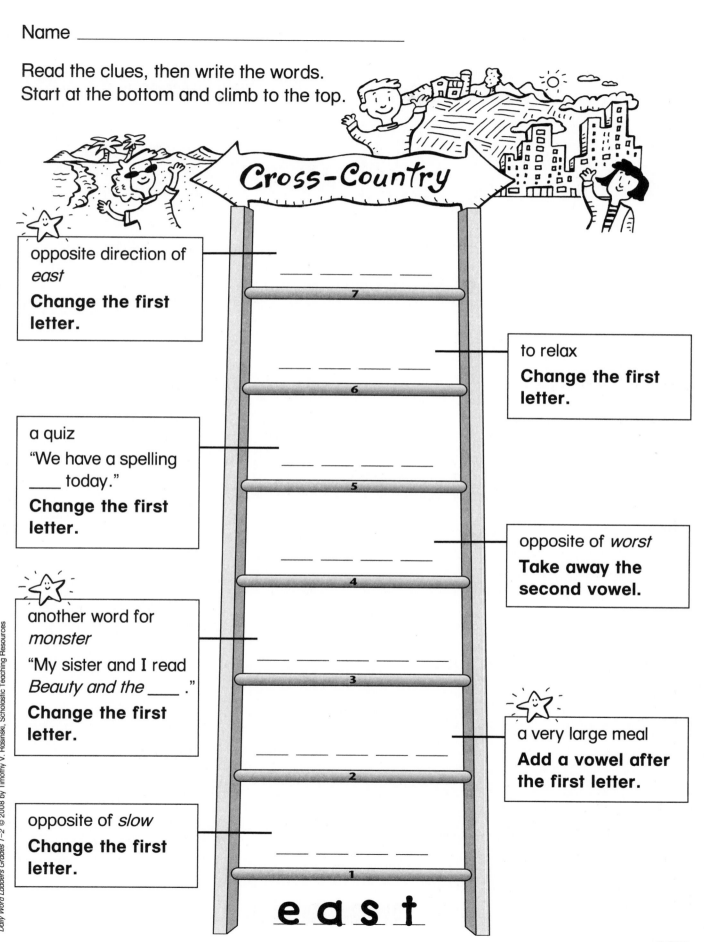

Cross-Country

opposite direction of *east*
Change the first letter.

to relax
Change the first letter.

a quiz
"We have a spelling ___ today."
Change the first letter.

opposite of *worst*
Take away the second vowel.

another word for *monster*
"My sister and I read *Beauty and the ___ .*"
Change the first letter.

a very large meal
Add a vowel after the first letter.

opposite of *slow*
Change the first letter.

7

6

5

4

3

2

1

e a s t

Name _____

Read the clues, then write the words.
Start at the bottom and climb to the top.

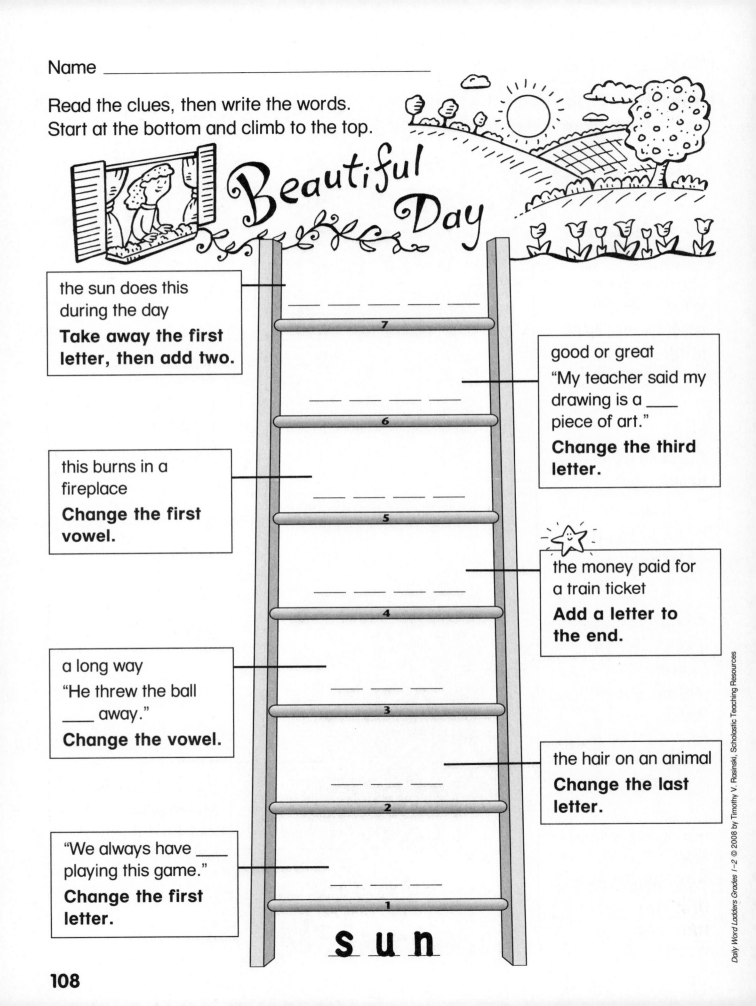

the sun does this during the day
Take away the first letter, then add two.

good or great
"My teacher said my drawing is a ____ piece of art."
Change the third letter.

this burns in a fireplace
Change the first vowel.

the money paid for a train ticket
Add a letter to the end.

a long way
"He threw the ball ____ away."
Change the vowel.

the hair on an animal
Change the last letter.

"We always have ____ playing this game."
Change the first letter.

s u n

Daily Word Ladders Grades 1–2 © 2008 by Timothy V. Rasinski, Scholastic Teaching Resources

Name _____

Read the clues, then write the words.
Start at the bottom and climb to the top.

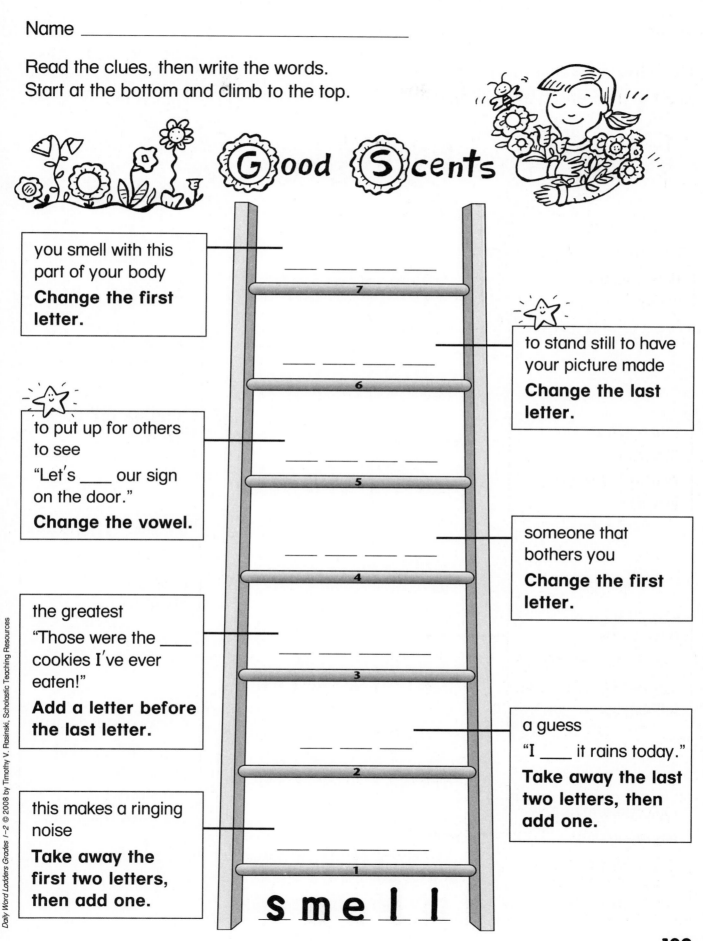

Good Scents

you smell with this part of your body
Change the first letter.

to stand still to have your picture made
Change the last letter.

to put up for others to see
"Let's ____ our sign on the door."
Change the vowel.

someone that bothers you
Change the first letter.

the greatest
"Those were the ____ cookies I've ever eaten!"
Add a letter before the last letter.

a guess
"I ____ it rains today."
Take away the last two letters, then add one.

this makes a ringing noise
Take away the first two letters, then add one.

7

6

5

4

3

2

1

s m e l l

Daily Word Ladders Grades 1–2 © 2008 by Timothy V. Rasinski, Scholastic Teaching Resources

Name _____

Read the clues, then write the words.
Start at the bottom and climb to the top.

On the Line

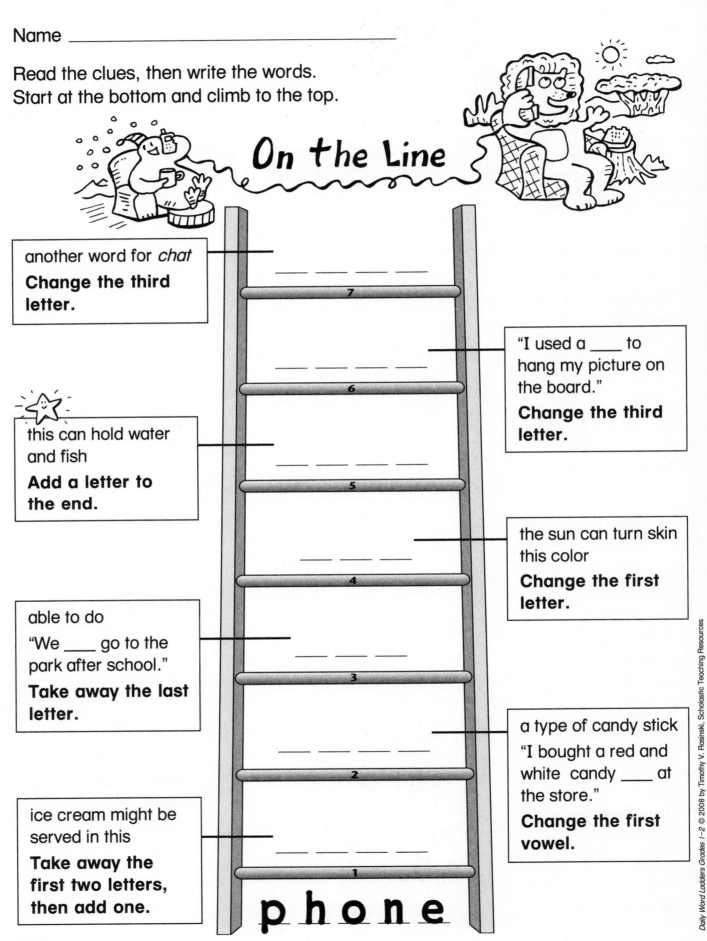

another word for *chat*
Change the third letter.

this can hold water and fish
Add a letter to the end.

able to do
"We ___ go to the park after school."
Take away the last letter.

ice cream might be served in this
Take away the first two letters, then add one.

7

6

5

4

3

2

1

"I used a ___ to hang my picture on the board."
Change the third letter.

the sun can turn skin this color
Change the first letter.

a type of candy stick
"I bought a red and white candy ___ at the store."
Change the first vowel.

p h o n e

110

Name _____

Read the clues, then write the words.
Start at the bottom and climb to the top.

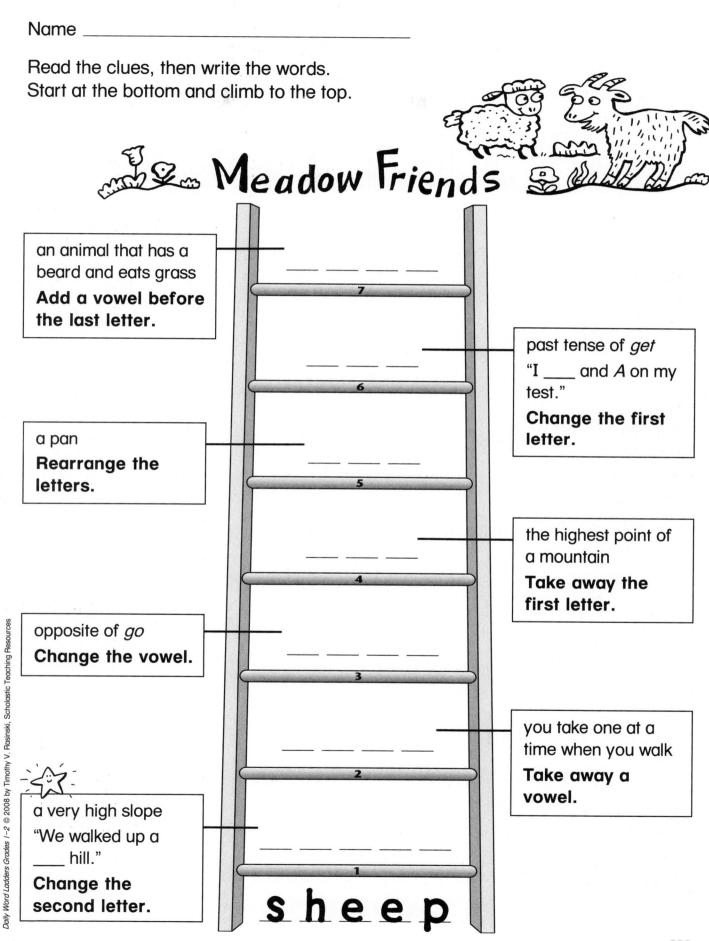

Meadow Friends

an animal that has a beard and eats grass
Add a vowel before the last letter.

7

6

past tense of *get*
"I ___ and *A* on my test."
Change the first letter.

a pan
Rearrange the letters.

5

the highest point of a mountain
Take away the first letter.

4

opposite of *go*
Change the vowel.

3

you take one at a time when you walk
Take away a vowel.

2

a very high slope
"We walked up a ___ hill."
Change the second letter.

1

s h e e p

Name _____

Read the clues, then write the words.
Start at the bottom and climb to the top.

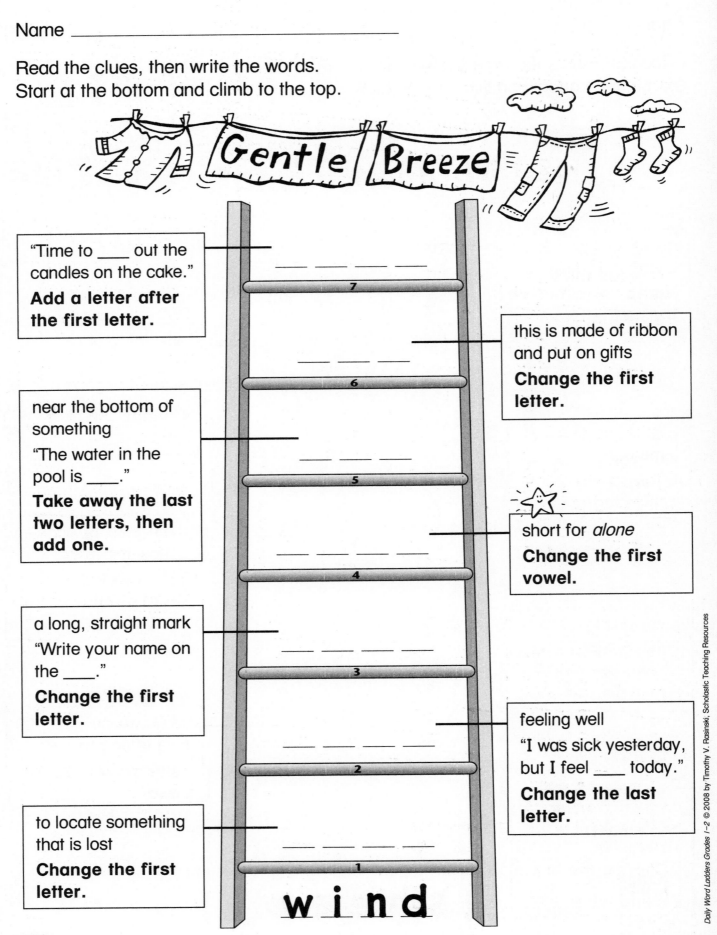

Gentle Breeze

"Time to ____ out the candles on the cake."
Add a letter after the first letter.

this is made of ribbon and put on gifts
Change the first letter.

near the bottom of something
"The water in the pool is ____."
Take away the last two letters, then add one.

short for *alone*
Change the first vowel.

a long, straight mark
"Write your name on the ____."
Change the first letter.

feeling well
"I was sick yesterday, but I feel ____ today."
Change the last letter.

to locate something that is lost
Change the first letter.

7

6

5

4

3

2

1

w i n d

Daily Word Ladders Grades 1–2 © 2008 by Timothy V. Rasinski, Scholastic Teaching Resources

Name _____

Read the clues, then write the words.
Start at the bottom and climb to the top.

Big and Cuddly

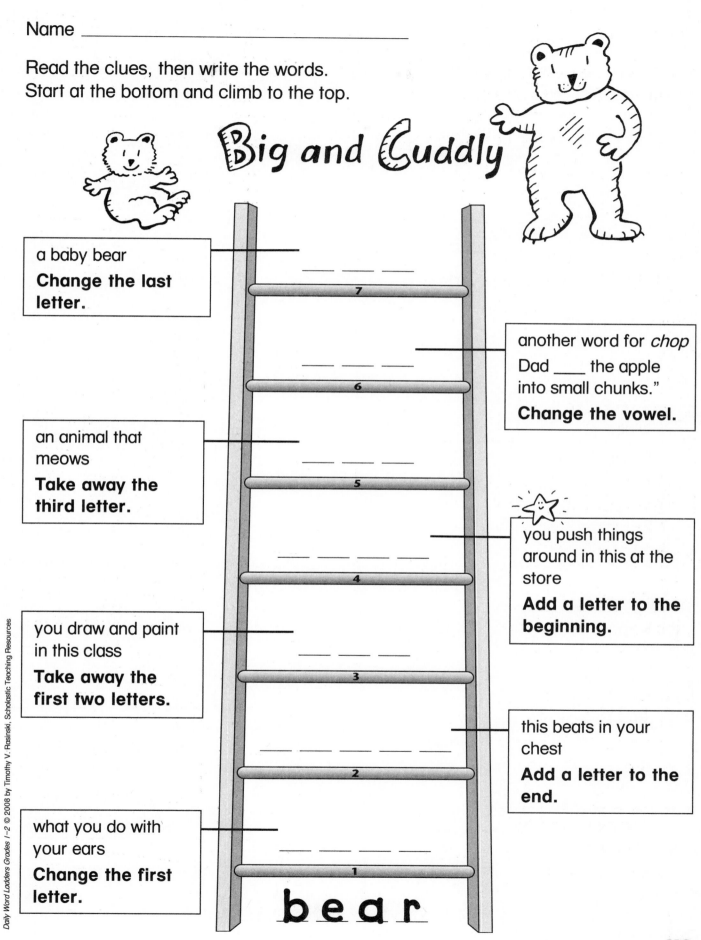

a baby bear
Change the last letter.

another word for *chop*
"Dad ___ the apple into small chunks."
Change the vowel.

an animal that meows
Take away the third letter.

you push things around in this at the store
Add a letter to the beginning.

you draw and paint in this class
Take away the first two letters.

this beats in your chest
Add a letter to the end.

what you do with your ears
Change the first letter.

7

6

5

4

3

2

1

b e a r

Name _____

Read the clues, then write the words.
Start at the bottom and climb to the top.

All in a Day

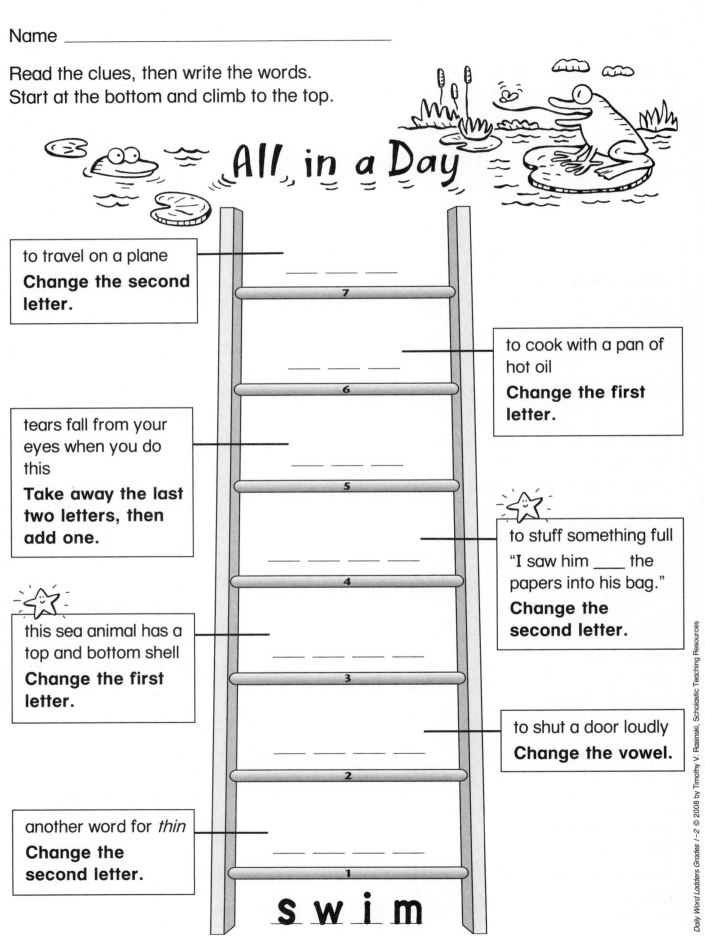

to travel on a plane
Change the second letter.

7 ___ ___ ___ ___

to cook with a pan of hot oil
Change the first letter.

6 ___ ___ ___

tears fall from your eyes when you do this
Take away the last two letters, then add one.

5 ___ ___ ___

to stuff something full
"I saw him ____ the papers into his bag."
Change the second letter.

4 ___ ___ ___ ___

this sea animal has a top and bottom shell
Change the first letter.

3 ___ ___ ___ ___

to shut a door loudly
Change the vowel.

2 ___ ___ ___ ___

another word for *thin*
Change the second letter.

1 ___ ___ ___ ___

s w i m

Daily Word Ladders Grades 1–2 © 2008 by Timothy V. Rasinski, Scholastic Teaching Resources

Name _____

Read the clues, then write the words.
Start at the bottom and climb to the top.

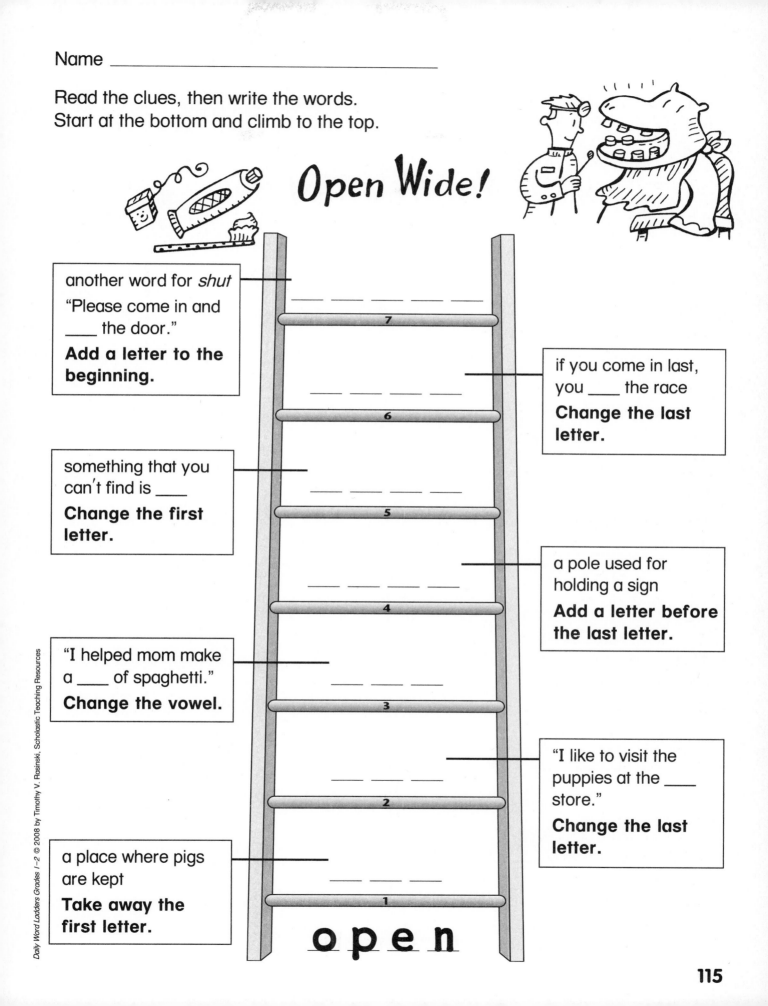

Open Wide!

another word for *shut*
"Please come in and ___ the door."
Add a letter to the beginning.

_ _ _ _ _   7

if you come in last, you ___ the race
Change the last letter.

_ _ _ _   6

something that you can't find is ___
Change the first letter.

_ _ _ _   5

a pole used for holding a sign
Add a letter before the last letter.

_ _ _ _   4

"I helped mom make a ___ of spaghetti."
Change the vowel.

_ _ _   3

"I like to visit the puppies at the ___ store."
Change the last letter.

_ _ _   2

a place where pigs are kept
Take away the first letter.

_ _ _   1

o p e n

Daily Word Ladders Grades 1–2 © 2008 by Timothy V. Rasinski, Scholastic Teaching Resources

Name _____

Read the clues, then write the words.
Start at the bottom and climb to the top.

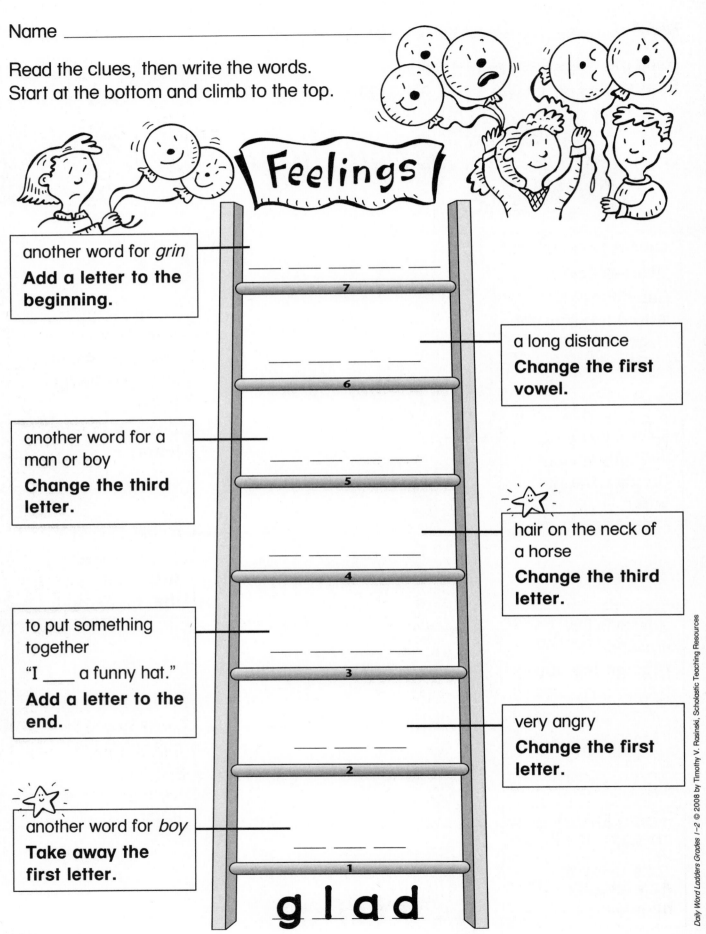

Feelings

another word for *grin*
Add a letter to the beginning.

7 _ _ _ _ _

a long distance
Change the first vowel.

6 _ _ _ _

another word for a man or boy
Change the third letter.

5 _ _ _ _

hair on the neck of a horse
Change the third letter.

4 _ _ _ _

to put something together
"I ___ a funny hat."
Add a letter to the end.

3 _ _ _ _

very angry
Change the first letter.

2 _ _ _ _

another word for *boy*
Take away the first letter.

1 _ _ _ _

g l a d

Name _____

Read the clues, then write the words.
Start at the bottom and climb to the top.

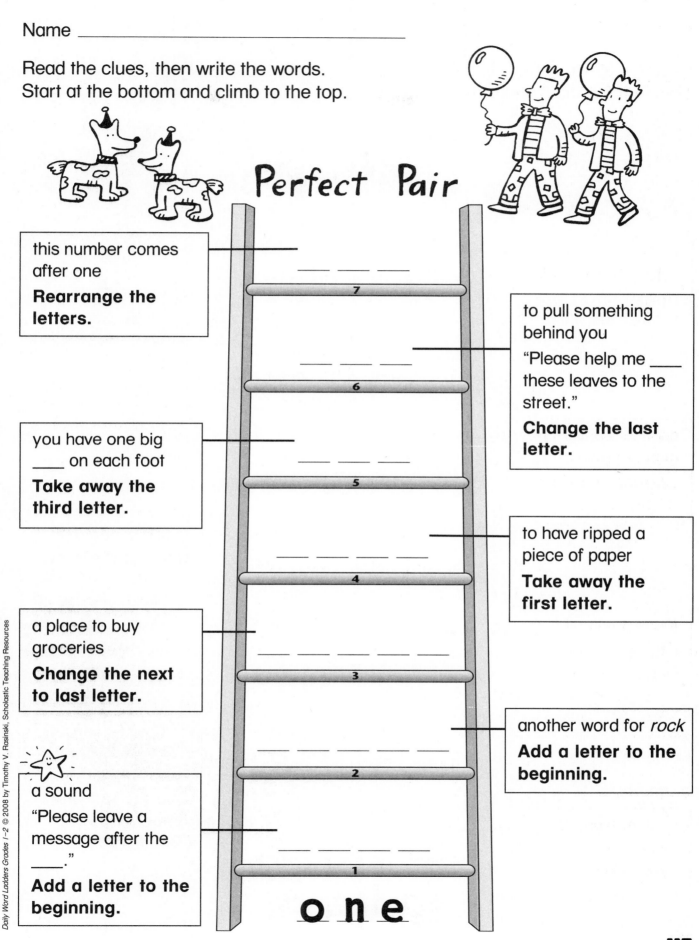

Perfect Pair

this number comes after one
Rearrange the letters.

_ _ _ (7)

to pull something behind you
"Please help me ___ these leaves to the street."
Change the last letter.

_ _ _ (6)

you have one big ___ on each foot
Take away the third letter.

_ _ _ (5)

to have ripped a piece of paper
Take away the first letter.

_ _ _ _ (4)

a place to buy groceries
Change the next to last letter.

_ _ _ _ (3)

another word for *rock*
Add a letter to the beginning.

_ _ _ _ (2)

a sound
"Please leave a message after the ___."
Add a letter to the beginning.

_ _ _ _ (1)

o n e

Name _____

Read the clues, then write the words.
Start at the bottom and climb to the top.

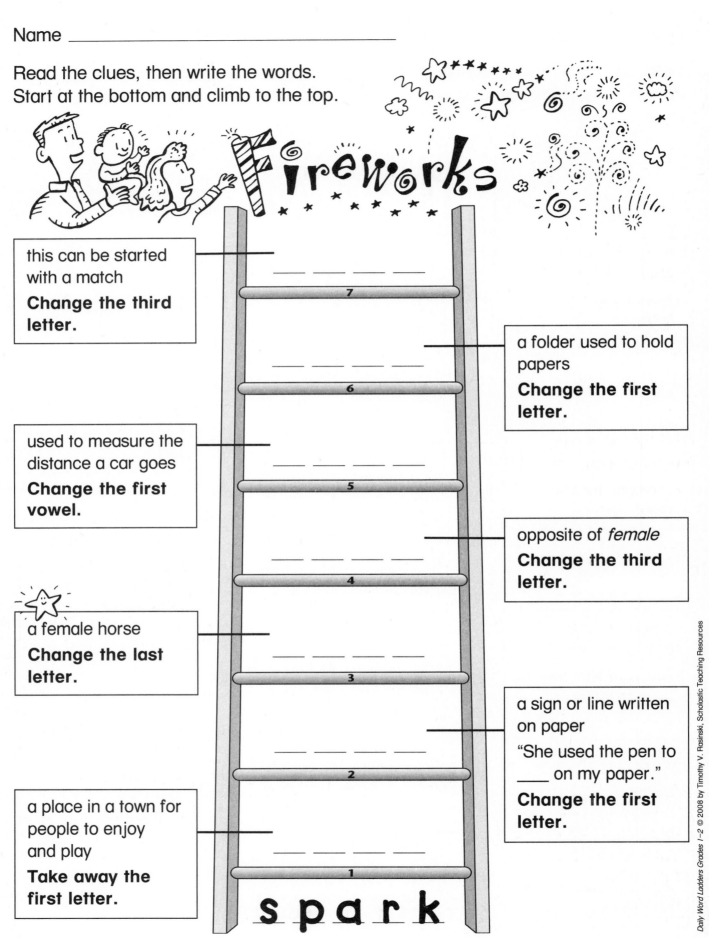

Fireworks

this can be started with a match
Change the third letter.

a folder used to hold papers
Change the first letter.

used to measure the distance a car goes
Change the first vowel.

opposite of *female*
Change the third letter.

a female horse
Change the last letter.

a sign or line written on paper
"She used the pen to ____ on my paper."
Change the first letter.

a place in a town for people to enjoy and play
Take away the first letter.

7

6

5

4

3

2

1

s p a r k

Daily Word Ladders Grades 1–2 © 2008 by Timothy V. Rasinski, Scholastic Teaching Resources

Name _____

Read the clues, then write the words.
Start at the bottom and climb to the top.

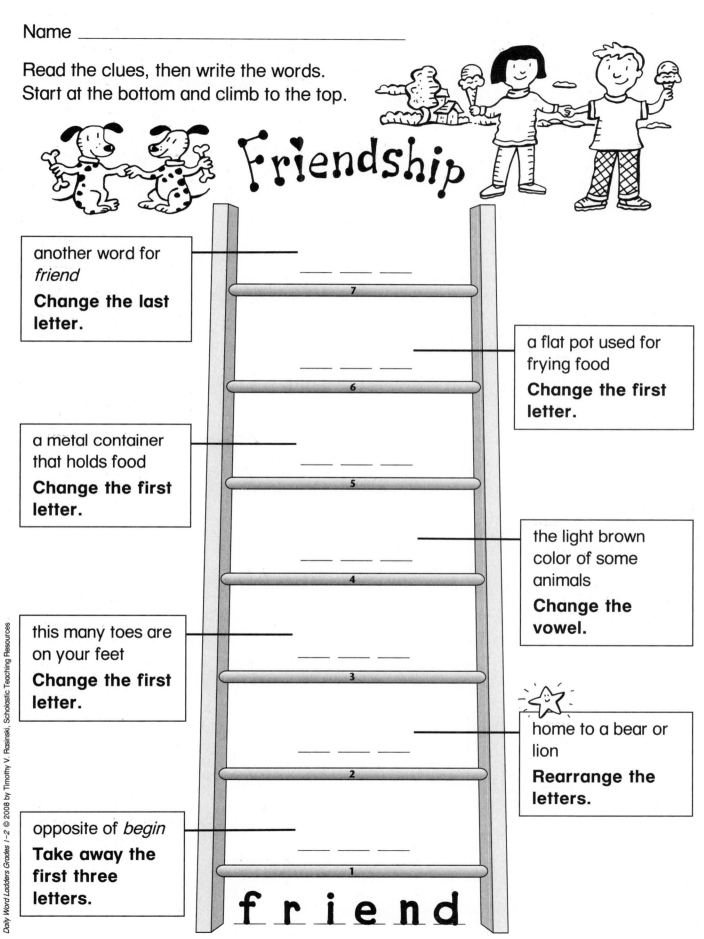

Friendship

another word for *friend*
Change the last letter.

7 _ _ _ _ _ _

a flat pot used for frying food
Change the first letter.

6 _ _ _ _ _

a metal container that holds food
Change the first letter.

5 _ _ _

the light brown color of some animals
Change the vowel.

4 _ _ _ _

this many toes are on your feet
Change the first letter.

3 _ _ _ _

home to a bear or lion
Rearrange the letters.

2 _ _ _ _

opposite of *begin*
Take away the first three letters.

1 _ _ _

f r i e n d

Name _____

Read the clues, then write the words.
Start at the bottom and climb to the top.

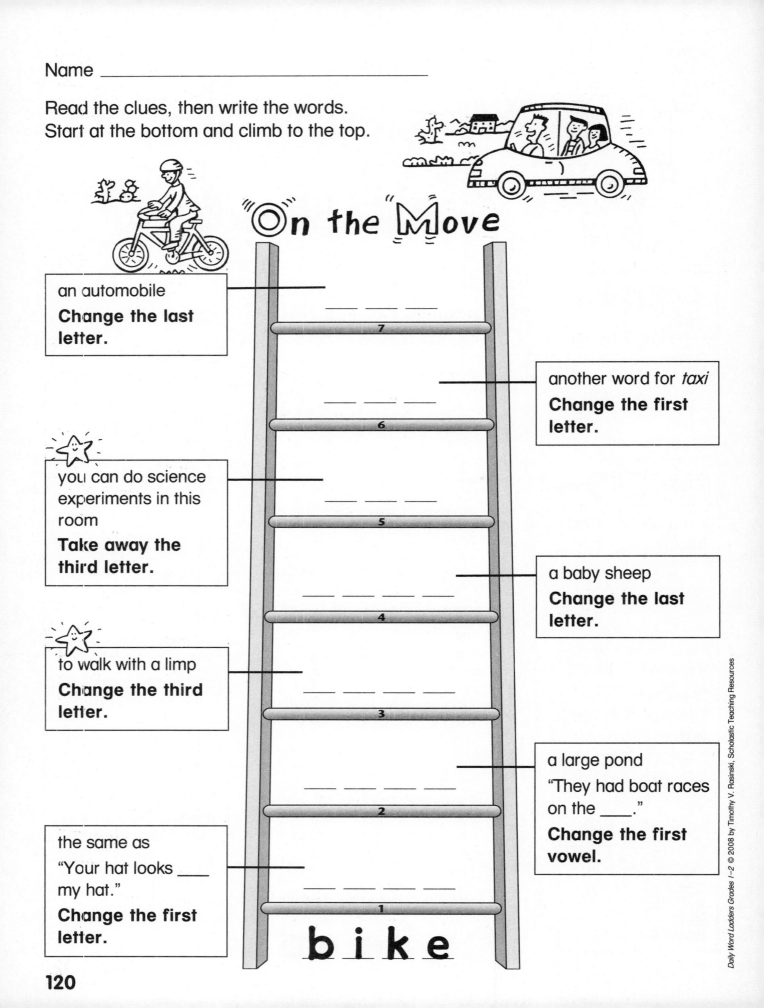

On the Move

an automobile
Change the last letter.

7 _ _ _ _

another word for *taxi*
Change the first letter.

6 _ _ _ _

you can do science experiments in this room
Take away the third letter.

5 _ _ _

a baby sheep
Change the last letter.

4 _ _ _ _

to walk with a limp
Change the third letter.

3 _ _ _ _

a large pond
"They had boat races on the ____."
Change the first vowel.

2 _ _ _ _

the same as
"Your hat looks ____ my hat."
Change the first letter.

1 _ _ _ _

b i k e

Daily Word Ladders Grades 1–2 © 2008 by Timothy V. Rasinski, Scholastic Teaching Resources

Name _____

Read the clues, then write the words.
Start at the bottom and climb to the top.

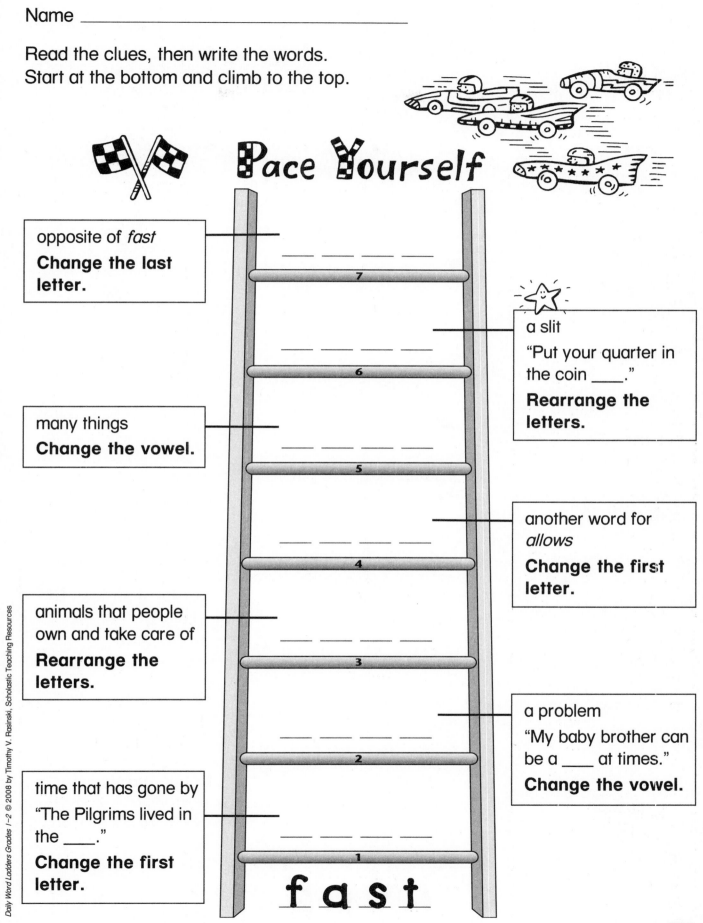

Pace Yourself

opposite of *fast*
Change the last letter.

— — — —
7

a slit
"Put your quarter in the coin ___."
Rearrange the letters.

— — — —
6

many things
Change the vowel.

— — — —
5

another word for *allows*
Change the first letter.

— — — — —
4

animals that people own and take care of
Rearrange the letters.

— — — —
3

a problem
"My baby brother can be a ___ at times."
Change the vowel.

— — — —
2

time that has gone by
"The Pilgrims lived in the ___."
Change the first letter.

— — — —
1

f a s t

Name _____

Read the clues, then write the words.
Start at the bottom and climb to the top.

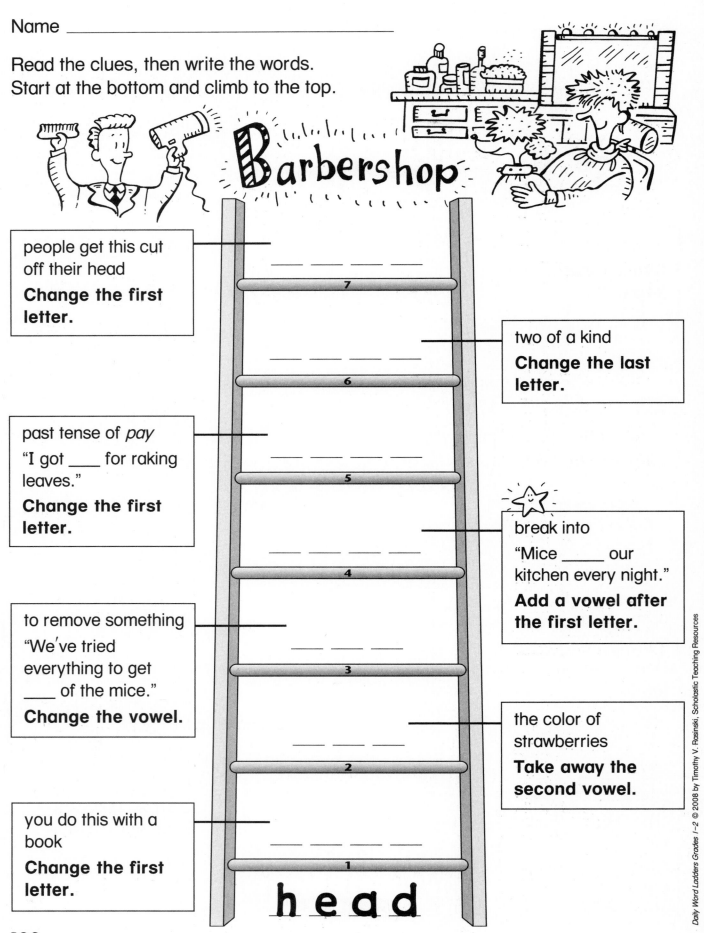

Barbershop

people get this cut off their head
Change the first letter.

two of a kind
Change the last letter.

past tense of *pay*
"I got ____ for raking leaves."
Change the first letter.

break into
"Mice _____ our kitchen every night."
Add a vowel after the first letter.

to remove something
"We've tried everything to get ___ of the mice."
Change the vowel.

the color of strawberries
Take away the second vowel.

you do this with a book
Change the first letter.

7

6

5

4

3

2

1

h e a d

Daily Word Ladders Grades 1–2 © 2008 by Timothy V. Rasinski, Scholastic Teaching Resources

Name _____

Read the clues, then write the words.
Start at the bottom and climb to the top.

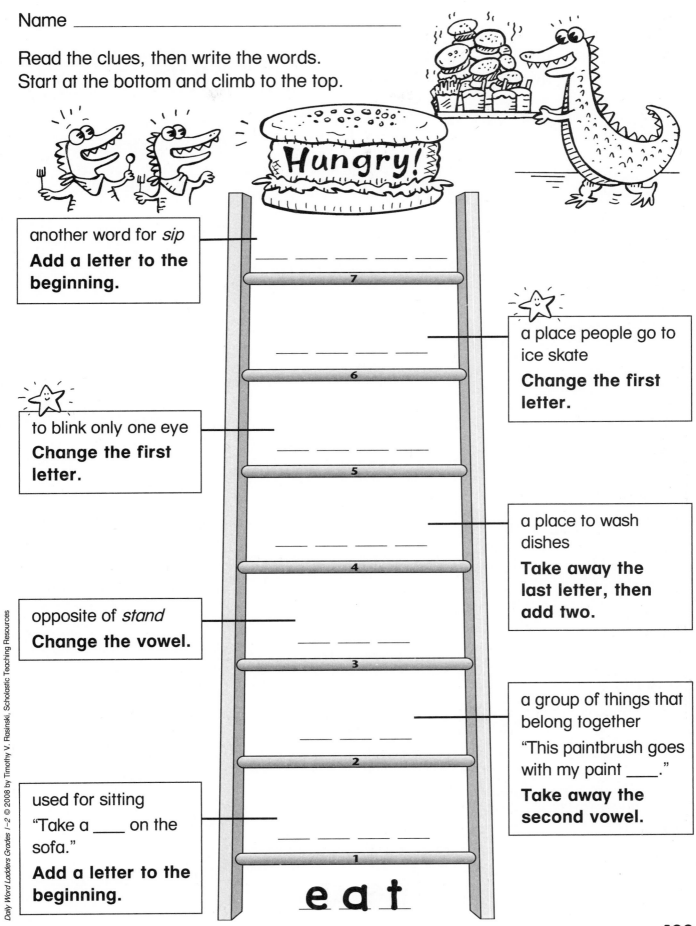

another word for *sip*
Add a letter to the beginning.

a place people go to ice skate
Change the first letter.

to blink only one eye
Change the first letter.

a place to wash dishes
Take away the last letter, then add two.

opposite of *stand*
Change the vowel.

a group of things that belong together
"This paintbrush goes with my paint ___."
Take away the second vowel.

used for sitting
"Take a ___ on the sofa."
Add a letter to the beginning.

7

6

5

4

3

2

1

e a t

Daily Word Ladders Grades 1–2 © 2008 by Timothy V. Rasinski, Scholastic Teaching Resources

Name _____

Read the clues, then write the words.
Start at the bottom and climb to the top.

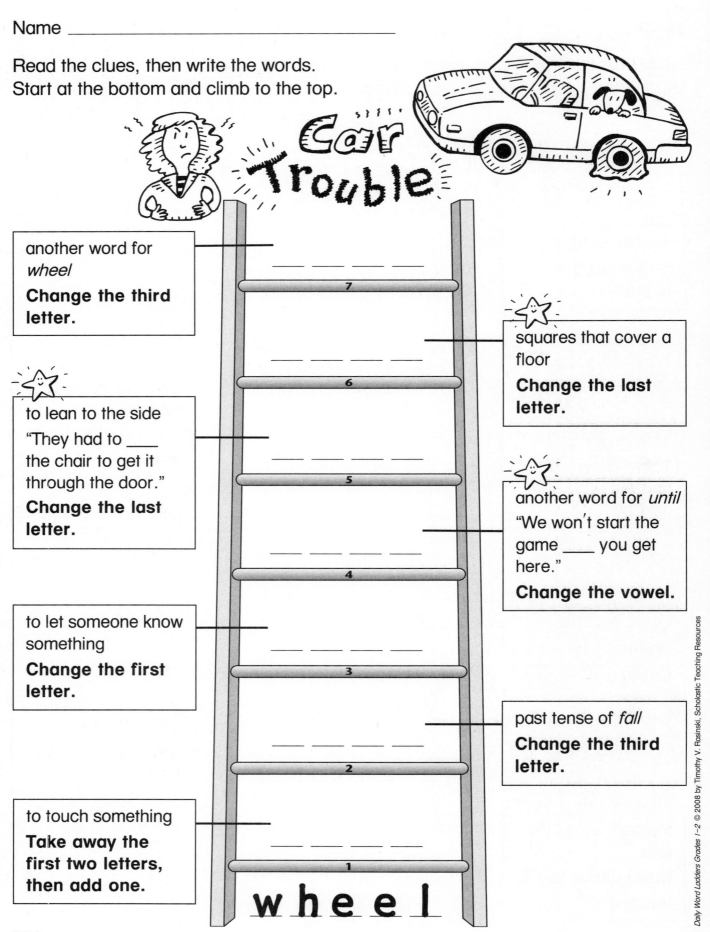

Car Trouble

another word for *wheel*
Change the third letter.

— — — — — 7

— — — — — 6

to lean to the side
"They had to ____ the chair to get it through the door."
Change the last letter.

— — — — — 5

— — — — 4

to let someone know something
Change the first letter.

— — — — — 3

— — — — 2

to touch something
Take away the first two letters, then add one.

— — — — — 1

squares that cover a floor
Change the last letter.

another word for *until*
"We won't start the game ____ you get here."
Change the vowel.

past tense of *fall*
Change the third letter.

w h e e l

Daily Word Ladders Grades 1–2 © 2008 by Timothy V. Rasinski, Scholastic Teaching Resources

Name _____

Read the clues, then write the words.
Start at the bottom and climb to the top.

Need a Lift?

vehicle used for moving big things
"They used the pickup ____ to move the washer."
Add a letter after the first letter.

to push in the ends of a bed cover
"My grandma likes to ____ me into bed at night."
Change the first letter.

a bird that quacks
Take away the last letter, then add two.

past tense of *dig*
Change the vowel.

a poodle or a hound is this
Change the last letter.

a female deer
Change the first letter.

the front end of a shoe
Change the last letter.

7

6

5

4

3

2

1

t o w

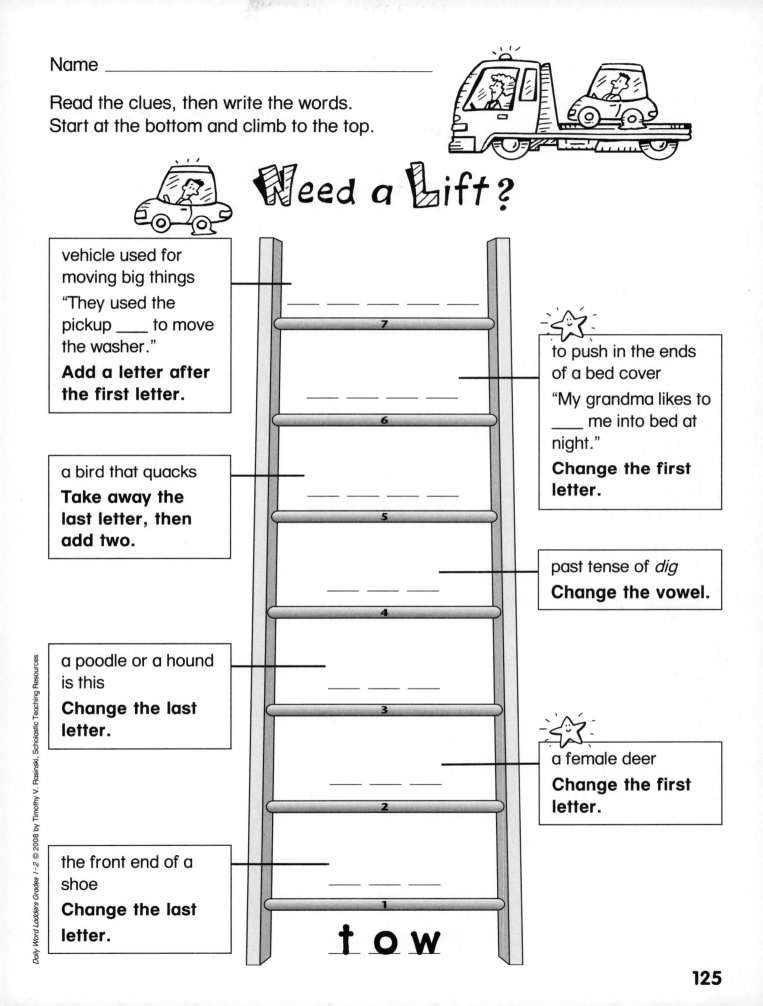

Name _____

Read the clues, then write the words.
Start at the bottom and climb to the top.

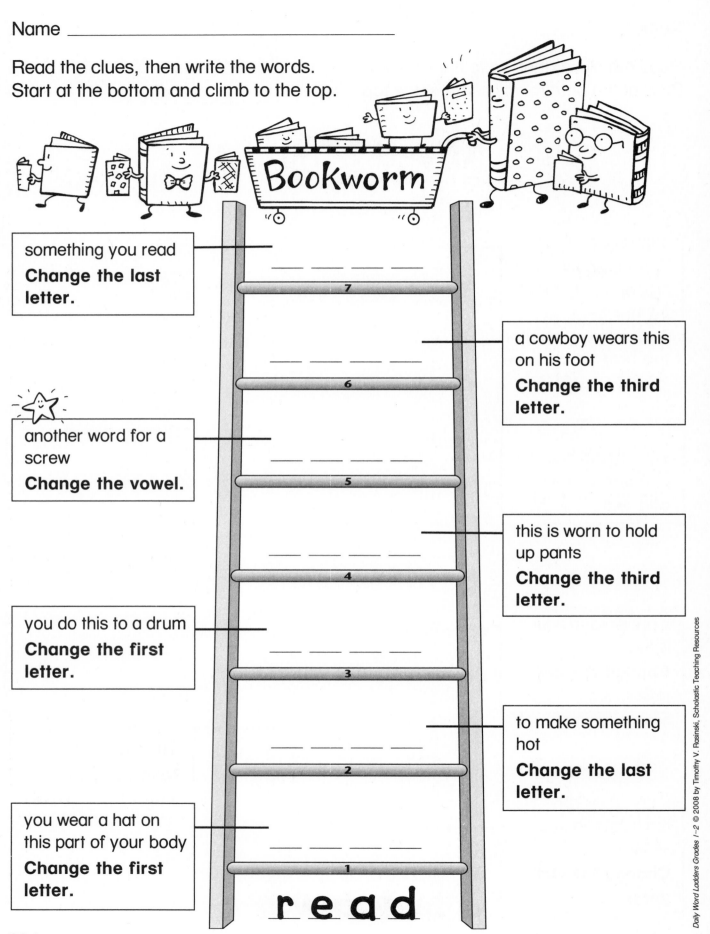

Bookworm

something you read
Change the last letter.

a cowboy wears this on his foot
Change the third letter.

another word for a screw
Change the vowel.

this is worn to hold up pants
Change the third letter.

you do this to a drum
Change the first letter.

to make something hot
Change the last letter.

you wear a hat on this part of your body
Change the first letter.

7

6

5

4

3

2

1

r e a d

Daily Word Ladders Grades 1–2 © 2008 by Timothy V. Rasinski, Scholastic Teaching Resources

Name _____

Read the clues, then write the words.
Start at the bottom and climb to the top.

A Little Light

this makes the light
that comes from a
candle
**Add a vowel to
the end.**

7 _ _ _ _ _

6 _ _ _ _

a type of evergreen
tree
**Change the last
letter.**

to be the right size
"This shirt is a
perfect ___."
**Change the first
letter.**

5 _ _ _ _

a small amount
Change the vowel.

a flying mammal that
lives in caves
**Take away the last
letter.**

4 _ _ _ _

3 _ _ _

2 _ _ _ _

you take a ___ to
get clean
**Take away the
next to last letter.**

a group of things
"Let's bake a ___
of cookies."
**Change the first
letter.**

1 **m a t c h**

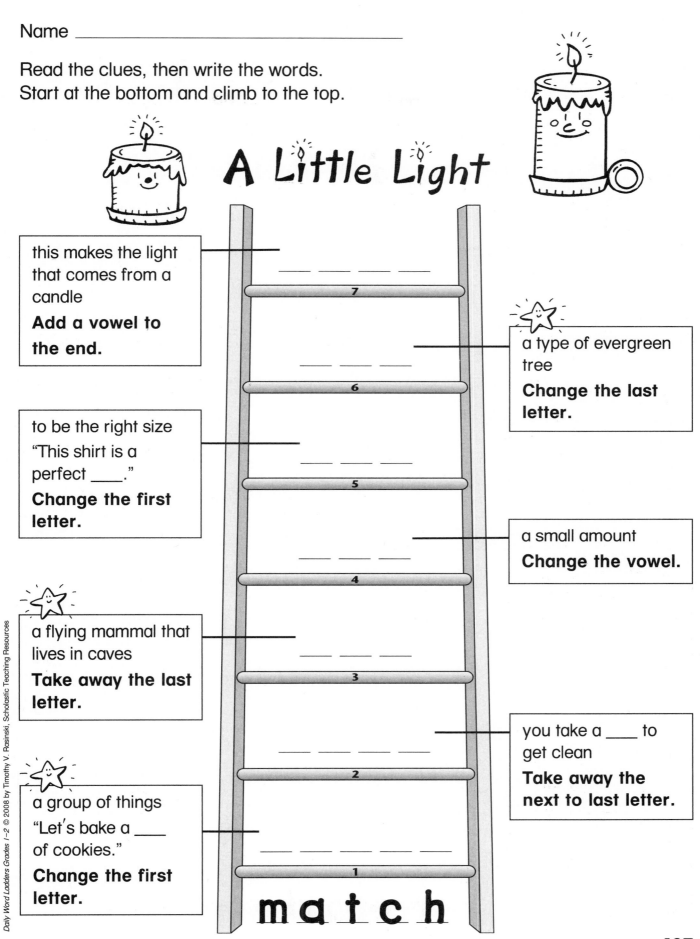

Name _____

Read the clues, then write the words.
Start at the bottom and climb to the top.

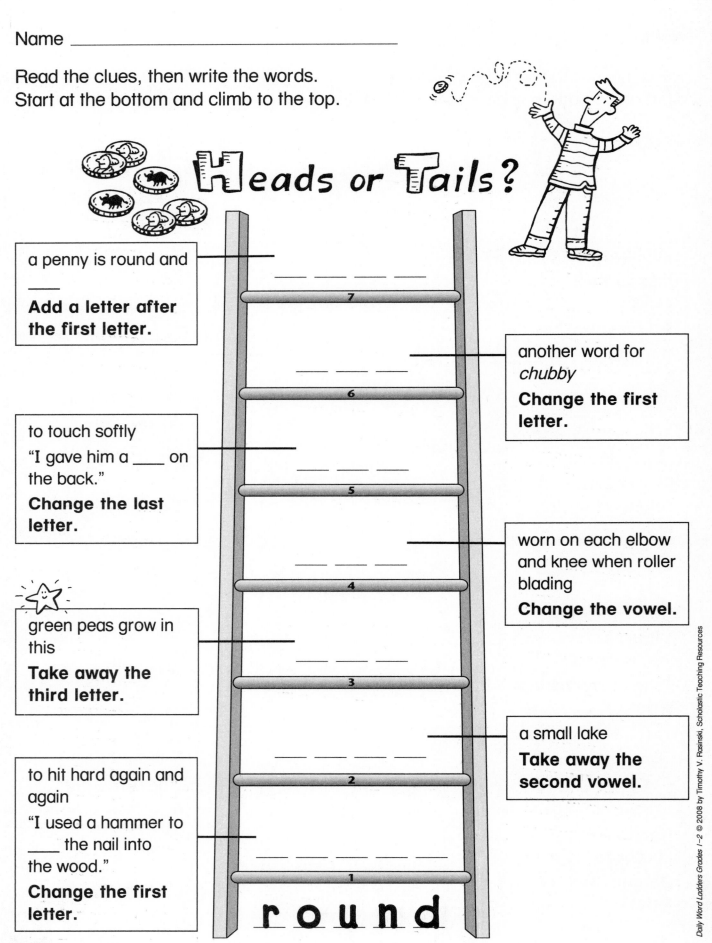

Heads or Tails?

a penny is round and
____

**Add a letter after
the first letter.**

_ _ _ _ _

7

another word for
chubby

**Change the first
letter.**

_ _ _ _

6

to touch softly

"I gave him a ____ on
the back."

**Change the last
letter.**

_ _ _ _

5

worn on each elbow
and knee when roller
blading

Change the vowel.

_ _ _ _

4

green peas grow in
this

**Take away the
third letter.**

_ _ _ _

3

a small lake

**Take away the
second vowel.**

_ _ _ _ _

2

to hit hard again and
again

"I used a hammer to
____ the nail into
the wood."

**Change the first
letter.**

_ _ _ _ _

1

r o u n d

Daily Word Ladders Grades 1–2 © 2008 by Timothy V. Rasinski, Scholastic Teaching Resources

Name _____

Read the clues, then write the words.
Start at the bottom and climb to the top.

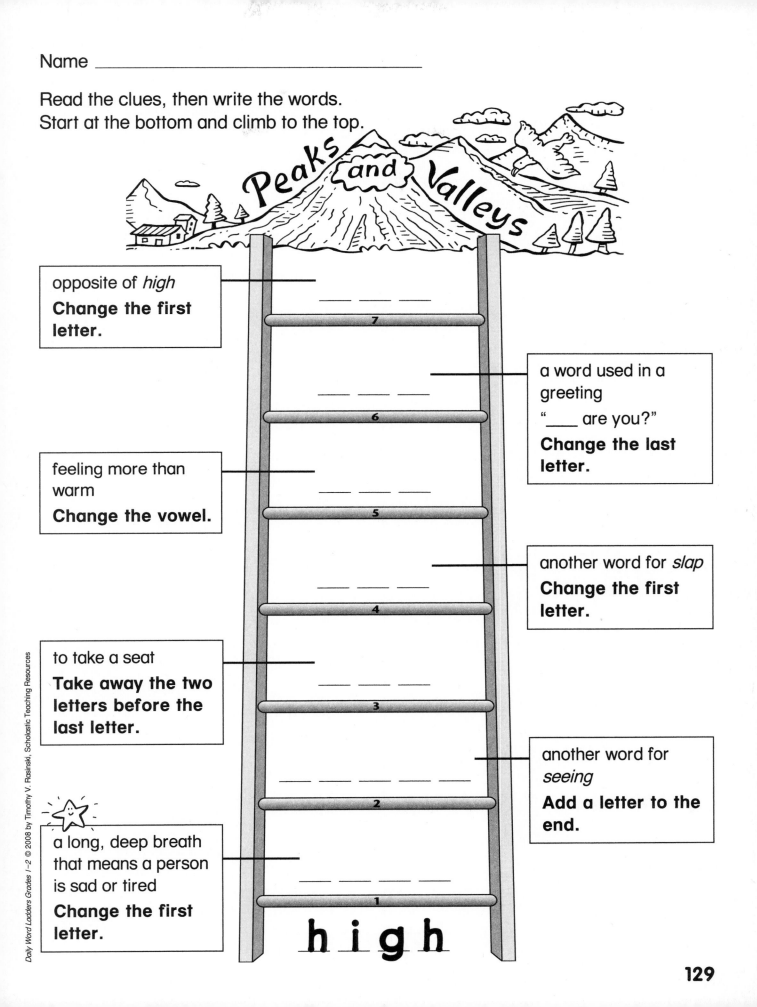

opposite of *high*
Change the first letter.

a word used in a greeting
"___ are you?"
Change the last letter.

feeling more than warm
Change the vowel.

another word for *slap*
Change the first letter.

to take a seat
Take away the two letters before the last letter.

another word for *seeing*
Add a letter to the end.

a long, deep breath that means a person is sad or tired
Change the first letter.

h i g h

Daily Word Ladders Grades 1–2 © 2008 by Timothy V. Rasinski, Scholastic Teaching Resources

Name _____

Read the clues, then write the words.
Start at the bottom and climb to the top.

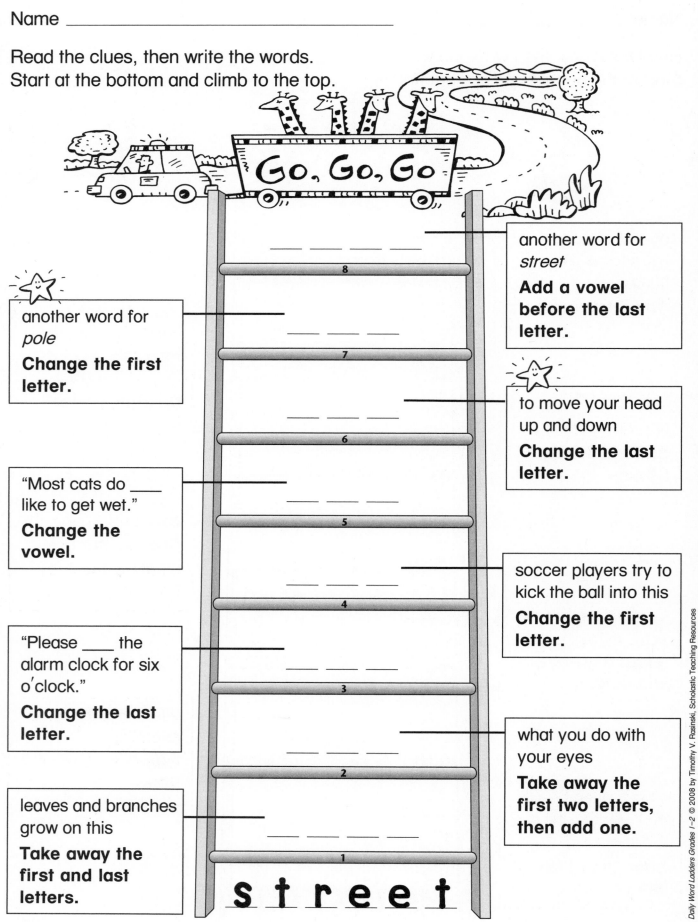

Go, Go, Go

__ __ __ __ __ __   8

another word for
street
**Add a vowel
before the last
letter.**

another word for
pole
**Change the first
letter.**

__ __ __   7

__ __ __   6

to move your head
up and down
**Change the last
letter.**

"Most cats do ____
like to get wet."
**Change the
vowel.**

__ __ __   5

__ __ __   4

soccer players try to
kick the ball into this
**Change the first
letter.**

"Please ____ the
alarm clock for six
o'clock."
**Change the last
letter.**

__ __ __   3

__ __ __   2

what you do with
your eyes
**Take away the
first two letters,
then add one.**

leaves and branches
grow on this
**Take away the
first and last
letters.**

__ __ __ __ __   1

s t r e e t

Daily Word Ladders Grades 1–2 © 2008 by Timothy V. Rasinski, Scholastic Teaching Resources

Name _____

Read the clues, then write the words.
Start at the bottom and climb to the top.

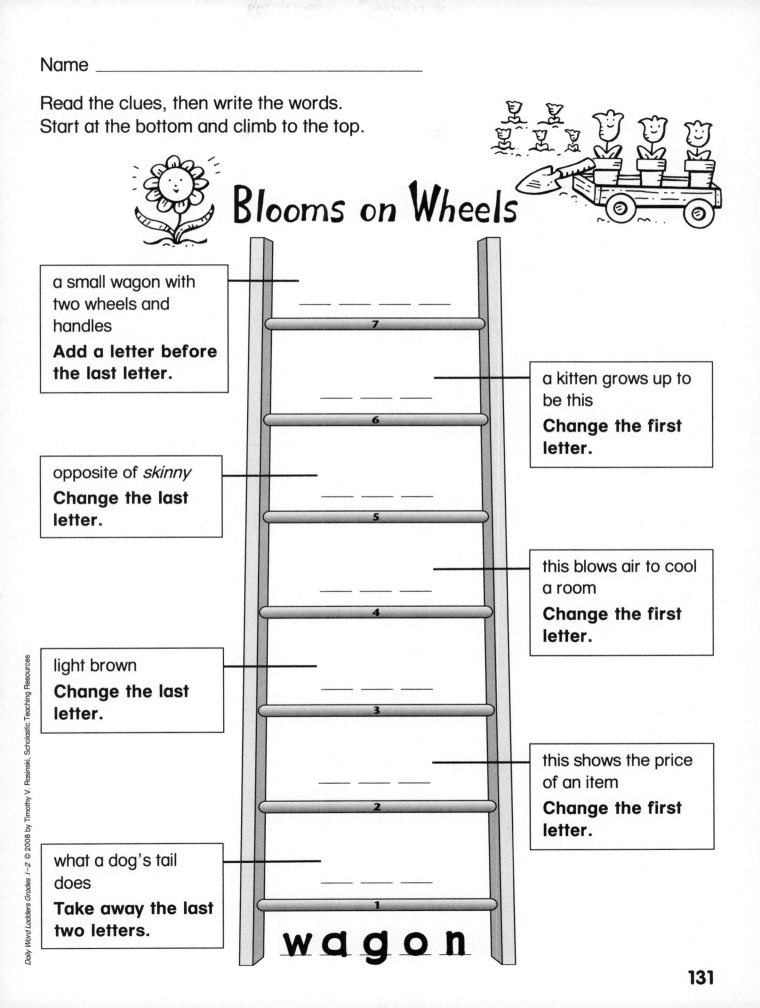

Blooms on Wheels

a small wagon with
two wheels and
handles
**Add a letter before
the last letter.**

7 _ _ _ _ _ _

a kitten grows up to
be this
**Change the first
letter.**

6 _ _ _ _

opposite of *skinny*
**Change the last
letter.**

5 _ _ _

this blows air to cool
a room
**Change the first
letter.**

4 _ _ _

light brown
**Change the last
letter.**

3 _ _ _

this shows the price
of an item
**Change the first
letter.**

2 _ _ _ _

what a dog's tail
does
**Take away the last
two letters.**

1 _ _ _ _

w a g o n

Name _____

Read the clues, then write the words.
Start at the bottom and climb to the top.

Life Saver

another word for *help*
Change the last letter.

to be sick or hurt
Change the second letter.

everything
Take away the first two letters.

another word for *little*
Change the vowel.

you use your nose to ____
Take away the first letter, then add two.

to call out
Change the last letter.

a short, sharp cry
"I heard a dog ____ last night."
Change the first letter.

7

6

5

4

3

2

1

h e l p

Daily Word Ladders Grades 1–2 © 2008 by Timothy V. Rosinski, Scholastic Teaching Resources

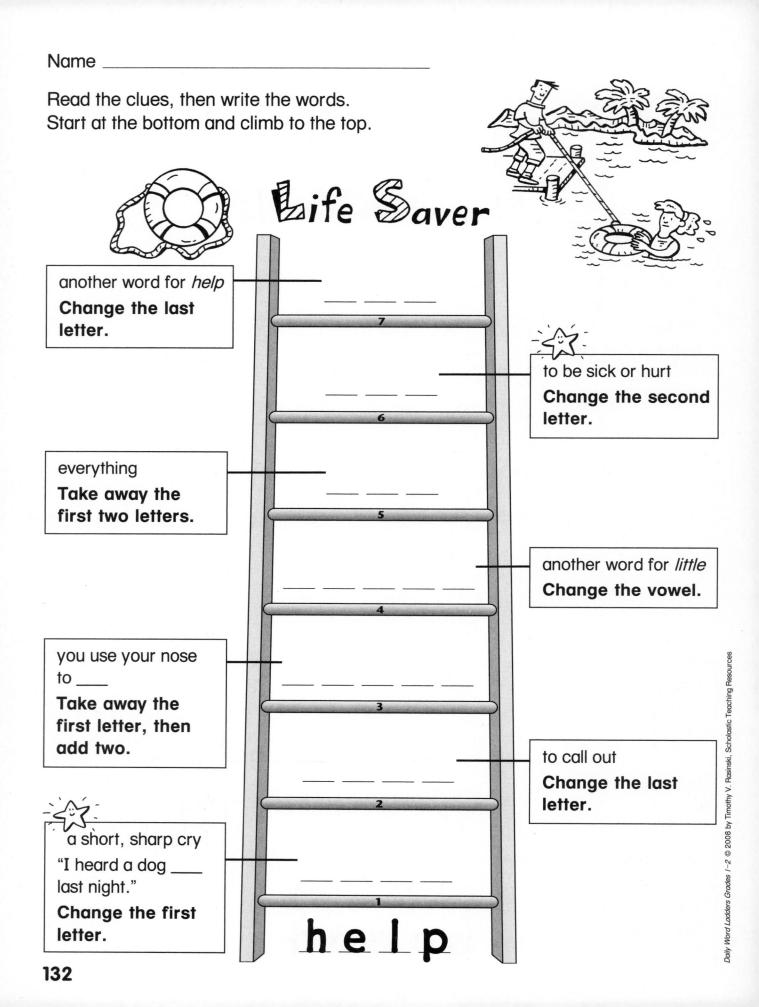

Name _____

Read the clues, then write the words.
Start at the bottom and climb to the top.

Bread and Butter

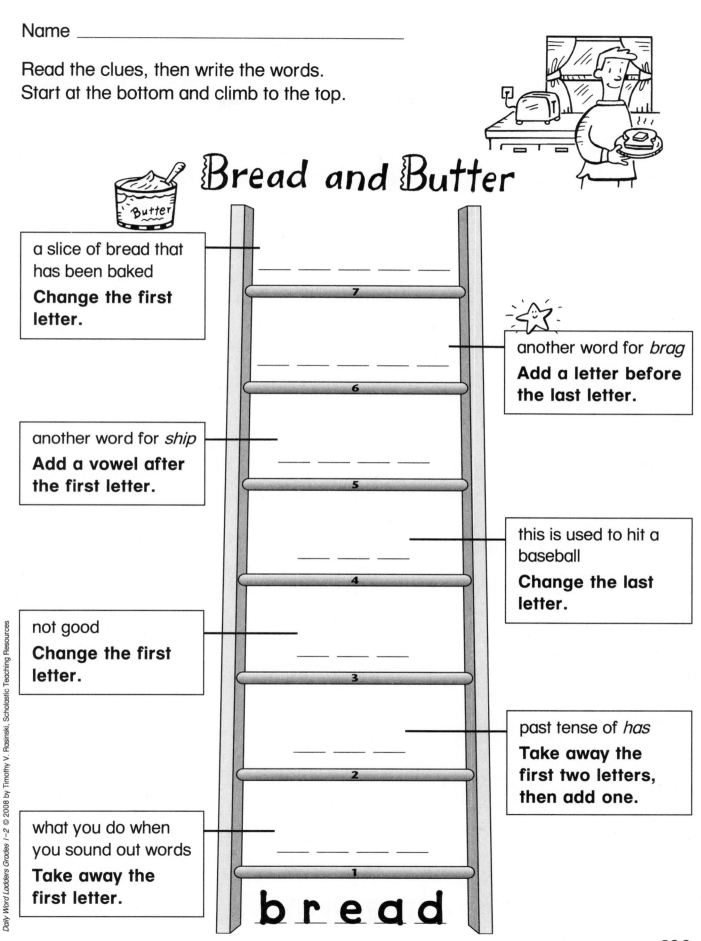

a slice of bread that has been baked
Change the first letter.

another word for *brag*
Add a letter before the last letter.

another word for *ship*
Add a vowel after the first letter.

this is used to hit a baseball
Change the last letter.

not good
Change the first letter.

past tense of *has*
Take away the first two letters, then add one.

what you do when you sound out words
Take away the first letter.

b r e a d

Name _____

Read the clues, then write the words.
Start at the bottom and climb to the top.

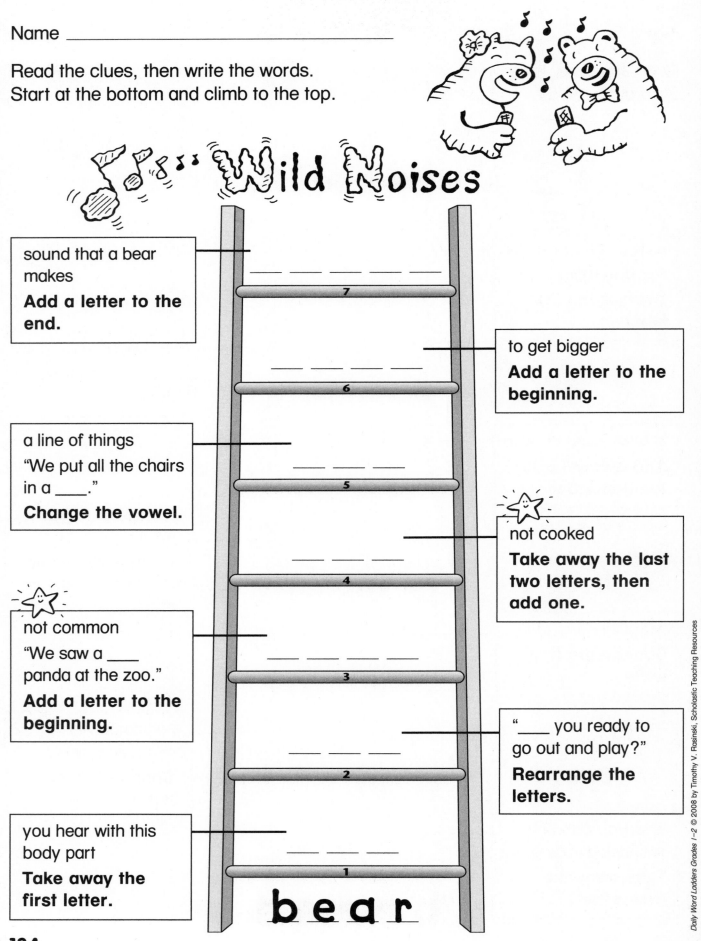

Wild Noises

sound that a bear makes
Add a letter to the end.

to get bigger
Add a letter to the beginning.

a line of things
"We put all the chairs in a ____."
Change the vowel.

not cooked
Take away the last two letters, then add one.

not common
"We saw a ____ panda at the zoo."
Add a letter to the beginning.

"____ you ready to go out and play?"
Rearrange the letters.

you hear with this body part
Take away the first letter.

7
6
5
4
3
2
1

b e a r

Daily Word Ladders Grades 1–2 © 2008 by Timothy V. Rasinski, Scholastic Teaching Resources

Name _____

Read the clues, then write the words.
Start at the bottom and climb to the top.

Open-Air Ride

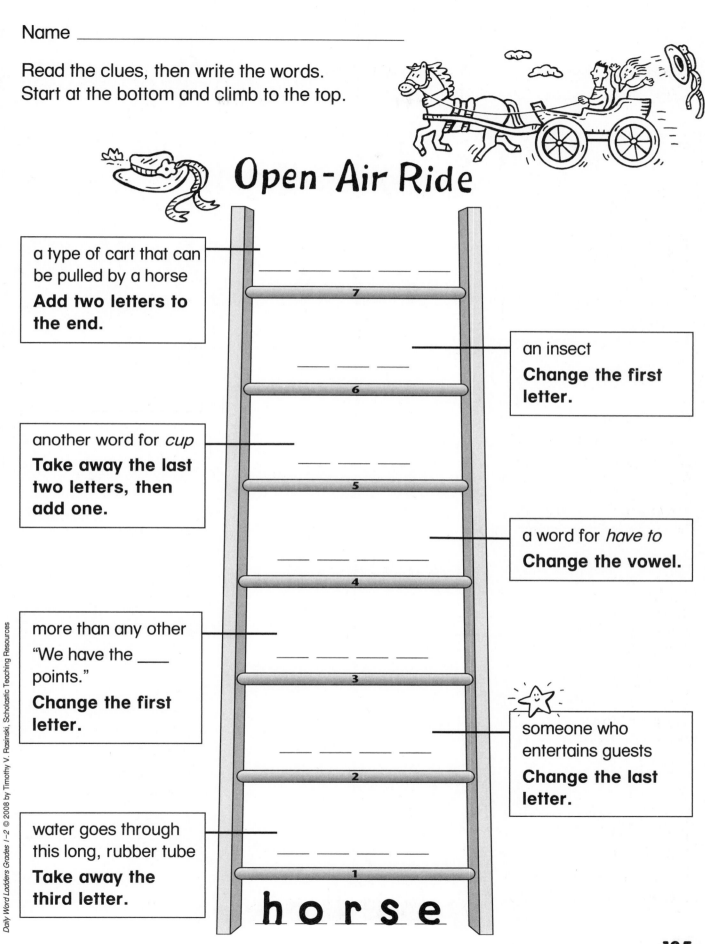

a type of cart that can be pulled by a horse
Add two letters to the end.

an insect
Change the first letter.

another word for *cup*
Take away the last two letters, then add one.

a word for *have to*
Change the vowel.

more than any other
"We have the ___ points."
Change the first letter.

someone who entertains guests
Change the last letter.

water goes through this long, rubber tube
Take away the third letter.

7

6

5

4

3

2

1

h o r s e

Daily Word Ladders Grades 1–2 © 2008 by Timothy V. Rasinski, Scholastic Teaching Resources

Name _____

Read the clues, then write the words.
Start at the bottom and climb to the top.

In the Sky

the color of the sky
Take away the first letter, then add two

7 _ _ _ _ _

a signal
Change the last letter.

6 _ _ _ _

you use a knife to do this
Change the first letter.

5 _ _ _ _

another word for *except*
Take away the last two letters, then add one.

4 _ _ _ _ _

a male cow
Change the vowel.

3 _ _ _ _

this rings at the beginning and end of school
Change the first letter.

2 _ _ _ _ _

another word for *shout*
Take away the last two letters.

1 _ _ _ _ _

y e l l o w

Daily Word Ladders Grades 1–2 © 2008 by Timothy V. Rasinski, Scholastic Teaching Resources

Name _____

Read the clues, then write the words.
Start at the bottom and climb to the top.

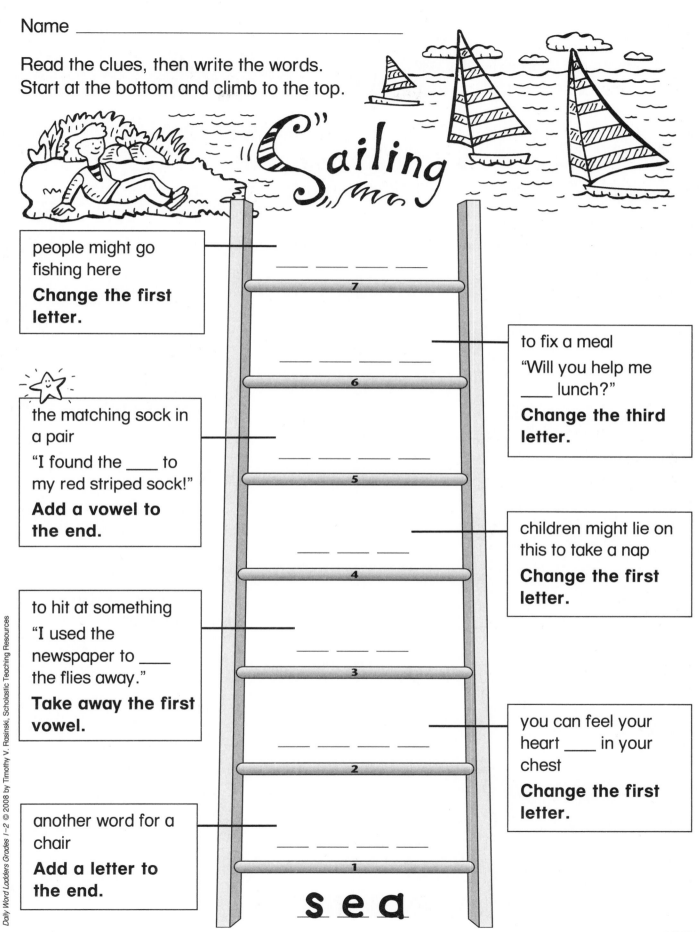

people might go fishing here
Change the first letter.

7 _ _ _ _

to fix a meal
"Will you help me ___ lunch?"
Change the third letter.

6 _ _ _ _

the matching sock in a pair
"I found the ___ to my red striped sock!"
Add a vowel to the end.

5 _ _ _ _

children might lie on this to take a nap
Change the first letter.

4 _ _ _

to hit at something
"I used the newspaper to ___ the flies away."
Take away the first vowel.

3 _ _ _

you can feel your heart ___ in your chest
Change the first letter.

2 _ _ _ _

another word for a chair
Add a letter to the end.

1 _ _ _

s e a

Name _____

Read the clues, then write the words.
Start at the bottom and climb to the top.

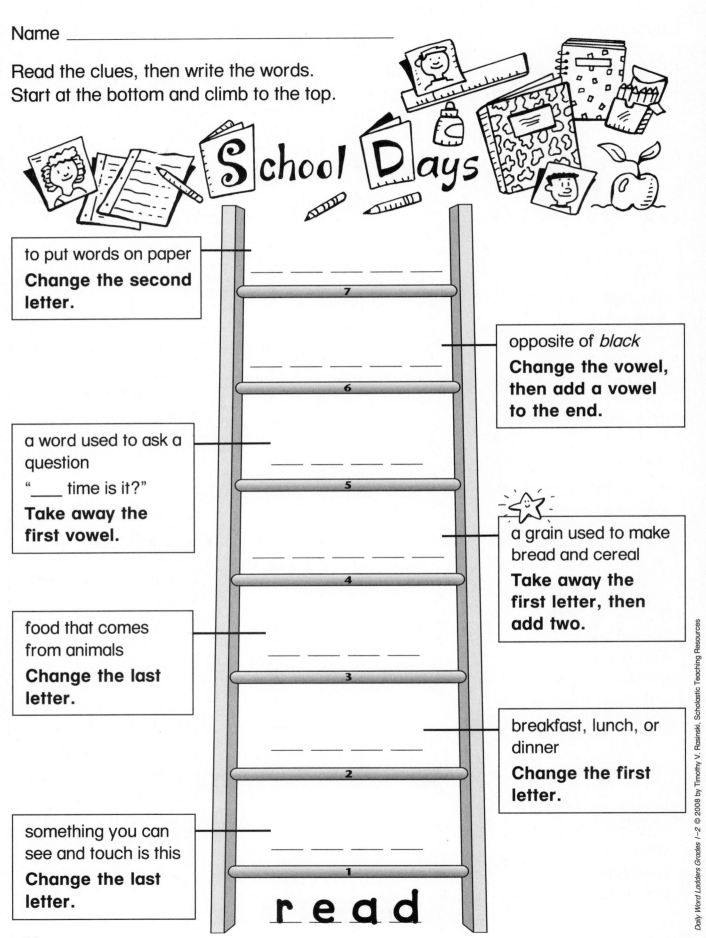

School Days

to put words on paper
Change the second letter.

7

opposite of *black*
Change the vowel, then add a vowel to the end.

6

a word used to ask a question
"___ time is it?"
Take away the first vowel.

5

a grain used to make bread and cereal
Take away the first letter, then add two.

4

food that comes from animals
Change the last letter.

3

breakfast, lunch, or dinner
Change the first letter.

2

something you can see and touch is this
Change the last letter.

1

r e a d

Daily Word Ladders Grades 1–2 © 2008 by Timothy V. Rasinski, Scholastic Teaching Resources

Name _____

Read the clues, then write the words.
Start at the bottom and climb to the top.

Toe-Tapping Tunes

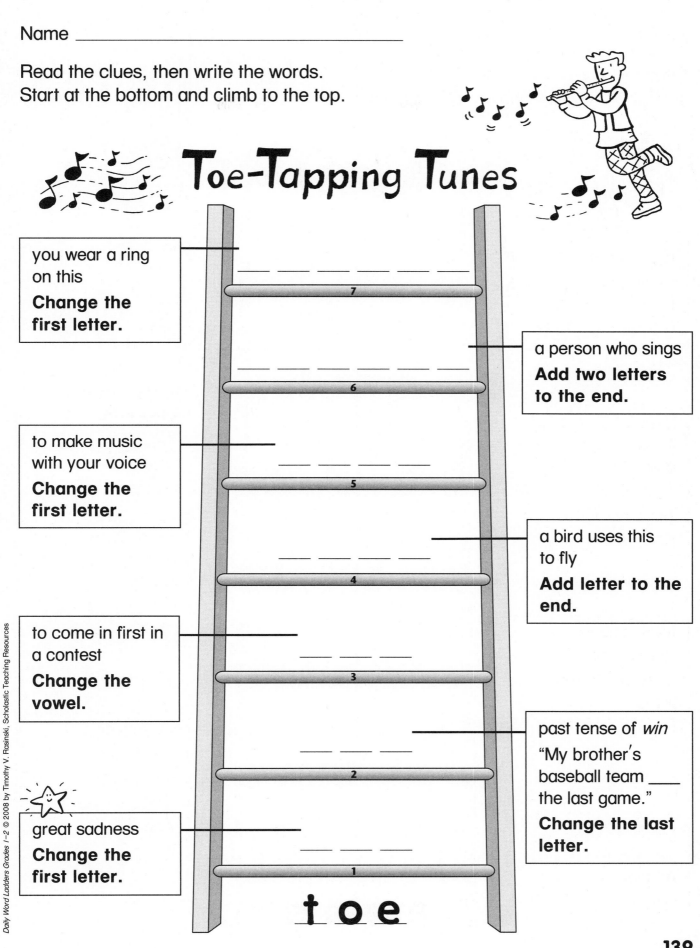

you wear a ring on this
Change the first letter.

a person who sings
Add two letters to the end.

to make music with your voice
Change the first letter.

a bird uses this to fly
Add letter to the end.

to come in first in a contest
Change the vowel.

past tense of *win*
"My brother's baseball team ____ the last game."
Change the last letter.

great sadness
Change the first letter.

t o e

Name _____

Read the clues, then write the words.
Start at the bottom and climb to the top.

You ARE
MY PAL

CATS
RULE

Wonderful Words

letters are put together to make this
Change the first letter.

the wire between a lamp and its plug
Add a letter before the last letter.

a type of fish
Change the last letter.

a small bed
Change the first letter.

coffee can be made in this
Change the first letter.

very much
"I like pepperoni pizza a whole ____."
Change the vowel.

to allow
Take away the last three letters.

7

6

5

4

3

2

1

l e t t e r

Daily Word Ladders Grades 1–2 © 2008 by Timothy V. Rasinski, Scholastic Teaching Resources

Name _____

Read the clues, then write the words.
Start at the bottom and climb to the top.

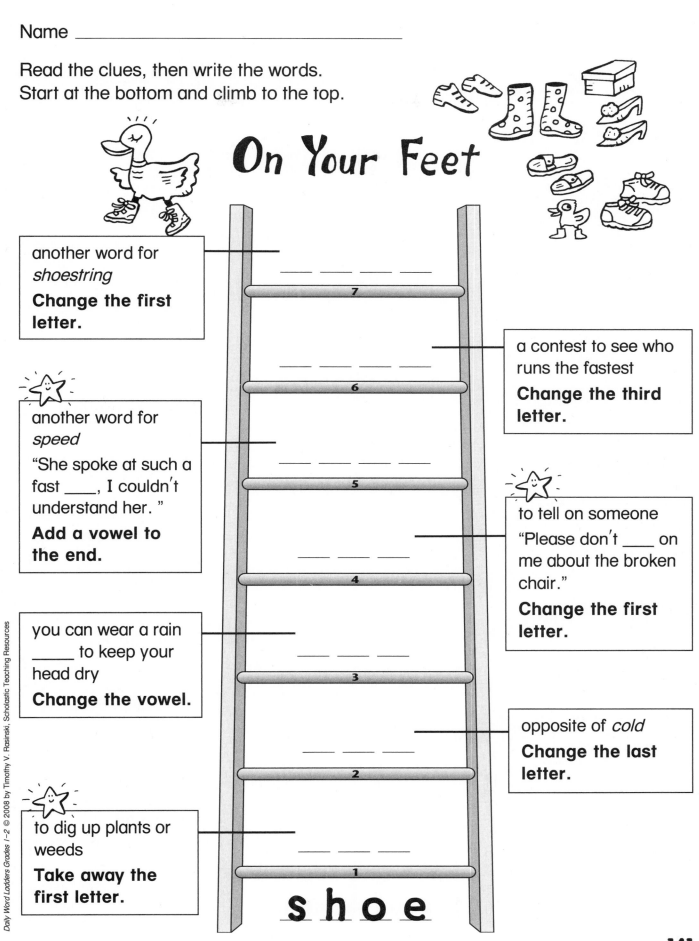

On Your Feet

another word for *shoestring*
Change the first letter.

a contest to see who runs the fastest
Change the third letter.

another word for *speed*
"She spoke at such a fast ____, I couldn't understand her. "
Add a vowel to the end.

to tell on someone
"Please don't ____ on me about the broken chair."
Change the first letter.

you can wear a rain ____ to keep your head dry
Change the vowel.

opposite of *cold*
Change the last letter.

to dig up plants or weeds
Take away the first letter.

7
6
5
4
3
2
1

s h o e

Daily Word Ladders Grades 1–2 © 2008 by Timothy V. Rasinski, Scholastic Teaching Resources

Name _____

Read the clues, then write the words.
Start at the bottom and climb to the top.

Just Peachy!

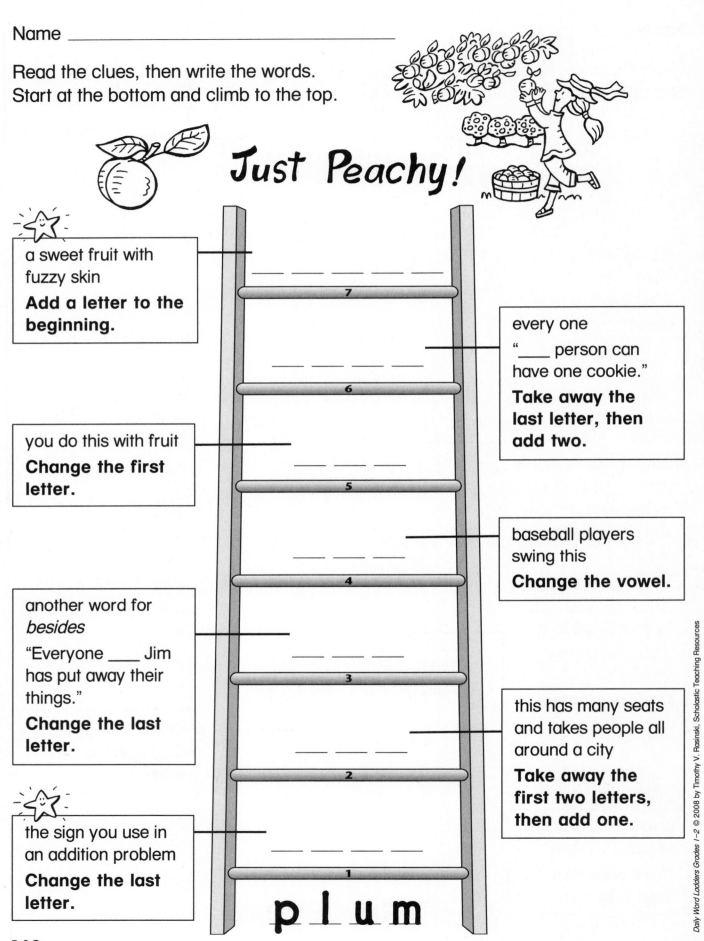

a sweet fruit with fuzzy skin

Add a letter to the beginning.

you do this with fruit

Change the first letter.

another word for *besides*

"Everyone ___ Jim has put away their things."

Change the last letter.

the sign you use in an addition problem

Change the last letter.

7

6

5

4

3

2

1

every one

"___ person can have one cookie."

Take away the last letter, then add two.

baseball players swing this

Change the vowel.

this has many seats and takes people all around a city

Take away the first two letters, then add one.

p l u m

Daily Word Ladders Grades 1–2 © 2008 by Timothy V. Rasinski, Scholastic Teaching Resources

Name _____

Read the clues, then write the words.
Start at the bottom and climb to the top.

More Is Better

the number after three
Add a letter to the beginning.

_ _ _ _ _ (7)

something that belongs to us
"That is ___ poster on the wall."
Change the last letter.

_ _ _ _ (6)

not in
Change the first letter.

_ _ _ _ (5)

another word for *stomach*
Change the vowel.

_ _ _ (4)

go for
"I'll ___ your coat for you."
Change the first letter.

_ _ _ (3)

opposite of *dry*
Change the last letter.

_ _ _ (2)

another word for *tiny*
Take away the first three letters, then add one.

_ _ _ (1)

t h r e e

Name _____

Read the clues, then write the words.
Start at the bottom and climb to the top.

Time's Up!

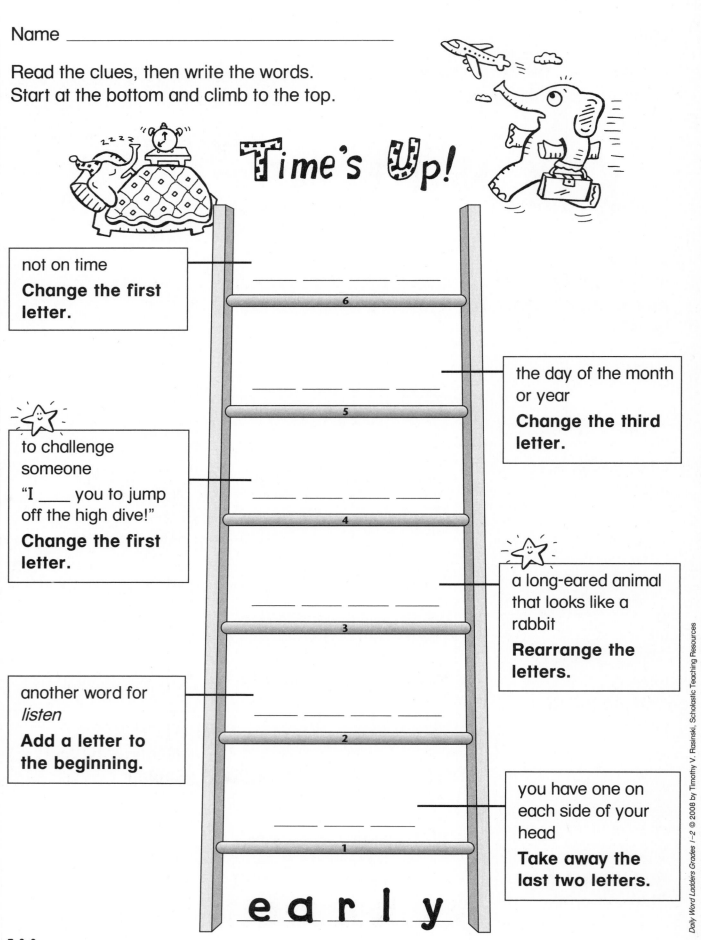

not on time
Change the first letter.

6 _ _ _ _ _ _

the day of the month or year
Change the third letter.

5 _ _ _ _ _ _

to challenge someone
"I ____ you to jump off the high dive!"
Change the first letter.

4 _ _ _ _ _ _

a long-eared animal that looks like a rabbit
Rearrange the letters.

3 _ _ _ _ _ _

another word for *listen*
Add a letter to the beginning.

2 _ _ _ _ _

you have one on each side of your head
Take away the last two letters.

1 _ _ _ _

e a r l y

Daily Word Ladders Grades 1–2 © 2008 by Timothy V. Rasinski, Scholastic Teaching Resources

Name _____

Read the clues, then write the words.
Start at the bottom and climb to the top.

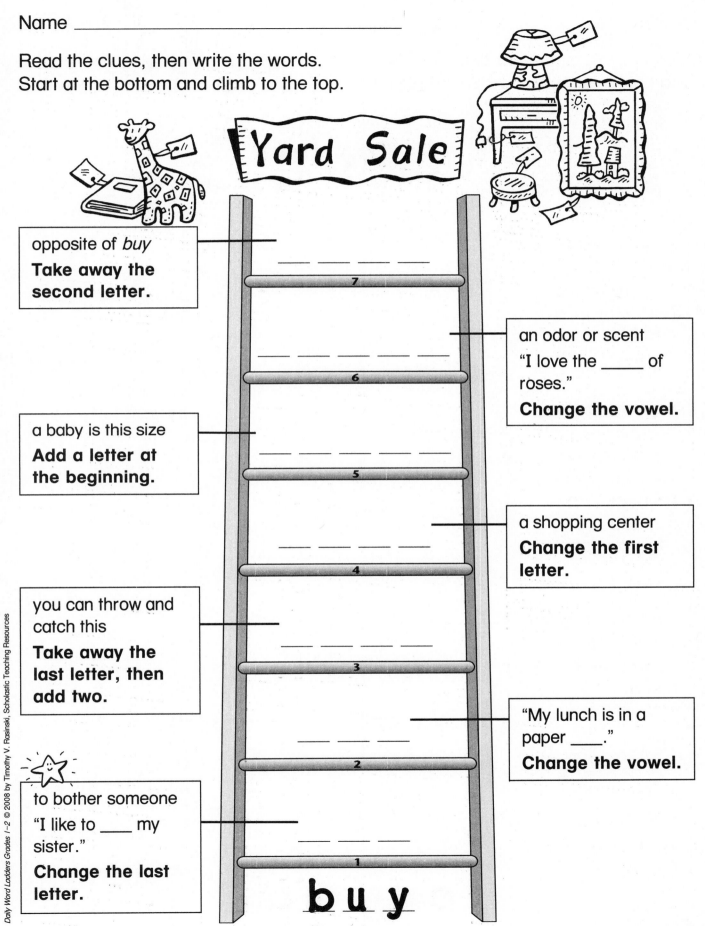

Yard Sale

opposite of *buy*
Take away the second letter.

an odor or scent
"I love the _____ of roses."
Change the vowel.

a baby is this size
Add a letter at the beginning.

a shopping center
Change the first letter.

you can throw and catch this
Take away the last letter, then add two.

"My lunch is in a paper ____."
Change the vowel.

to bother someone
"I like to ____ my sister."
Change the last letter.

7

6

5

4

3

2

1

b u y

Daily Word Ladders Grades 1–2 © 2008 by Timothy V. Rasinski, Scholastic Teaching Resources

Name _____

Read the clues, then write the words.
Start at the bottom and climb to the top.

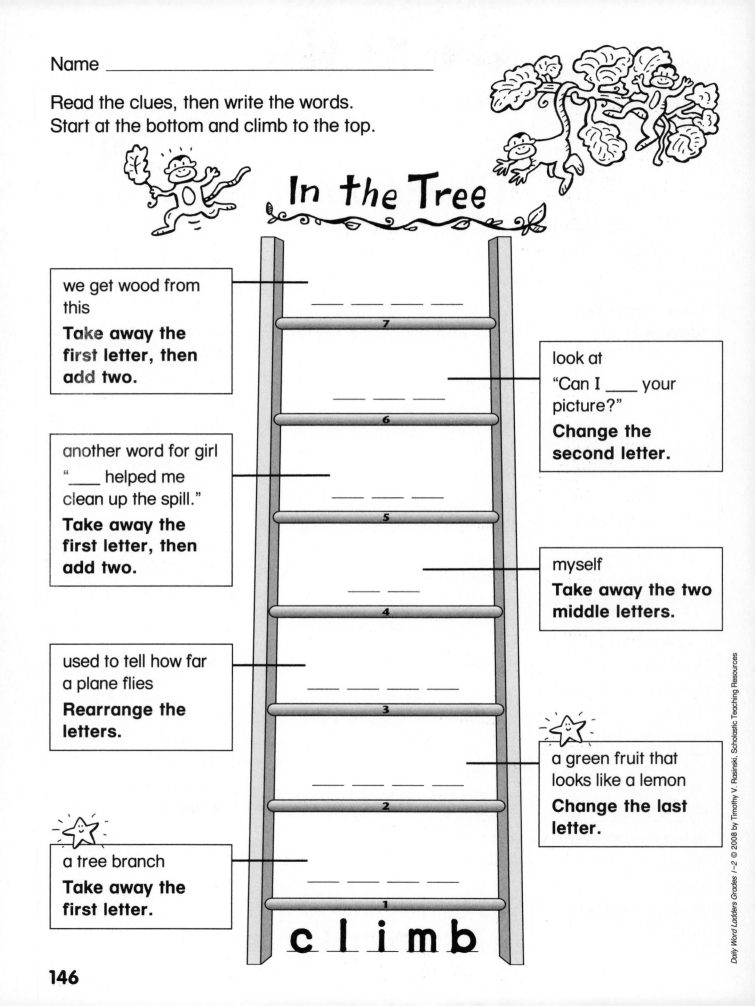

In the Tree

we get wood from this
Take away the first letter, then add two.

_ _ _ _ _
7

_ _ _ _
6

look at
"Can I ____ your picture?"
Change the second letter.

another word for girl
"____ helped me clean up the spill."
Take away the first letter, then add two.

_ _ _ _
5

_ _ _
4

myself
Take away the two middle letters.

used to tell how far a plane flies
Rearrange the letters.

_ _ _ _ _
3

_ _ _ _ _
2

a green fruit that looks like a lemon
Change the last letter.

a tree branch
Take away the first letter.

_ _ _ _ _
1

c l i m b

Daily Word Ladders Grades 1–2 © 2008 by Timothy V. Rasinski, Scholastic Teaching Resources

Name _____

Read the clues, then write the words.
Start at the bottom and climb to the top.

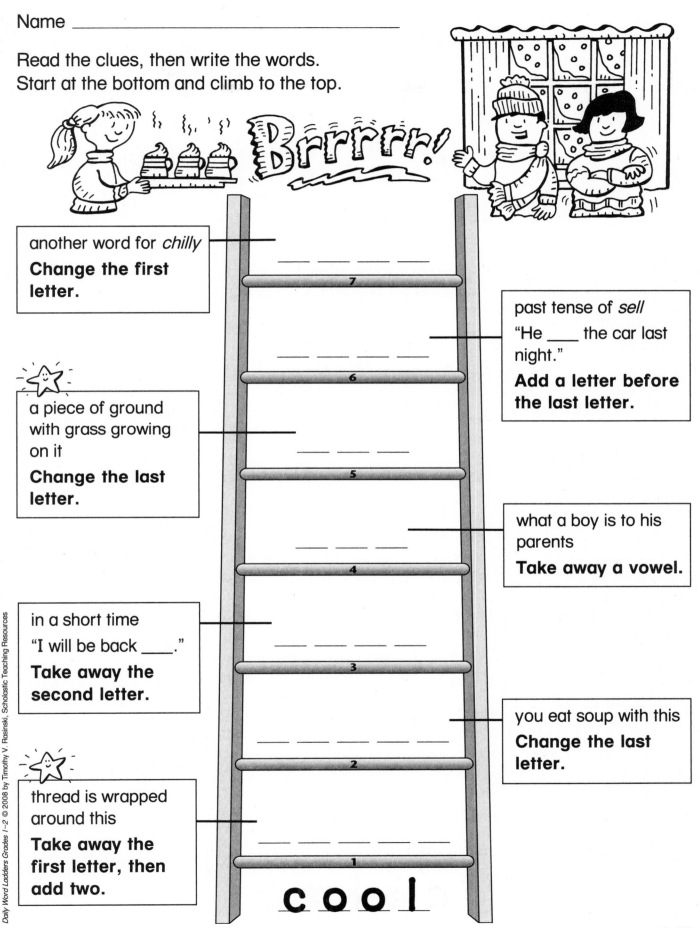

another word for *chilly*
Change the first letter.

a piece of ground with grass growing on it
Change the last letter.

in a short time
"I will be back ____."
Take away the second letter.

thread is wrapped around this
Take away the first letter, then add two.

past tense of *sell*
"He ____ the car last night."
Add a letter before the last letter.

what a boy is to his parents
Take away a vowel.

you eat soup with this
Change the last letter.

c o o l

Name _____

Read the clues, then write the words.
Start at the bottom and climb to the top.

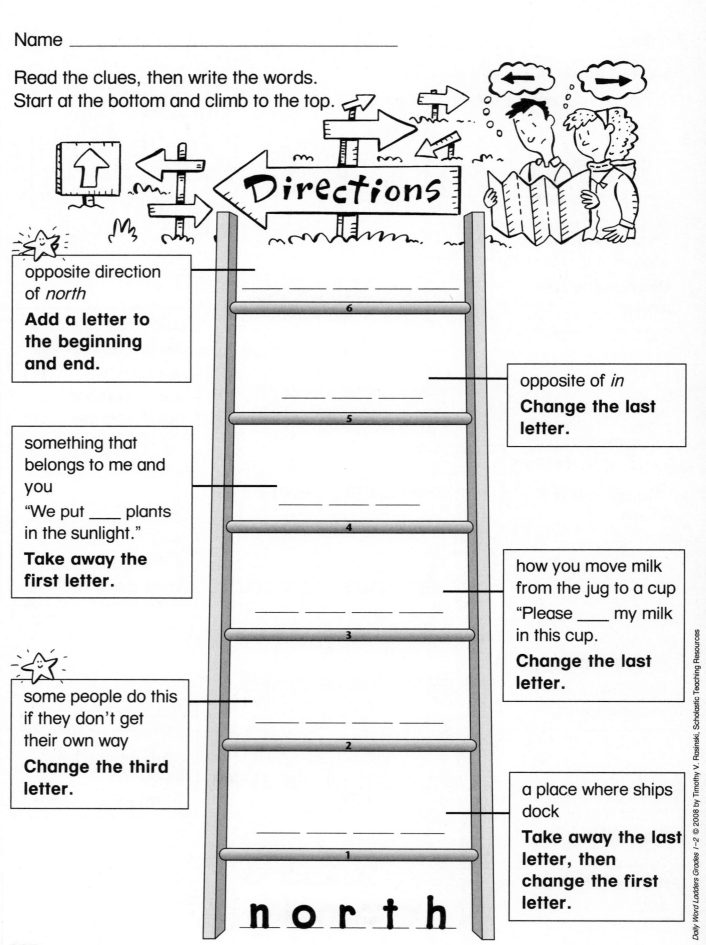

opposite direction of *north*
Add a letter to the beginning and end.

opposite of *in*
Change the last letter.

something that belongs to me and you
"We put ____ plants in the sunlight."
Take away the first letter.

how you move milk from the jug to a cup
"Please ____ my milk in this cup.
Change the last letter.

some people do this if they don't get their own way
Change the third letter.

a place where ships dock
Take away the last letter, then change the first letter.

n o r t h

6

5

4

3

2

1

Daily Word Ladders Grades 1–2 © 2008 by Timothy V. Rasinski, Scholastic Teaching Resources

Name _____

Read the clues, then write the words.
Start at the bottom and climb to the top.

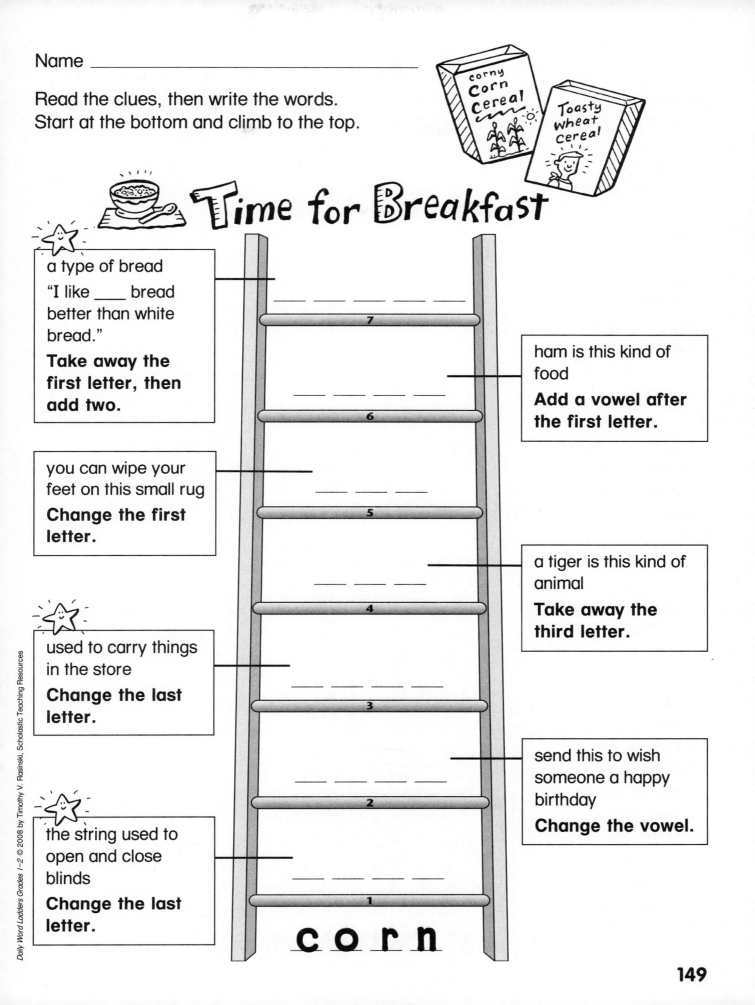

Time for Breakfast

a type of bread

"I like ____ bread better than white bread."

Take away the first letter, then add two.

_ _ _ _ _ _   7

ham is this kind of food

Add a vowel after the first letter.

_ _ _ _   6

you can wipe your feet on this small rug

Change the first letter.

_ _ _ _   5

a tiger is this kind of animal

Take away the third letter.

_ _ _ _   4

used to carry things in the store

Change the last letter.

_ _ _ _   3

send this to wish someone a happy birthday

Change the vowel.

_ _ _ _   2

the string used to open and close blinds

Change the last letter.

_ _ _ _   1

c o r n

Daily Word Ladders Grades 1–2 © 2008 by Timothy V. Rasinski, Scholastic Teaching Resources

Name _____

Read the clues, then write the words.
Start at the bottom and climb to the top.

A Clear View

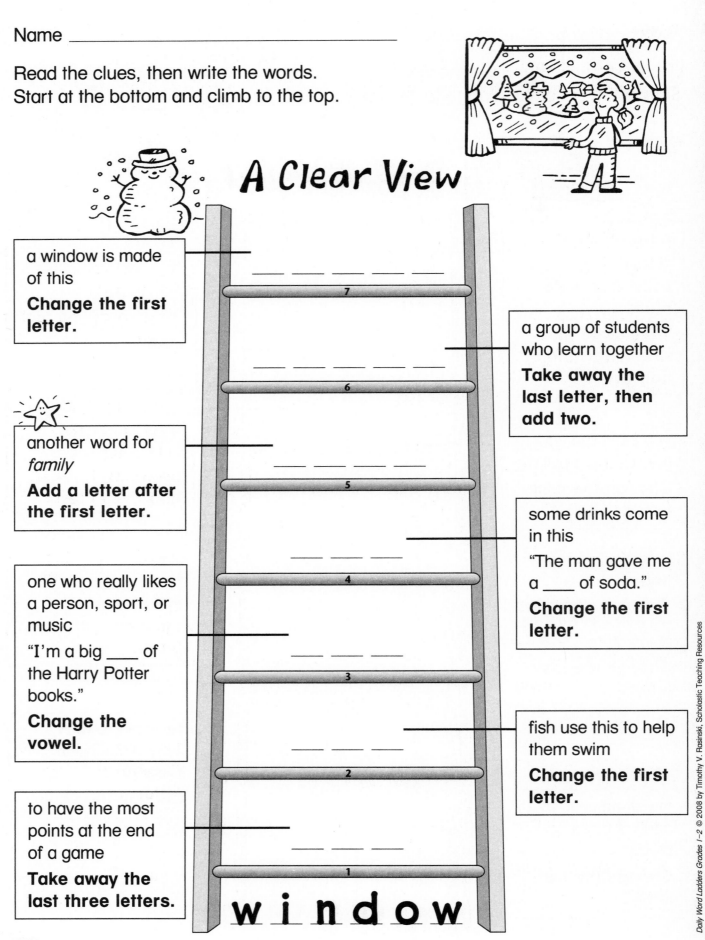

a window is made of this
Change the first letter.

a group of students who learn together
Take away the last letter, then add two.

another word for *family*
Add a letter after the first letter.

some drinks come in this
"The man gave me a ___ of soda."
Change the first letter.

one who really likes a person, sport, or music
"I'm a big ___ of the Harry Potter books."
Change the vowel.

fish use this to help them swim
Change the first letter.

to have the most points at the end of a game
Take away the last three letters.

w i n d o w

Daily Word Ladders Grades 1–2 © 2008 by Timothy V. Rasinski, Scholastic Teaching Resources

Name _____

Read the clues, then write the words.
Start at the bottom and climb to the top.

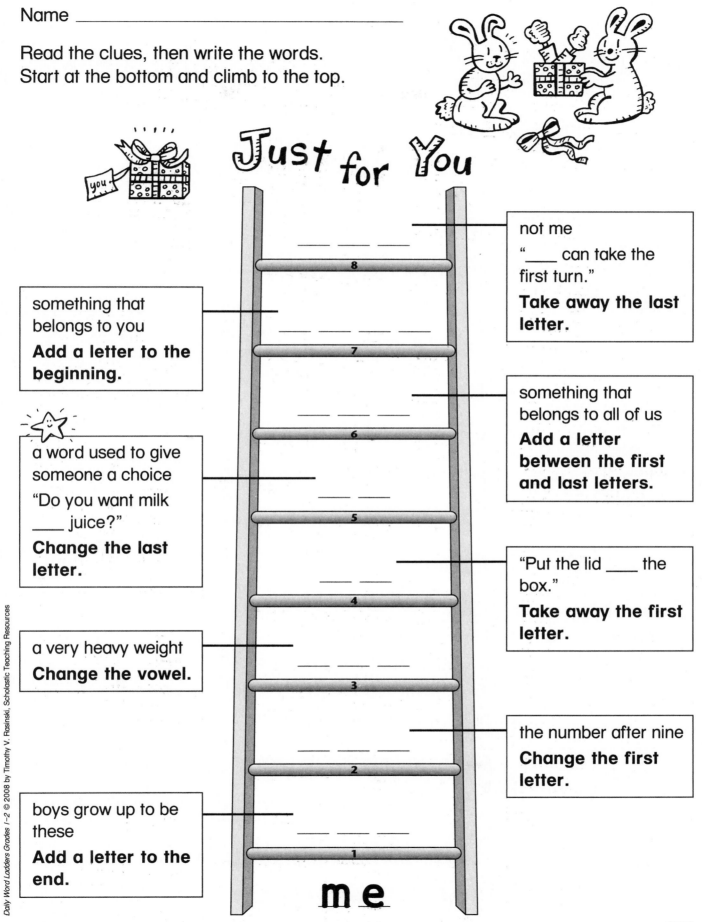

Just for You

8 _ _ _ _

not me
"___ can take the first turn."
Take away the last letter.

something that belongs to you
Add a letter to the beginning.

7 _ _ _ _

something that belongs to all of us
Add a letter between the first and last letters.

6 _ _ _ _

a word used to give someone a choice
"Do you want milk ___ juice?"
Change the last letter.

5 _ _ _

"Put the lid ___ the box."
Take away the first letter.

4 _ _ _

a very heavy weight
Change the vowel.

3 _ _ _

the number after nine
Change the first letter.

2 _ _ _

boys grow up to be these
Add a letter to the end.

1 _ _ _

m e

Name _____

Read the clues, then write the words.
Start at the bottom and climb to the top.

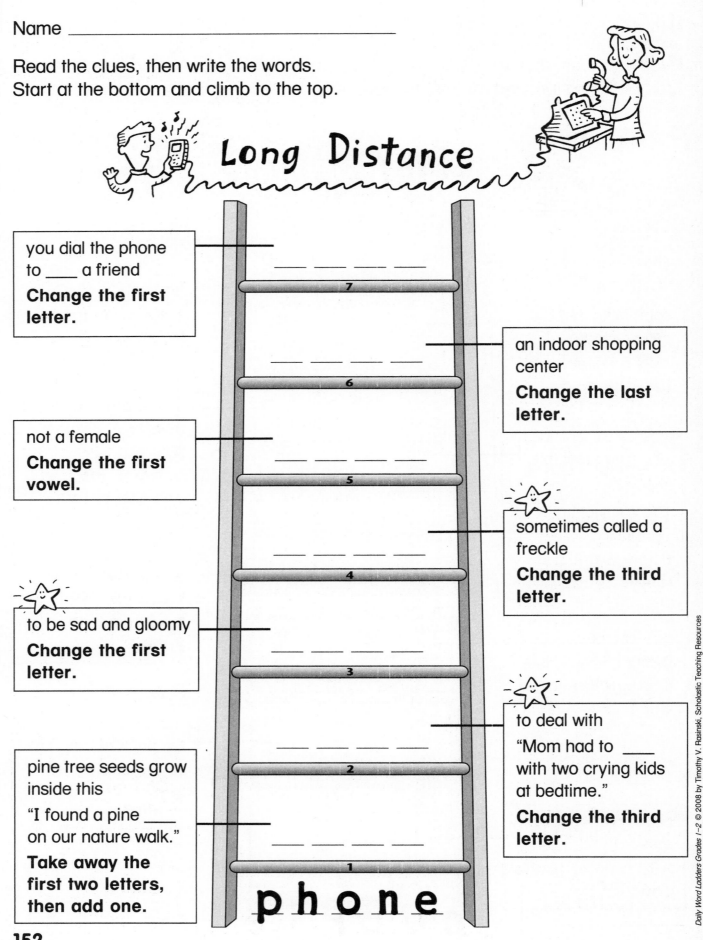

Long Distance

you dial the phone
to ____ a friend
**Change the first
letter.**

an indoor shopping
center
**Change the last
letter.**

not a female
**Change the first
vowel.**

sometimes called a
freckle
**Change the third
letter.**

to be sad and gloomy
**Change the first
letter.**

to deal with
"Mom had to ____
with two crying kids
at bedtime."
**Change the third
letter.**

pine tree seeds grow
inside this
"I found a pine ____
on our nature walk."
**Take away the
first two letters,
then add one.**

7

6

5

4

3

2

1

p h o n e

Daily Word Ladders Grades 1–2 © 2008 by Timothy V. Rasinski, Scholastic Teaching Resources

Name _____

Read the clues, then write the words.
Start at the bottom and climb to the top.

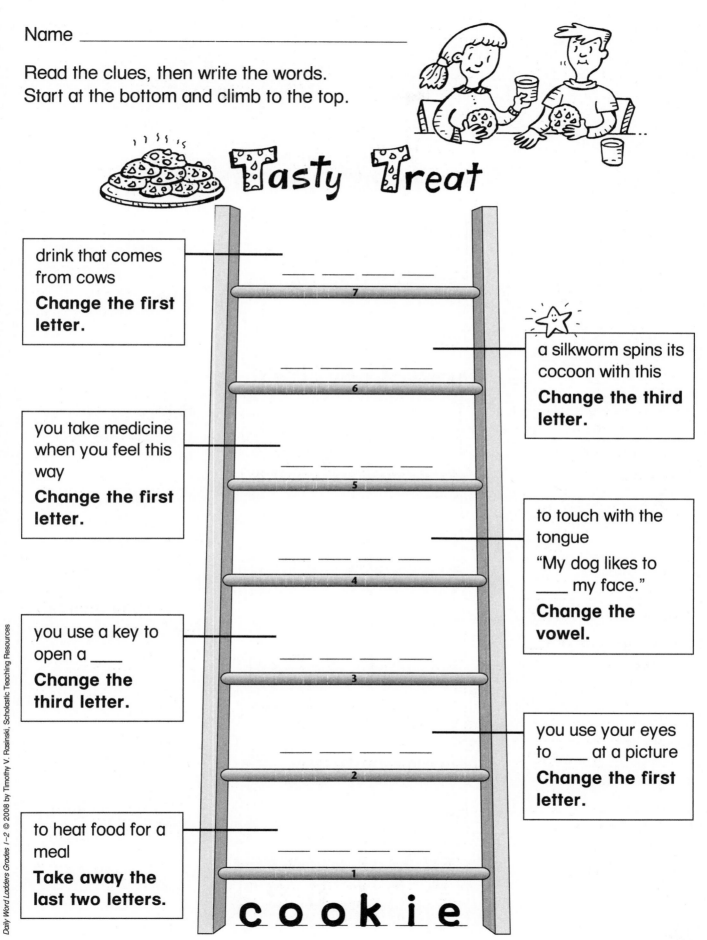

Tasty Treat

drink that comes from cows
Change the first letter.

a silkworm spins its cocoon with this
Change the third letter.

you take medicine when you feel this way
Change the first letter.

to touch with the tongue
"My dog likes to ___ my face."
Change the vowel.

you use a key to open a ___
Change the third letter.

you use your eyes to ___ at a picture
Change the first letter.

to heat food for a meal
Take away the last two letters.

c o o k i e

Name _____

Read the clues, then write the words.
Start at the bottom and climb to the top.

A Bundle of Surprises

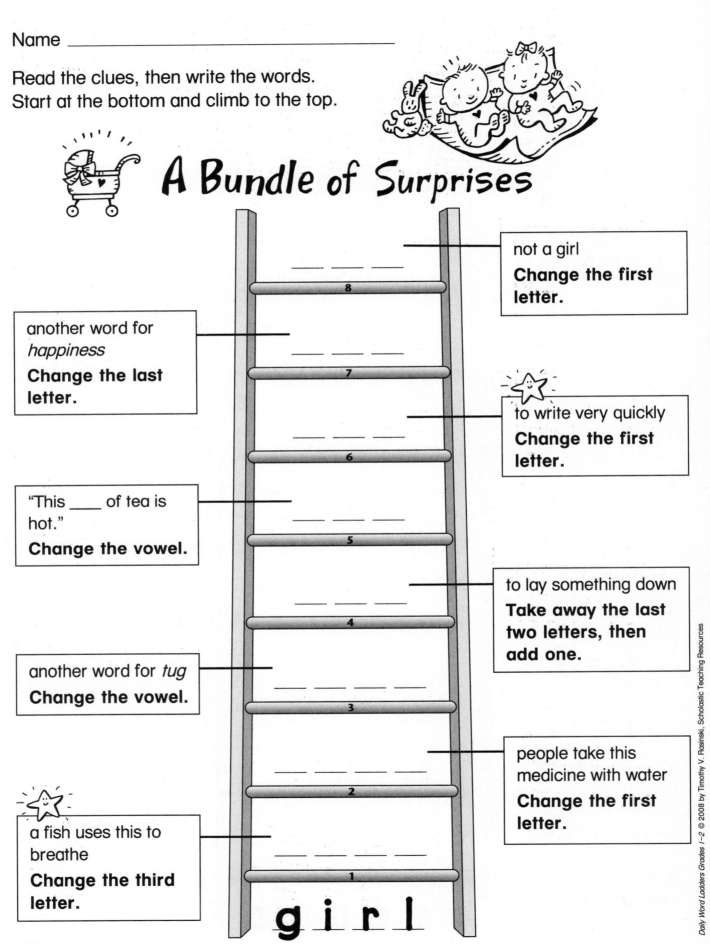

not a girl
Change the first letter.

_____ 8

another word for *happiness*
Change the last letter.

_____ 7

to write very quickly
Change the first letter.

_____ 6

"This ___ of tea is hot."
Change the vowel.

_____ 5

to lay something down
Take away the last two letters, then add one.

_____ 4

another word for *tug*
Change the vowel.

_____ 3

people take this medicine with water
Change the first letter.

_____ 2

a fish uses this to breathe
Change the third letter.

_____ 1

g i r l

Daily Word Ladders Grades 1–2 © 2008 by Timothy V. Rasinski, Scholastic Teaching Resources

Name _____

Read the clues, then write the words.
Start at the bottom and climb to the top.

Fried Snacks

to cook something in oil
Change the first letter.

_ _ _ _ _   8

opposite of *wet*
Change the second letter.

_ _ _ _   7

opposite of *night*
Change the first letter.

_ _ _ _   6

another word for *inlet*
"Many ships dock in the San Francisco ____."
Change the vowel.

_ _ _ _   5

opposite of *sell*
Change the last letter.

_ _ _ _   4

the bread that a hot dog is put in
Take away the last two letters.

_ _ _   3

a lot
"I have a ____ of books at home."
Change the vowel.

_ _ _ _   2

a long wooden seat found at the park
Take away the first two letters, then add one.

_ _ _ _ _   1

F r e n c h

Name _____

Read the clues, then write the words.
Start at the bottom and climb to the top.

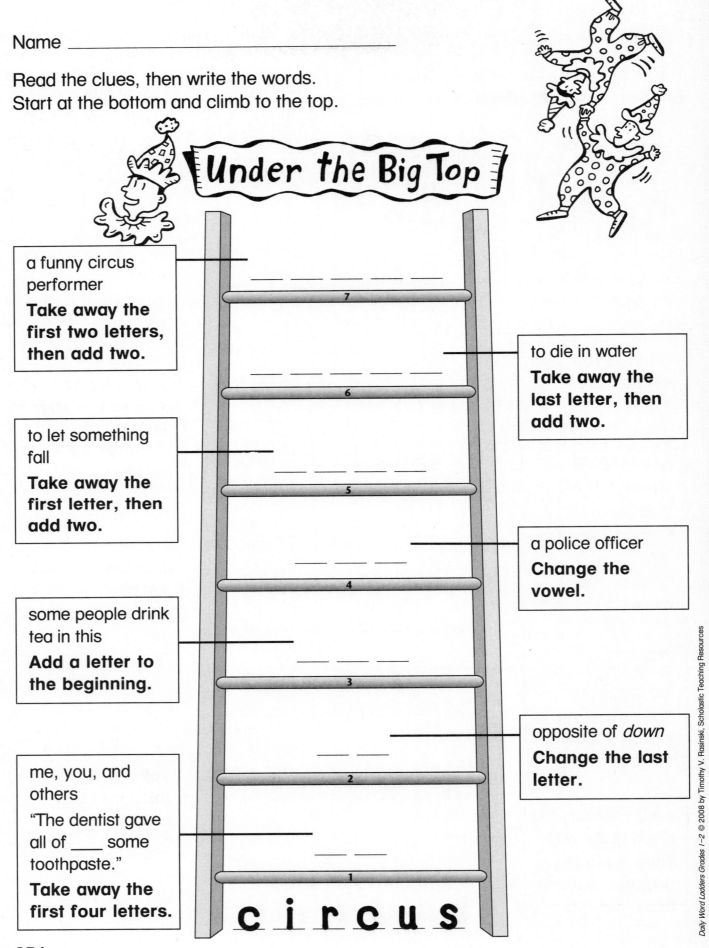

Under the Big Top

a funny circus performer

Take away the first two letters, then add two.

to die in water

Take away the last letter, then add two.

to let something fall

Take away the first letter, then add two.

a police officer

Change the vowel.

some people drink tea in this

Add a letter to the beginning.

opposite of *down*

Change the last letter.

me, you, and others

"The dentist gave all of ____ some toothpaste."

Take away the first four letters.

c i r c u s

Daily Word Ladders Grades 1–2 © 2008 by Timothy V. Rasinski, Scholastic Teaching Resources

Name _____

Read the clues, then write the words.
Start at the bottom and climb to the top.

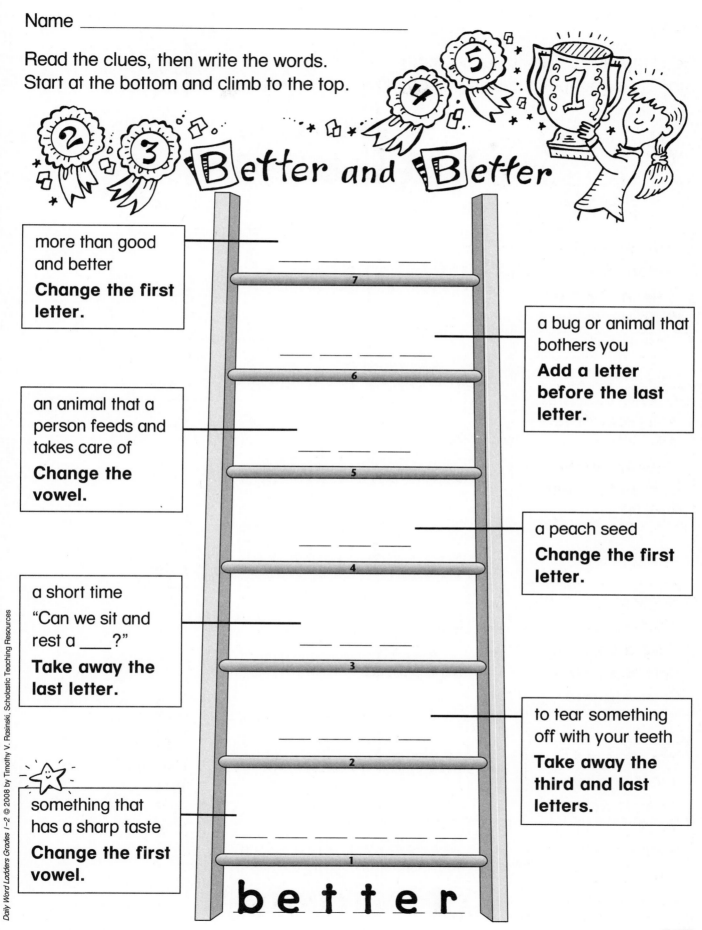

Better and Better

more than good and better
Change the first letter.

7 _ _ _ _ _

a bug or animal that bothers you
Add a letter before the last letter.

6 _ _ _ _ _

an animal that a person feeds and takes care of
Change the vowel.

5 _ _ _ _

a peach seed
Change the first letter.

4 _ _ _ _

a short time
"Can we sit and rest a ___?"
Take away the last letter.

3 _ _ _ _

to tear something off with your teeth
Take away the third and last letters.

2 _ _ _ _ _

something that has a sharp taste
Change the first vowel.

1 _ _ _ _ _ _

b e t t e r

Daily Word Ladders Grades 1–2 © 2008 by Timothy V. Rasinski, Scholastic Teaching Resources

Name _____

Read the clues, then write the words.
Start at the bottom and climb to the top.

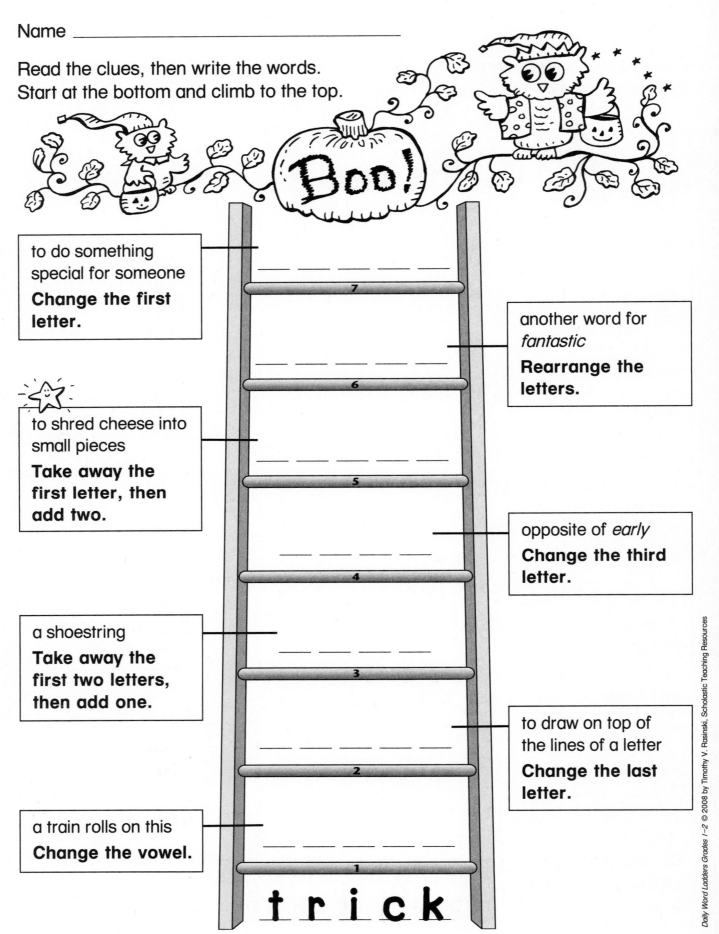

Boo!

to do something
special for someone
**Change the first
letter.**

7 _ _ _ _ _ _

another word for
fantastic
**Rearrange the
letters.**

6 _ _ _ _ _ _

to shred cheese into
small pieces
**Take away the
first letter, then
add two.**

5 _ _ _ _ _

opposite of *early*
**Change the third
letter.**

4 _ _ _ _

a shoestring
**Take away the
first two letters,
then add one.**

3 _ _ _ _

to draw on top of
the lines of a letter
**Change the last
letter.**

2 _ _ _ _ _

a train rolls on this
Change the vowel.

1

t r i c k

Daily Word Ladders Grades 1–2 © 2008 by Timothy V. Rasinski, Scholastic Teaching Resources

Name _____

Read the clues, then write the words.
Start at the bottom and climb to the top.

Up, Up and Away

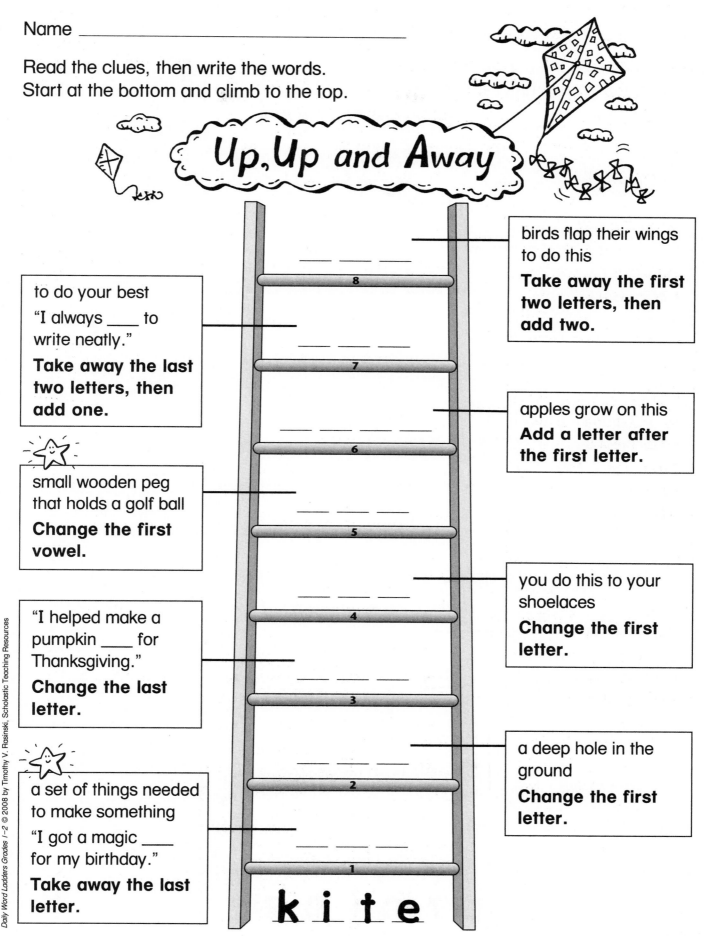

birds flap their wings to do this
Take away the first two letters, then add two.

8 ___ ___ ___ ___

to do your best
"I always ___ to write neatly."
Take away the last two letters, then add one.

7 ___ ___ ___

apples grow on this
Add a letter after the first letter.

6 ___ ___ ___ ___

small wooden peg that holds a golf ball
Change the first vowel.

5 ___ ___ ___

you do this to your shoelaces
Change the first letter.

4 ___ ___ ___ ___

"I helped make a pumpkin ___ for Thanksgiving."
Change the last letter.

3 ___ ___ ___

a deep hole in the ground
Change the first letter.

2 ___ ___ ___

a set of things needed to make something
"I got a magic ___ for my birthday."
Take away the last letter.

1 ___ ___ ___ ___

k i t e

Name _____

Read the clues, then write the words.
Start at the bottom and climb to the top.

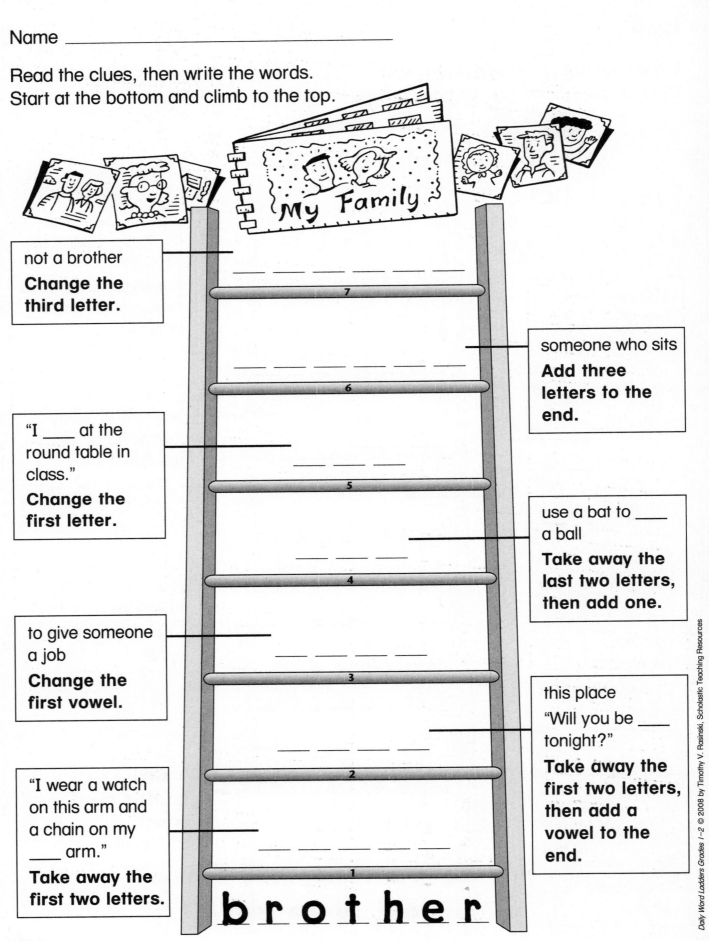

My Family

not a brother
**Change the
third letter.**
_____ _____ _____ _____ _____ _____

7

someone who sits
**Add three
letters to the
end.**
_____ _____ _____ _____

6

"I ___ at the
round table in
class."
**Change the
first letter.**
_____ _____ _____

5

use a bat to ___
a ball
**Take away the
last two letters,
then add one.**
_____ _____ _____

4

to give someone
a job
**Change the
first vowel.**
_____ _____ _____ _____

3

this place
"Will you be ___
tonight?"
**Take away the
first two letters,
then add a
vowel to the
end.**
_____ _____ _____ _____

2

"I wear a watch
on this arm and
a chain on my
___ arm."
**Take away the
first two letters.**
_____ _____ _____ _____ _____

1

b r o t h e r

Daily Word Ladders Grades 1–2 © 2008 by Timothy V. Rasinski, Scholastic Teaching Resources

Name _____

Read the clues, then write the words.
Start at the bottom and climb to the top.

On the Set

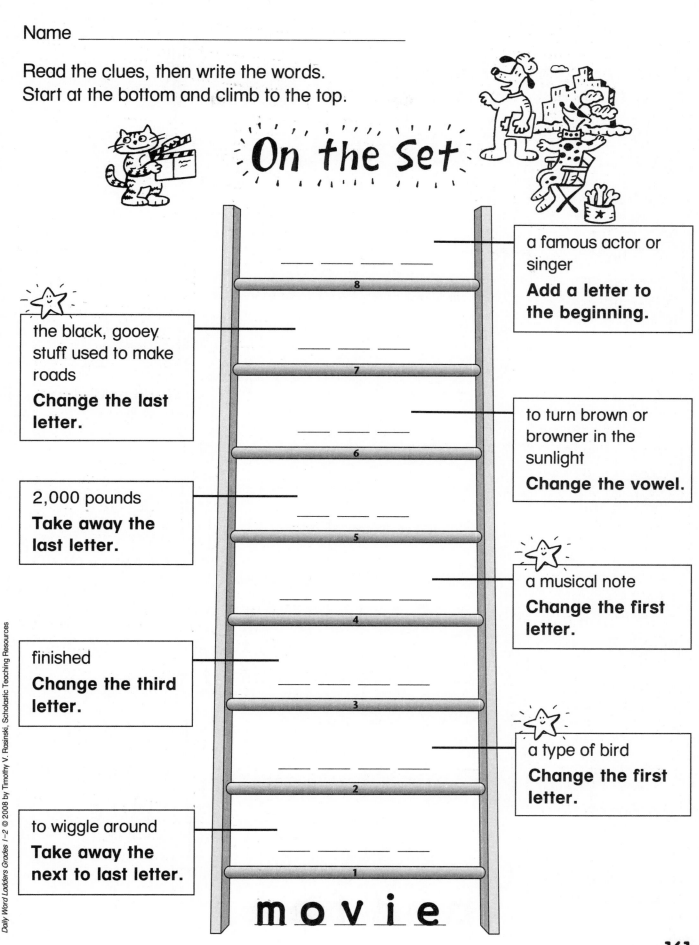

a famous actor or singer
Add a letter to the beginning.

the black, gooey stuff used to make roads
Change the last letter.

to turn brown or browner in the sunlight
Change the vowel.

2,000 pounds
Take away the last letter.

a musical note
Change the first letter.

finished
Change the third letter.

a type of bird
Change the first letter.

to wiggle around
Take away the next to last letter.

m o v i e

Name _____

Read the clues, then write the words.
Start at the bottom and climb to the top.

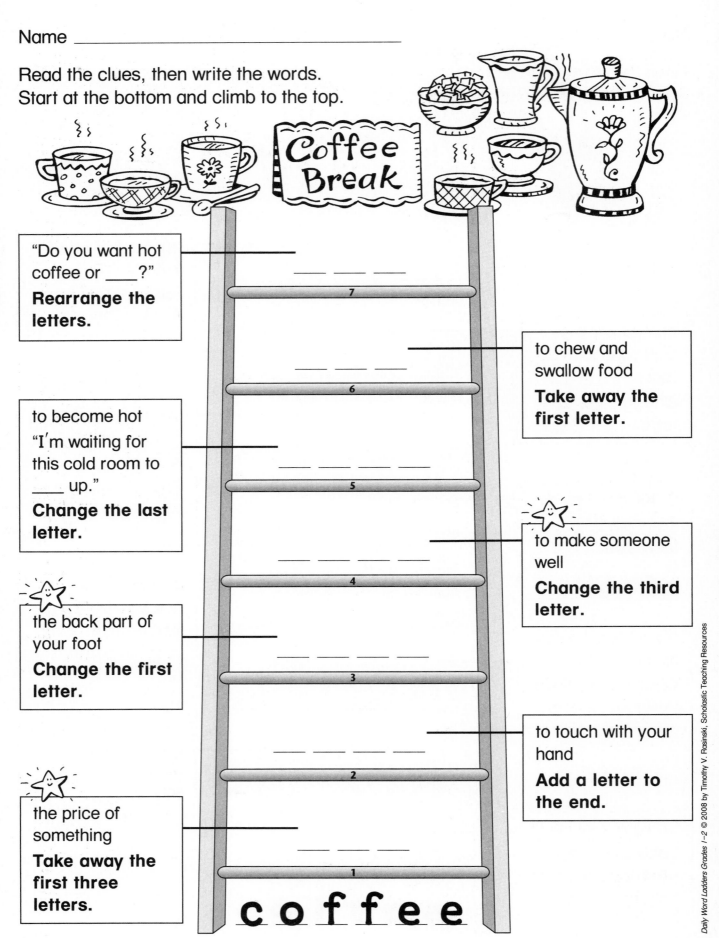

Coffee Break

"Do you want hot coffee or ____?"
Rearrange the letters.

to chew and swallow food
Take away the first letter.

to become hot
"I'm waiting for this cold room to ____ up."
Change the last letter.

to make someone well
Change the third letter.

the back part of your foot
Change the first letter.

to touch with your hand
Add a letter to the end.

the price of something
Take away the first three letters.

c o f f e e

7

6

5

4

3

2

1

Daily Word Ladders Grades 1–2 © 2008 by Timothy V. Rasinski, Scholastic Teaching Resources

Name _____

Read the clues, then write the words.
Start at the bottom and climb to the top.

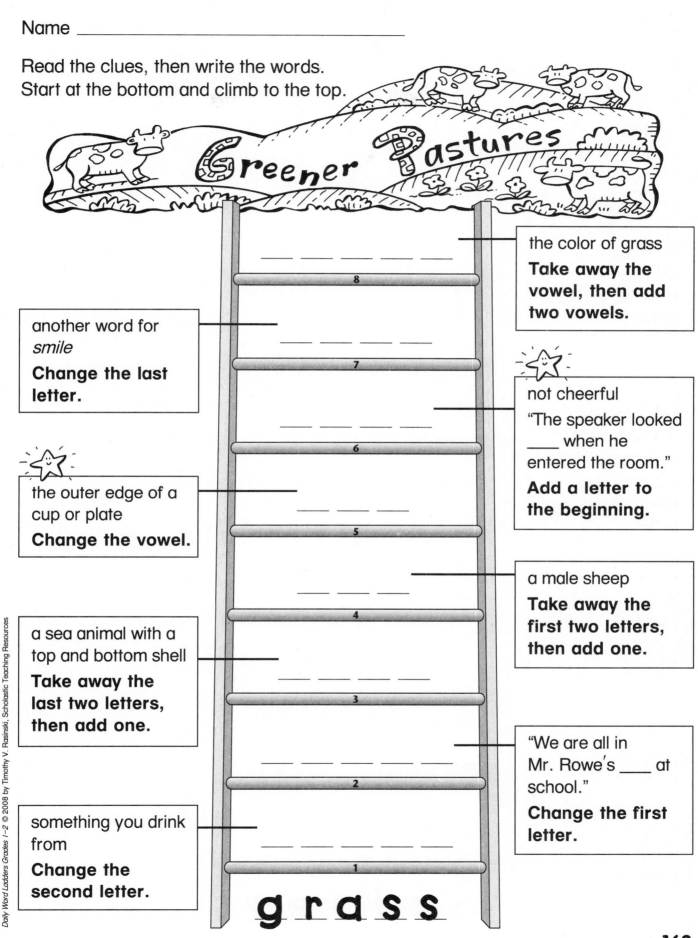

Greener Pastures

the color of grass
Take away the vowel, then add two vowels.

another word for *smile*
Change the last letter.

not cheerful
"The speaker looked ___ when he entered the room."
Add a letter to the beginning.

the outer edge of a cup or plate
Change the vowel.

a male sheep
Take away the first two letters, then add one.

a sea animal with a top and bottom shell
Take away the last two letters, then add one.

"We are all in Mr. Rowe's ___ at school."
Change the first letter.

something you drink from
Change the second letter.

8

7

6

5

4

3

2

1

g r a s s

Name _____

Read the clues, then write the words.
Start at the bottom and climb to the top.

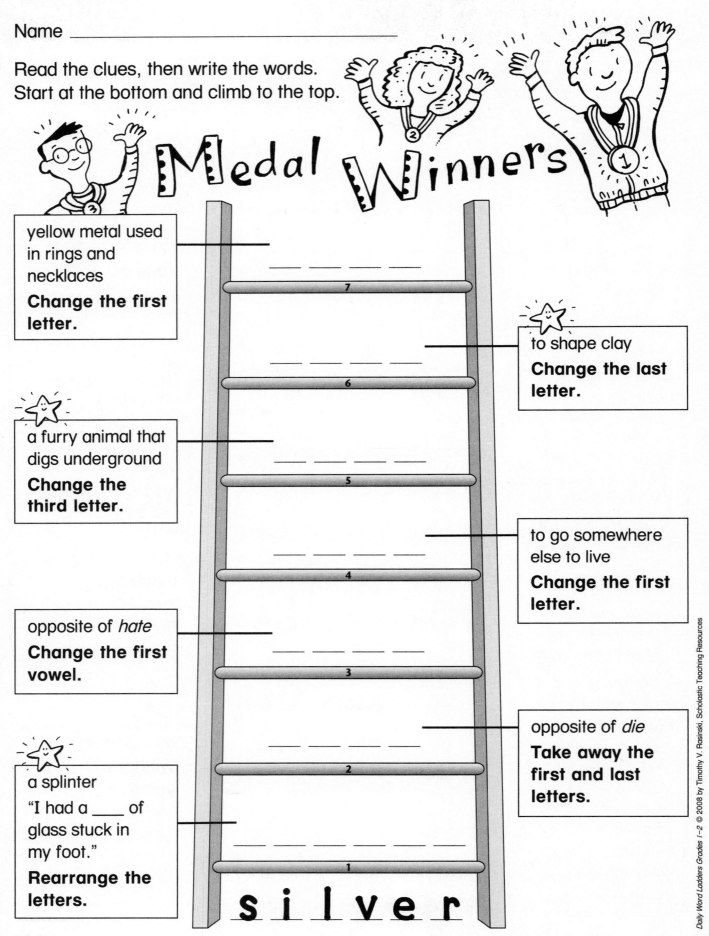

Medal Winners

yellow metal used in rings and necklaces
Change the first letter.

7 _ _ _ _

to shape clay
Change the last letter.

6 _ _ _ _

a furry animal that digs underground
Change the third letter.

5 _ _ _ _

to go somewhere else to live
Change the first letter.

4 _ _ _ _

opposite of *hate*
Change the first vowel.

3 _ _ _ _

opposite of *die*
Take away the first and last letters.

2 _ _ _ _ _

a splinter
"I had a ____ of glass stuck in my foot."
Rearrange the letters.

1 _ _ _ _ _ _

s i l v e r

Daily Word Ladders Grades 1–2 © 2008 by Timothy V. Rasinski, Scholastic Teaching Resources

Name _____

Read the clues, then write the words.
Start at the bottom and climb to the top.

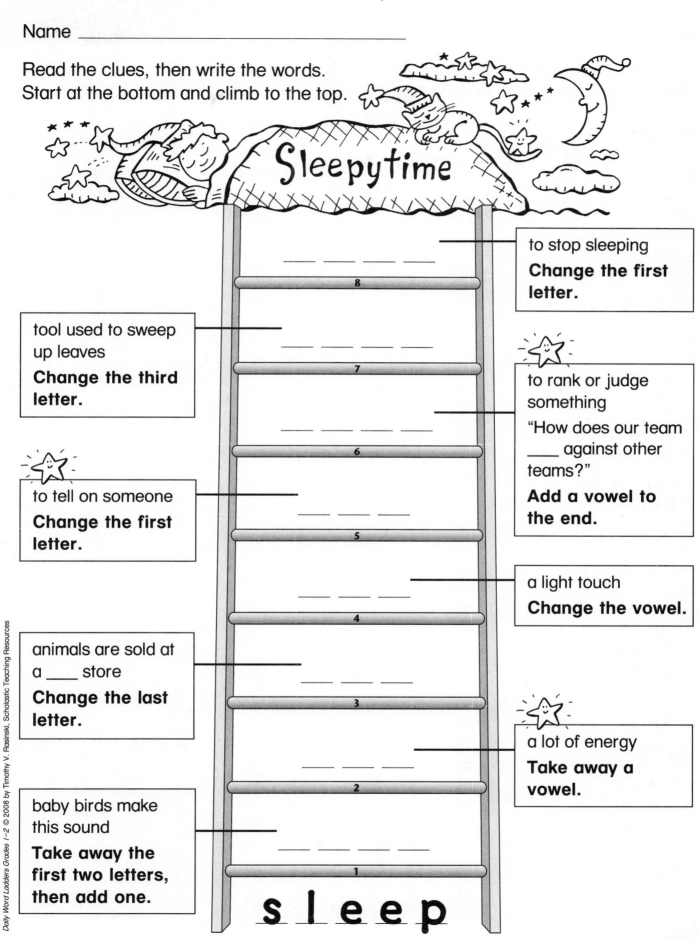

Sleepytime

8 _ _ _ _ _

to stop sleeping
Change the first letter.

tool used to sweep up leaves
Change the third letter.

7 _ _ _ _ _

to rank or judge something
"How does our team ___ against other teams?"
Add a vowel to the end.

6 _ _ _ _

to tell on someone
Change the first letter.

5 _ _ _

a light touch
Change the vowel.

4 _ _ _

animals are sold at a ___ store
Change the last letter.

3 _ _ _

a lot of energy
Take away a vowel.

2 _ _ _ _

baby birds make this sound
Take away the first two letters, then add one.

1 _ _ _ _ _

s l e e p

Name _____

Read the clues, then write the words.
Start at the bottom and climb to the top.

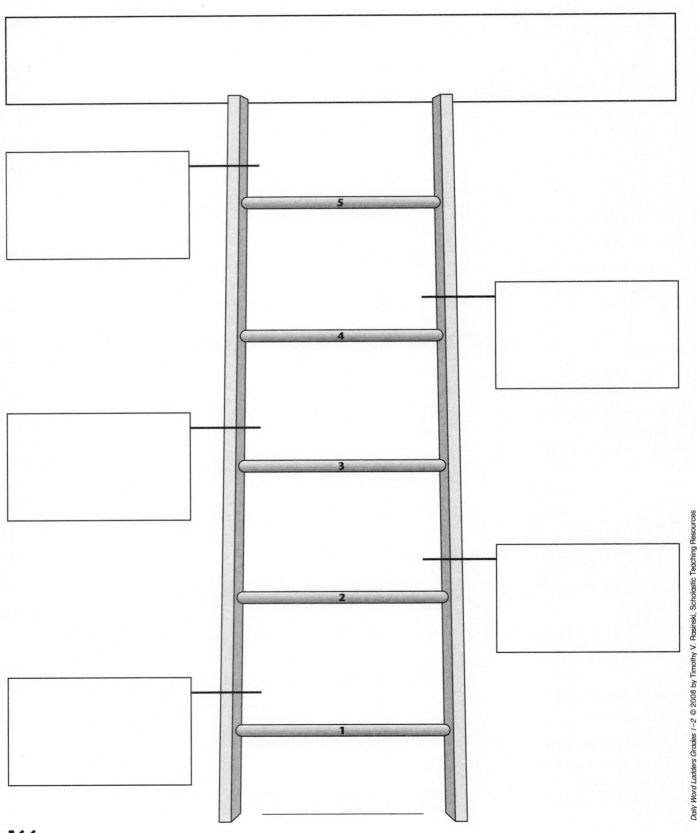

Daily Word Ladders Grades 1–2 © 2008 by Timothy V. Rasinski, Scholastic Teaching Resources

Name _____

Read the clues, then write the words.
Start at the bottom and climb to the top.

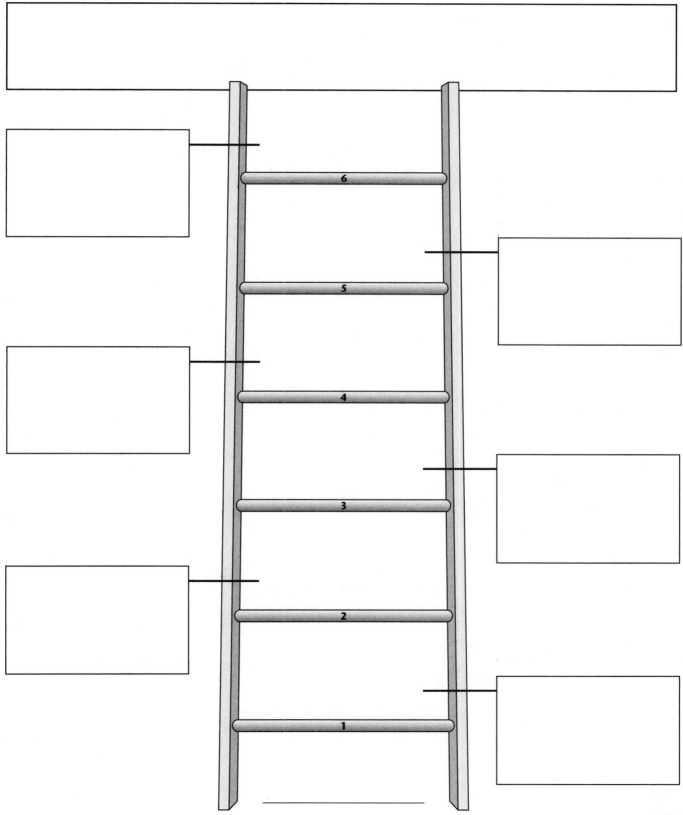

Daily Word Ladders Grades 1–2 © 2008 by Timothy V. Rasinski, Scholastic Teaching Resources

Name _____

Read the clues, then write the words.
Start at the bottom and climb to the top.

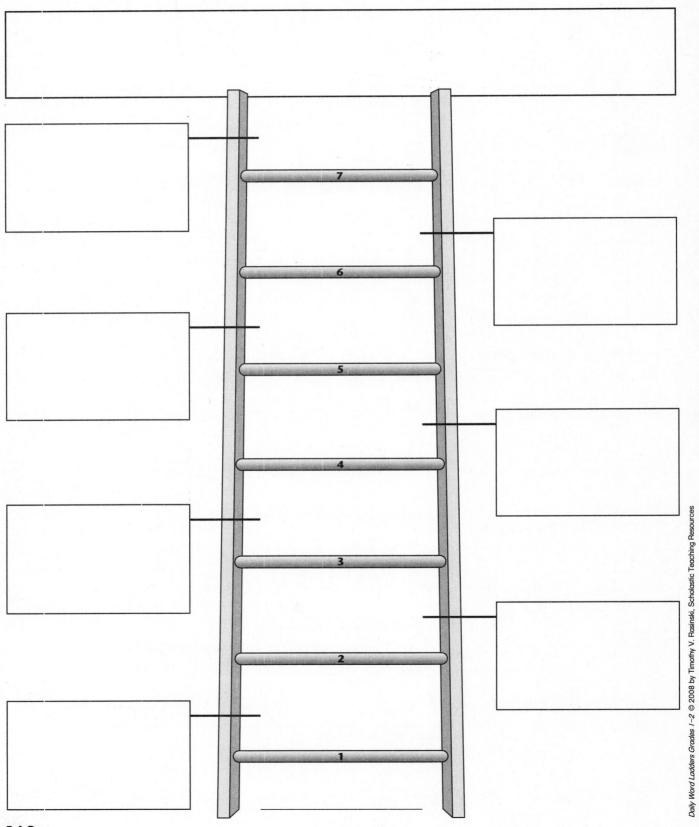

Daily Word Ladders Grades 1–2 © 2008 by Timothy V. Rasinski, Scholastic Teaching Resources

Answer Key

Farm Fun, page 8
cow, cot, pot, pet, pit, pig

Dinner's Ready, page 9
bite, bit, hit, hat, fat, eat

Inside Out, page 10
in, fin, fan, fat, cat, cut, out

Color Change, page 11
red, bed, bet, pet, pit, pin, pink

Animal Enemies, page 12
dog, dot, pot, pop, top, tap, cap, cat

Air Travel, page 13
plane, plan, pan, pen, men, met, jet

A Matter of Size, page 14
big, bit, bill, ball, mall, small

Around the Clock, page 15
tick, sick, sack, rack, rock, tock

Family Ties, page 16
mom, mop, top, tap, tan, man, mad, dad

Fun on a Bun, page 17
hot, lot, let, pet, pit, pig, dig, dog

Opposites Attract, page 18
fat, fit, hit, his, this, thin

Sweet Sounds, page 19
ear, eat, rat, ran, rang, ring

Give a Dog a Bone, page 20
tail, sail, said, sad, bad, bag, wag

Here to There, page 21
walk, wall, fall, full, fun, run

Get Well Soon, page 22
ill, pill, hill, sill, silk, sick

In the Can, page 23
trash, crash, cash, cast, cat, can

America's Pastime, page 24
base, case, care, bare, bale, ball

Hop to It!, page 25
frog, jog, jug, tug, tag, tad, toad

On the Playground, page 26
sit, hit, hat, had, hand, sand, stand

Fur Facts, page 27
hair, hail, fail, fall, ball, bald

Ship Shape, page 28
ship, slip, slap, sap, sat, set, sea

Pail Problem, page 29
pail, tail, tall, tale, sale, pale

Fancy Footwear, page 30
sock, rock, row, how, show, shoe

In the Doghouse, page 31
dog, hog, hag, bag, bar, barn, bark

Counting Up, page 32
few, dew, den, men, man, many

Personality Change, page 33
good, gold, cold, bold, bald, bad

Cross-Country, page 107
east, fast, feast, beast, best, test, rest, west

Beautiful Day, page 108
sun, fun, fur, far, fare, fire, fine, shine

Good Scents, page 109
smell, bell, bet, best, pest, post, pose, nose

On the Line, page 110
phone, cone, cane, can, tan, tank, tack, talk

Meadow Friends, page 111
sheep, steep, step, stop, top, pot, got, goat

Gentle Breeze, page 112
wind, find, fine, line, lone, low, bow, blow

Big and Cuddly, page 113
bear, hear, heart, art, cart, cat, cut, cub

All in a Day, page 114
swim, slim, slam, clam, cram, cry, fry, fly

Open Wide!, page 115
open, pen, pet, pot, post, lost, lose, close

Feelings, page 116
glad, lad, mad, made, mane, male, mile, smile

Perfect Pair, page 117
one, tone, stone, store, tore, toe, tow, two

Fireworks, page 118
spark, park, mark, mare, male, mile, file, fire

Friendship, page 119
friend, end, den, ten, tan, can, pan, pal

On the Move, page 120
bike, like, lake, lame, lamb, lab, cab, car

Pace Yourself, page 121
fast, past, pest, pets, lets, lots, slot, slow

Barbershop, page 122
head, read, red, rid, raid, paid, pair, hair

Hungry!, page 123
eat, seat, set, sit, sink, wink, rink, drink

Car Trouble, page 124
wheel, feel, fell, tell, till, tilt, tile, tire

Need a Lift?, page 125
tow, toe, doe, dog, dug, duck, tuck, truck

Bookworm, page 126
read, head, heat, beat, belt, bolt, boot, book

A Little Light, page 127
match, batch, bath, bat, bit, fit, fir, fire

Heads or Tails?, page 128
round, pound, pond, pod, pad, pat, fat, flat

Peaks and Valleys, page 129
high, sigh, sight, sit, hit, hot, how, low

Go, Go, Go, page 130
street, tree, see, set, net, not, nod, rod, road

Fried Snacks, page 155
French, bench, bunch, bun, buy, bay, day, dry, fry

Under the Big Top, page 156
circus, us, up, cup, cop, drop, drown, clown

Better and Better, page 157
better, bitter, bite, bit, pit, pet, pest, best

Boo!, page 158
trick, track, trace, lace, late, grate, great, treat

Up, Up and Away, page 159
kite, kit, pit, pie, tie, tee, tree, try, fly

My Family, page 160
brother, other, here, hire, hit, sit, sitter, sister

On the Set, page 161
movie, move, dove, done, tone, ton, tan, tar, star

Coffee Break, page 162
coffee, fee, feel, heel, heal, heat, eat, tea

Greener Pastures, page 163
grass, glass, class, clam, ram, rim, grim, grin, green

Medal Winners, page 164
silver, sliver, live, love, move, mole, mold, gold

Sleepytime, page 165
sleep, peep, pep, pet, pat, rat, rate, rake, wake

Notes